TUNE UP:

your

SPANISH

The Top
10
Ways to
Improve
your
Spoken
Spanish

Mary McVey Gill
Brenda Wegmann

McGraw·Hill

New York   Chicago   San Francisco   Lisbon   London   Madrid   Mexico City
Milan   New Delhi   San Juan   Seoul   Singapore   Sydney   Toronto

The *McGraw·Hill* Companies

Library of Congress Cataloging-in-Publication Data

Gill, Mary McVey.
    Tune up your Spanish : the top ten ways to improve your spoken Spanish / Mary
McVey Gill and Brenda Wegmann.
        p.   cm.
    ISBN 0-07-143227-2 (book only : alk. paper)
    ISBN 0-07-143226-4 (book and CD package)
    1. Spanish language—Conversation and phrase books—English.   I. Wegmann,
Brenda, 1941–   II. Title.

PC4121.G56   2004
468.3'421—dc22   2004053854

Also in this series
Tune Up Your French, *Natalie Schorr*
Series editor: Natalie Schorr

1 2 3 4 5 6 7 8 9 0 AGM/AGM 3 2 1 0 9 8 7 6 5 4

ISBN 0-07-143226-4 (book and CD package)
ISBN 0-07-143227-2 (book only)

Interior design by Pamela Juárez

This book is printed on acid-free paper.

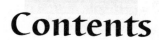

Contents

Acknowledgments **v**

Introduction: *¡Viva el español, idioma sin par!* **vii**
  Hooray for Spanish, a Peerless Language!

Tune-Up 1: *¡Vamos a charlar!*   1
Getting the Spanish out of Your Mouth and into Conversation

Tune-Up 2: *Sonido y sentido*   37
Active Listening . . . or Hang in There!

Tune-Up 3: *¡Buen provecho!*   63
Eating and Drinking: Not Just Tacos and Margaritas!

Tune-Up 4: *Amor, pasión y aventura*   95
The Fine Arts of Love and Romance

Tune-Up 5: *¡Viajar es vivir!*   127
Traveling the Many Worlds of Spanish-Speaking Cultures

Tune-Up 6: *De compras*   161
Shopping and Money

Tune-Up 7: *¿En serio o en broma?*   183
Understanding How Language, Culture, and Humor Interact

Tune-Up 8: *De la casa a la plaza*   211
The Intimate Life of Family and Friends

Tune-Up 9: *El español: voz de muchos pueblos*   241
The Many Ways of Speaking Spanish

Tune-Up 10: *Don Quijote, La Malinche, Bolívar...*   269
Understanding Icons, Heroes, and Antiheroes

Appendix A: Regional Variations for "You"   293
Appendix B: Pronunciation Around the Globe   297
Answer Key   301
Index of Top Five and Top Ten Lists   323

Acknowledgments

Many thanks go to Natalie Schorr and Julia Anderson Bauer for their contributions to the design and production of this book. We also wish to express our heartfelt gratitude to Christopher Brown, whose editorial expertise, patience, and inspiration have guided us through the many phases of this project.

Introduction

¡Viva el español, idioma sin par!
Hooray for Spanish, a Peerless Language!

This is not a book for the total beginner. If you have studied Spanish or been exposed to it in the past and you would like to improve it, or if you feel that your Spanish is lying dormant somewhere in the back of your mind, then this book is for you. Awaken and refresh the Spanish you know (or once knew), build on it, and extend it. But, wait a minute—is learning Spanish worth your time and effort? Read through the following list to find out how the Spanish advantage can enhance your life.

TOP TEN Reasons to Learn Spanish (*Diez razones para aprender español*)

1. **Hay veintiún países de habla española que esperan tu llegada.** There are twenty-one Spanish-speaking countries that are awaiting your arrival.

2. **El español es el cuarto idioma de importancia con respecto al número de hablantes (después del chino, del**

inglés y del hindú). Spanish is the fourth language in importance with respect to the number of speakers (after Chinese, English, and Hindi).

3. **Los hispanos son el grupo minoritario más numeroso de Estados Unidos y una presencia creciente en Canadá.** Hispanics are the most numerous minority group in the United States and a growing presence in Canada.

4. **El español es bello, melodioso y expresivo.** Spanish is beautiful, melodious, and expressive.

5. **Después del inglés, el español es la segunda lengua más usada en el Internet.** After English, Spanish is the second most used language on the Internet.

6. **El español es uno de los idiomas más importantes para los negocios.** Spanish is one of the most important languages for business.

7. **Existe una magnífica literatura en español.** There exists a magnificent literature in Spanish.

8. **Hay un número incontable de lindas canciones y exquisitas películas producidas en España y en Latinoamérica.** There is a countless number of lovely songs and exquisite movies produced in Spain and Latin America.

9. **Miles de restaurantes españoles y latinoamericanos le brindan sus menús.** Thousands of Spanish and Latin American restaurants extend their menus to you.

10. **Abundan los destinos turísticos de belleza excepcional en España y Latinoamérica, con atracciones históricas y culturales.** Tourist destinations of exceptional beauty abound in Spain and Latin America, with historic and cultural attractions.

Let's get started learning Spanish by making some observations about the language in this "Top Ten" list.

Observaciones (Observations)

Once you decide to learn Spanish, take advantage of opportunities to observe it. You can pick up a lot about a language by observation.

1. **Two words for "language."** Did you notice in the list that Spanish has two common words for "language," (*el idioma, la lengua*), while English has two common words for *decir* ("say," "tell")? Like England, Spain was once an imperial power, exposed to diverse influences from around the globe. Consequently, both languages are rich in synonyms.

2. **Contrasting singulars and plurals.** Notice that "business" is singular in English but plural in Spanish: *los negocios*. Think about the word's meaning for a moment. Is there any reason why it has to be one or the other? On the other hand, "politics" is plural in English but singular in Spanish: *la política*. Even the common greetings "Good day" and "Good evening" are different in the two languages because in Spanish these English singulars are plural: *Buenos días. Buenas tardes.*

3. **Which goes first: noun or adjective?** Observing can tell you a great deal about patterns and structures. In case you don't remember (or never learned) about where to put adjectives (descriptive words), look at items 9 and 10 under "Top Ten Reasons to Learn Spanish." How do you say the following in Spanish: "Spanish and Latin American restaurants?" "Tourist destinations?" Say these aloud in Spanish. Does the adjective usually go *before* or *after* the thing or person it's describing? Right. *Restaurantes españoles y latinoamericanos, destinos turísti-*

cos. The adjectives usually go *after* the nouns, just the opposite of English order. Only when an adjective is considered an essential part of what you are describing do you put it before the noun, as in items 7 and 8: *magnífica literatura, lindas canciones, exquisitas películas*. This happens only about 1 percent of the time, so don't worry about it. In common everyday conversation, put the descriptive word *after* what is being described. Nouns first, adjectives second.

Information, Contexts, Words, and Phrases

This is not a book that will teach you grammar. As it has become painfully obvious from the failure of many grammar-driven courses, studying the grammar of a language is not a guarantee of communicating well in it. Instead, you will see and hear patterns, then imitate and internalize them. That is what this book is all about. It gives you information (tips about Spanish and Spanish-speaking cultures), presents a context in which the language is spoken, and provides words, phrases, and key sentences that will open many doors for you.

The Magic of Cognates

Research shows that vocabulary is the single most important factor in language acquisition. You must acquire a critical mass of words and basic patterns to plug them into. Fortunately, many words in Spanish will seem like familiar friends to you because English and Spanish share a large number of *cognates*, words similar in form and meaning, and many of the most common and useful ones have been included in this book. So, tune up your Spanish by reading, repeating, listening to the compact disk, and learning more about this fascinating language and its cultures!

¡Vamos a charlar!

Getting the Spanish out of Your Mouth and into Conversation

Preview

1. What do you say if your taxi driver takes off like James Bond in a car chase or someone is firing Spanish at you a mile a minute?

2. How can you get rid of "gringo" vowel sounds?

3. What Spanish sound does not exist at all in English?

4. Which Spanish letter is pronounced like the *th* in the word *then*?

5. How do you introduce yourself in Spanish?

6. What is meant by *la buena educación*?

7. How many ways can you say "thank you"?

8. When do you give the *besito* or the *abrazo*?

9. To get someone's attention, when would you say *¡Oiga!* and when would you say *¡Disculpe!*?

10. What can you say to a stranger to start a conversation?

Many English speakers say that they feel like a different person when they speak Spanish. This is not surprising. Every language has not only its own sounds, gestures, and cultural characteristics, but also its own unique rhythm (*ritmo*), and Spanish is no exception. English and Spanish are both international languages that are spoken by people from many cultures, but each of these languages has its own peculiar characteristics.

Getting the Feel of Spanish

To learn to speak Spanish well, try to imitate Spanish speakers: the way they look and move and sound. Watch ads or soap operas (*telenovelas*) on TV, go to a concert or salsa club, see a Spanish or Latin American movie. What do you notice about Spanish speakers? Do they stand still when they talk? What do they do with their hands and arms? Do their faces look the same as the faces of English-speaking actors and performers? Don't be afraid that if you try to imitate Spanish speakers, you will lose your own English-speaking identity. It will snap right back in place as soon as you speak English, like a comfortable set of clothes.

A Word About the Different Kinds of Spanish

As you may know from watching and listening to American, Australian, British, Canadian, and Irish movies, there are many types of English, each with its distinctive accent and vocabulary. The same is true of Spanish; these differences are explored in Chapter 9. In this book, you'll be practicing standard Latin American Spanish, which you can use everywhere to make yourself understood.

The Friendly Sounds of Spanish

Almost all of the sounds in Spanish (except for the initial trilled *r* or the double *r*) also exist in English, so you already know how to say them. As an English speaker learning Spanish, you have a great advantage. This is not the same in reverse: English has many sounds that are not present in Spanish, and consequently Spanish speakers have a much harder time pronouncing English.

Even though Spanish sounds are not so difficult for English speakers, the correlation between the sounds and the letters of the alphabet are somewhat different and can be tricky.

Read the following with special care to pronounce the *ll* (the double *l*) like the *y* in "yes," the *ñ* like the *ny* in "canyon," and the *c* before *e* or *i* like *s*. Open your mouth WIDE for all vowels.

TOP TEN Spanish Phrases for a Tourist in Need

1. **¡Más despacio, por favor!** Slow down, please! (Use this when someone fires Spanish at you like a machine gun or your taxi driver takes off like James Bond in a car chase.)

2. **¿Cómo llego a la playa (al centro)?** How do I get to the beach (downtown)?

3. **No comprendo.** I don't understand.

4. **¿Cómo?** What?

5. **¿Cómo se dice... en español?** How do you say . . . in Spanish?

6. **¡Hay una enorme araña en mi cuarto!** There's an enormous spider in my room!

7. **Necesito ayuda (un taxi, un banco).** I need help (a taxi, a bank). (You don't need *yo* with *necesito*, because the subject "I" is clear from the *-o* verb ending.)

8. **¿Dónde está la farmacia (el hospital)?** Where is the pharmacy (the hospital)? (Notice that the *ph* combination is not used in Spanish at all. The letter *f* takes its place.)

9. **¿Dónde están los baños (sanitarios, aseos)?** Where are the bathrooms (washrooms, restrooms)? (The word for "bathroom" has many variations, depending on the region.)

10. **¡Un momento, por favor!** One moment, please!

Getting the Rhythm

Spanish, like English, is an *emphatic* language: every word has *one* stressed syllable that must be emphasized or pronounced more clearly than the others. Think how strange it would sound in English if you were to say "syl-LA-ble" instead of "SYL-la-ble." How do you know which Spanish syllable to emphasize? Just by looking. There are two rules to follow in emphasizing syllables in Spanish.

1. If a Spanish word has a written accent mark, stress the syllable with the accent mark.

2. If a Spanish word ends in a vowel, *n*, or *s*, stress the second-to-last syllable. Otherwise, stress the last syllable.

Let's look at the rules more closely.

Words That Have an Accent Mark

The accent mark *always* occurs in the syllable that you should emphasize. Practice this by saying the following words to tell how wonderful something is. Move your hand (or slap the table) to the rhythm of the words.

TOP TEN Expressive Ways to Say "Wonderful!"

1. **¡Fantástico!** Fantastic!

2. **¡Magnífico!** Magnificent! (used more frequently in Spanish)

3. **¡Chévere!** Terrific! (carries a Caribbean flavor but is used in many other parts of Latin America)

4. **¡Bárbaro!** Super! (either very good or very bad)

5. **¡Lindísimo!** Lovely! (takes the common word *lindo* to the nth degree)

6. **¡Espléndido!** Splendid!

7. **¡Buenísimo!** Good! (takes *bueno* to the nth degree)

8. **¡Increíble!** Incredible! Unbelievable!

9. **¡Bacán!** Cool! (popular approval word in many parts of Latin America)

10. **¡Padrísimo!** Awesome! (This is the word for "father" changed into a superlative adjective—literally, very, very father, used very commonly in Mexico.)

So, in Spanish you can add *-ísimo(-a)* to a descriptive word to increase its expressive power. If the word refers to something masculine, use *-ísimo*. If it refers to something feminine, use *-ísima*. Pronounce the following phrases, saying the syllable with the accent mark on the *í* more emphatically (for example, *ma-LI-si-mo*); notice how expressive it sounds. Be sure to pronounce the *ll* like the *y* in "yes" and the *g* before an *e* or *i* like an *h*.

TOP FIVE Examples of Expressiveness with *-ísimo* Endings

1. **un doctor malo, muy malo, malísimo** a bad doctor, very bad, very, very bad

2. **una mujer bella, muy bella, bellísima** a beautiful woman, very beautiful, very, very beautiful

3. **un traje elegante, muy elegante, elegantísimo** an elegant suit, very elegant, very, very elegant

4. **un restaurante caro, muy caro, carísimo** an expensive restaurant, very expensive, very, very expensive

5. **una persona generosa, muy generosa, generosísima** a generous person, a very generous person, a very, very generous person

English does not have written accent marks, so how do you know which syllable to stress in English? Usually, you just guess or you may look up an unfamiliar word in the dictionary—a word like "antithesis" or "misogynist." Fortunately, in Spanish you don't have to do that. To pronounce a Spanish word with no written accent mark, follow these simple rules:

The Dominant Rhythm: Words That End in a Vowel, *N*, or *S*

Most words have the emphasis on the second-to-last syllable. Pronounce the following, beating out the rhythm with your hand.

Two-syllable words (/ —) as in *CHI-cas, CO-men, CA-sa*
Las chicas comen en casa. The girls eat at home.

Three-syllable words (— / —) as in *a-MI-gos, ca-MI-nan, es-TA-dio*
Los amigos caminan al estadio. The friends walk to the stadium.

Four-syllable words (— — / —) as in *pro-fe-SO-res, par-ti-CI-pan, be-ne-FI-cio*
Los profesores participan en el beneficio. The teachers participate in the benefit.

The Secondary Rhythm: Words That End in a Consonant Other than *N* or *S*

Pronounce the following words and drum out the beat with your hand as you say them.

Two-syllable words (— /) as in *ho-TEL, ciu-DAD, doc-TOR, re-LOJ*
Three-syllable words (— — /) as in *hos-pi-TAL*
Four-syllable words (— — — /) as in *fe-li-ci-DAD*
Five-syllable words (— — — — /) as in *o-por-tu-ni-DAD*

How did you do on that last word? No matter how long or short the word is: just go for the stressed syllable and say it emphatically!

Don't Pronounce the *H*! *(¡No pronuncie la hache!)*

The most important rule for good pronunciation in Spanish is "Don't pronounce the *h*!" A little bit of history will help to understand why.

Spanish is much easier to read and to spell than many other languages. This is no accident. Ever since its founding in 1700, the Spanish Royal Academy (*la Real Academia Española*) has been changing the rules of writing to make it more similar to the spoken language. Because of that, Spanish is very phonetic: it sounds pretty much the way it is written. If you learn to read Spanish, your reading will reinforce your speaking and help you retain the language during times when you do not have oral contact with it.

While in English there are many silent letters (like the final *e* in "late" or the *gh* in "through"), in Spanish there is only the *h*. Perhaps out of respect for history, the Academy has never dropped it.

Read the following useful Spanish words and phrases; the stressed syllable for each word is in capital letters. Make sure to pronounce the *qu* in *¿qué tal?* like a *k* . . . and don't pronounce the *h*!

TOP FIVE Useful Words with *H*

1. **HOM-bre: ¡Hombre! ¡Qué gusto verte!** Man, what a pleasure to see you!

2. **HO-la: Hola, ¿qué tal?** Hi, how's it going?

3. **HA-bla: ¿Habla usted inglés?** Do you speak English?

4. **hay: ¿Hay café? ¿Hay tazas?** Is there any coffee? Are there any cups?

5. **a-HO-ra: ¿Nos vamos ahora?** Are we going now? Shall we get going now?

Notice that the word *hombre* means "man," but it is used when speaking to men or women as an expression of enthusiasm or emotion, similar to "Wow!," "Boy!," or "Man!" in English slang. The word *hay* ("there is" or "there are") is very useful and is the normal way of asking waiters or store clerks if they have something in stock or available. We usually ask, "Do you have . . .?" in these situations: *¿Hay vino?* ("Is there/Do you have any wine?") *¿Hay enchiladas?* ("Are there/Do you have any enchiladas?")

There are no double consonants with the same sound as there are in English words like "committee": the Spanish equivalent is *comité*. In short, what you see is what you say, except for the silent *h*.

🎼 Rehearsal Time

Ritmos. Got the rhythm? Can you find the right syllable to stress in the following Spanish words? Underline the stressed syllable. Check your answers in the Answer Key.

1. plan-tas

2. cho-co-la-te

3. es-pa-ñol

4. e-xa-men

5. bal-cón

6. ter-mó-me-tro

7. in-ter-na-cio-nal

8. u-ni-ver-si-dad

9. in-dus-trio-so

10. in-ter-pre-ta-ción

Now practice pronouncing the words. For the long ones, take a deep breath and go for the stressed syllable. *¡Échale ganas!* ("Go for it!"; literally, "Put some effort into it!")

¿Cómo se llama usted?: Names and Introductions and How to Pronounce Them

Before looking at some Spanish names and how to introduce yourself, let's review how the sounds and letters are pronounced. (If you already know this, you may want to skim this part and move on to "*La buena educación*: Show That You Are *bien educado[-a]*".)

Vowels: Say Them the Spanish Way (with Mouth Wide Open)

English vowels can be pronounced in many different ways, but in Spanish there are essentially just five vowel sounds and they are always the same. These sounds are tense: short and crisp. They keep their full value *even in unstressed syllables*. They do not get dragged out and slide down in tone to "uh" in unaccented syllables as they do in English.

Listen to the sounds of the letter *a* in the English word "bananas." Say it in the normal American English way: "buh-NAnuhs." The unaccented syllables both come out as "uh" with only the stressed middle syllable keeping a true *a* sound. This word also exists in Spanish. Now say it in the Spanish way with every *a* pronounced as a short crisp *ah: bah-NAH-nahs*. Notice that your mouth has to open wide for this. It's hard work, but it sounds so much more Spanish!

To say Spanish vowels properly, keep the vowels short. Exaggerate and you will probably do it just right. Remember to open your mouth WIDE.

Five Vowels: Crisp and Clear

A as in "almond," or "Ah!" at the doc's office: **Ana, amable**
E as the *a* in "ate" or "April" (crisp and short): **Eduardo, Chile**
I as the *e* in "eel" or "eating": **Isabel, Lima**
O as in "Oh no!" (crisp and short, not "O-oo noh-oo!"): **Olga, Colombia**
U as in "boot" or "lute" (never as in "Utah"): **Usted, Cuba**

In Spanish, the letter *y* is a consonant pronounced like the *y* in the English word "yes" when it comes at the beginning of a word (like *yo* or *Yucatán*), but it can also be a vowel when it stands on its own (*y* meaning "and") or comes at the end of a word (for instance, *muy* meaning "very"). As a vowel, it has the same sound as the letter *i* in Spanish. The English sound *i* as in "ice cream" exists in Spanish too: *ai* or *ay* as in the word *hay* ("there is" or "there are").

Many words have a different meaning depending on the unstressed vowel at the end, so clear pronunciation is important to meaning. Read the following word pairs and take care to say the last vowel crisply and clearly with no sliding, so the sound and meaning come through. Remember to open your mouth wide; it might help to practice in the mirror.

TOP FIVE Examples of Word Endings that Change the Meaning

1. **abuelo, abuela** grandfather, grandmother

2. **barro, barra** mud, bar (as in *una barra de chocolate*)

3. **copo, copa** snowflake, wine glass, or alcoholic drink (as in *una copa de vino*)

4. **puerto, puerta** port, door

5. **velo, vela** veil, candle

Tricky Consonants

Because Spanish sounds are not very difficult for English speakers, many learners don't take the time to learn exact pronunciation. This works fine for consonants like *f*, *l*, *m*, *n*, and *x* (and even for *p* and *t*, which are almost the same as in English, but without the small puff of air used by English speakers). However, some consonants are quite different. Turn fuzzy knowledge into exact knowledge. This will help you to speak with confidence.

Let's start with *los siete demonios* ("the seven devils"), consonants with a very different sound, and learn some common names of people and places at the same time. This will help you when you travel and meet Hispanic people to recognize and pronounce their names correctly.

Los siete demonios: g / j / ll / ñ / r / rr / v

g, j While the *h* is never pronounced in Spanish, the sound of *h* as in the English "hat" is common. The *j*, called *la jota* in Spanish, is always pronounced as *h*: *jardín* ("garden"), *jugo* ("juice"). The letter *g* before *e* or *i* also has an *h* sound:

geografía ("geography"), *gigante* ("giant"). In all other positions the *g* sounds like the hard *g* in "go": *gasolina, globo.*

gu To get the hard *g* sound before an *e* or *i*, you need a *u* after the *g*: *guía* ("guide"), *guerra* ("war"), *Guillermo* ("William"). If a *u* has two dots (called *un diéresis*) over it, you pronounce it as a *w*—for example, *lingüista* ("linguist").

ll The *ll* has the sound of *y* in the English word "yes": *llave* ("key"), *llamada* ("call" or "phone call"), *brillante* ("brilliant"), *Puerto Vallarta.*

ñ The *eñe* exists only in Spanish and sounds like the *ny* in "canyon." The European Union put a lot of pressure on members of the Spanish Academy a few years ago to give up this letter in the interest of standardizing the European keyboard, but the Spanish refused. *La señora sueña por la mañana.* ("The lady dreams in the morning.")

r The single *r* is trilled like the double *rr* when it comes at the beginning of a word (see *rr* in the next section). In other positions, it is similar to the British upper-class *r*. Think of Queen Victoria coming back to life and going to Cancún, Mexico, during spring vacation and saying, "I am very, very shocked!" It would sound like "veddy, veddy," and that is the way the Spanish single *r* sounds in the middle or at the end of a word. In North American English, it is similar to the *dd* or *tt* sound in the middle of the words "ladder" and "letter" when you are speaking normally (i.e., not carefully). The tip of your tongue flaps against your upper gums behind your front teeth.

Now use the same sound in the middle of *para* ("for"): *Tengo algo para ti.* ("I have something for you.") Say "ladder." Now say *María, Laura.* This flap *r* makes your accent sound very Spanish, especially when it comes between two vowels, so it is worthwhile to practice it.

rr This is the most challenging sound in Spanish, the one that does not exist in English: the trilled *r*, which sounds like a motor or a mini-air hammer. This comes naturally to some

English speakers and is impossible for others, but most people can acquire a pretty good simulation with some practice. The tongue is in the same position as for the flap *r* but you breathe out and just keep it flapping very fast. This is always the sound of the double *rr* and also for the single *r* when it begins a word: *perro* ("dog"), *corre* ("run"), *terremoto* ("earthquake"), *Roberto* ("Robert"). *El perro corre. Roberto corre también. Roberto corre tras el perro durante el terremoto.*

Give the trilled *r* sound your best shot. But don't get discouraged if it doesn't sound perfect. They say that even some native speakers can't pronounce it very well. Maybe that's why the following tongue twister (*trabalenguas*) exists in different versions and is so popular among children in Latin America. When you say it fast, it sounds like a moving train. Practice it a few times and come up with something as close as you can to the trilled *r* sound.

R con R, cigarro	*R* with *R*, cigar
R con R, barril	*R* with *R*, barrel
Rápido corren los carros	Fast go the cars
que van en el ferrocarril	that run on the railroad train

v This is pronounced exactly like the letter *b* in Spanish. At the beginning of a word, the sound of both *b* and *v* in Spanish is like the *b* in the English word "boy," but a little softer: *Bueno. ¡Vamos! Victoria, Víctor.* In other positions, the sound is even more relaxed: *abajo* ("underneath"), *lobos* ("wolves"), *Evita.*

There is another consonant that can cause problems: *c*. The Spanish *c* has an *s* sound before *e* or *i* and a hard *c* sound in all other positions: *ciudad, Barcelona* (soft); *canta, clínica* (hard). Because this parallels English usage, it doesn't cause much of a problem.

Read the following Spanish names aloud, pronouncing them as clearly as you can. Remember that Spanish syllables are open, generally starting with a consonant and ending with a vowel.

TOP TEN Typical Spanish Names Containing Tricky Consonants

1. **Ángel** (a popular name for boys, related to religion)

2. **Guillermo** (equivalent of William, with nicknames *Memo* in Mexico or *Guille* in South America)

3. **Héctor** (from the classics, like many boys' names in Spanish, such as *César* or *Homero*)

4. **Jaime** (one equivalent of James; others are *Diego* and *Santiago*)

5. **Jesús** (a common religious name for boys; the feminine counterpart is *Jesusa*—these do not imply any disrespect)

6. **Bárbara** (written just as in English, but the flap *r* makes it sound very different)

7. **Concepción** (a popular name for girls, derived from a religious concept, the Immaculate Conception of the Virgin Mary, the mother of Jesus; in Mexico and Central America, the nickname is *Concha* or *Conchita*)

8. **Genoveva** (equivalent of Genevieve)

9. **Margarita** (equivalent of Margaret; *una margarita* refers to a daisy or the tequila drink)

10. **Refugio** (another popular name for girls, derived from a religious concept, the Virgin Mary being the *refuge* of the helpless)

The Letter Q and Sounds That Animals Make

Animal sounds are represented differently by speakers of different languages, as you will find out if you listen to the stories and songs of Spanish-speaking children. What does the rooster say in Spanish? *Qui-qui-ri-quí*. The letter *q* is always followed by a *u* and pronounced like the English *k*. To get the "qua" sound (of "quality") in Spanish, use *cua*, as in *cuaderno* ("notebook") or *cuadro* ("picture"). This is also what the frog says: *cua cua*.

Read aloud the animal sounds as Spanish speakers say them and compare them with the English.

TOP TEN Sounds That Animals Make

1. **gallo** (rooster): **qui-qui-ri-quí**

2. **rana** (frog): **cua cua** (variant: **croac croac**)

3. **gallina** (hen): **cloc cloc**

4. **gato** (cat): **miau miau**

5. **oveja** (sheep): **beee beee**

6. **pájaro** (bird): **fliu fliu**

7. **perro** (dog): **güau güau**

8. **pollo** (baby chick): **pío pío**

9. **puerco** (pig): **joinc joinc**

10. **vaca** (cow): **muuu muuu**

Read this old traditional children's song that talks about baby chicks and imitates their sound.

Los pollitos dicen:
¡pío, pío, pío!
cuando tienen hambre
cuando tienen frío.

The little chicks say:
peep, peep, peep!
when they are hungry
when they are cold.

La gallina busca
el maíz y el trigo.
Duermen los pollitos
bajo su abrigo.

The hen looks for
the corn and wheat grains.
The little chicks sleep
under the shelter of her wing.

Refining Your Spanish Accent with *D* and *Z*

Two consonants that often go unpracticed because they seem so similar to their English counterparts are *d* and *z*. But there are subtle differences; learn them and you can make your Spanish sound more like a native speaker's.

d   This sounds a lot like the English *d* at the beginning of a word: *Daniel, dinero*. However, in between vowels or at the end of a word, *d* is pronounced like the *th* in "then": *to-dos, es-ta-do, Da-vid*. These words sound like *to-thos, es-ta-thos, Da-vith*, with the *th* as in the word "then" and *not* as in the word "teeth." *Es de Estados Unidos*. (He or she is from the United States.) Say it first with the English *d*, then with the Spanish *th* sound and listen to the difference.

z   This does not have the *z* sound of "buzz"; it has the *s* sound of "sun": *zapatos* (sa-pa-tos), *zona* (so-na), *luz* (lus). While the Spanish *z* always has the *s* sound, the Spanish *s* takes on a sound similar to the English *z* when it precedes the letter *m*: *mismo*.

Show you have mastered these tricky consonants as you read the following list.

TOP TEN Famous Places in Spain and Latin America

1. **Cartagena: una ciudad histórica en la costa de Colombia** a historic city on the coast of Colombia

2. **Granada: una bella ciudad en el sur de España** a beautiful city in the south of Spain

3. **Guanajuato: una ciudad mexicana famosa por su arquitectura colonial** a Mexican city famous for its colonial architecture

4. **Mazatlán: un destino turístico en la costa del Pacífico, en México** a tourist destination on the Pacific coast of Mexico

5. **Medellín: una ciudad importante de Colombia** an important city in Colombia

6. **Managua: la capital de Nicaragua** the capital of Nicaragua

7. **Querétero: una hermosa ciudad colonial de México** a lovely colonial city in Mexico

8. **Quito: la capital de Ecuador** the capital of Ecuador

9. **Sevilla: la ciudad española que muchos llaman «Sevilla, la maravilla»** the Spanish city called by many "the marvel"

10. **Tegucigalpa: la capital de Honduras** the capital of Honduras

---

Las presentaciones: How to Introduce Yourself in Spanish

Now that you've learned a bit about how to pronounce Spanish names, you might want to learn how to get to know some of the people who use them. In most parts of the Spanish-speaking world, you do not have to wait until someone else introduces you. It is considered normal to take the initiative and introduce yourself.

TOP TEN Useful Phrases for Introductions in Spanish

1. **Hola. Me llamo...** Hi. My name is . . . (Literally, I call myself . . . ; this is the most common way of telling what your name is.)

2. **Hola. Mi nombre es...** Hi. My name is . . . (much less common than the above)

3. **¿Cómo se llama usted?** What's your name? (Literally, How do you call yourself?; the most common way to ask this.)

4. **¿Cuál es su nombre?** What's your name? (much less common than the above)

5. **Mucho gusto.** Pleased to meet you. (Literally, A great deal of pleasure.)

6. **El gusto es mío.** The pleasure is mine.

7. **Encantado(-a).** Delighted. (Use the -*o* ending if you are male, -*a* if female.)

8. **Encantado(-a) de conocerlo(-la).** Delighted (literally, enchanted) to meet you. (Again, use the -*o* ending if you are male, the -*a* if you are female. Use the *lo* at the end of *conocer* if the person you are meeting is male, the *la* if female.)

9. **Un placer.** A pleasure.

10. **Igualmente.** Likewise. I am also pleased to meet you. (Literally, Equally.)

Rehearsal Time

Presentaciones. (Introductions.) Complete these introductions with the missing words. Check your answers in the Answer Key.

JORGE: Hola. Mi (1) _____ es Jorge. ¿ (2) _____
    es su nombre?
LAURA: Me (3) _____ Laura.
JORGE: Mucho (4) _____, Laura.
LAURA: El (5) _____ es mío, Jorge.

HÉCTOR: Hola. Me (6) _____ Héctor Benavides. ¿Cuál
    es su (7) _____?
GUILLERMO: Mi nombre (8) _____ Guillermo
    Jiménez.
HÉCTOR: Encantado de (9) _____.
GUILLERMO: (10) _____.

La pronunciación. How sure are you now about Spanish pronunciation? Circle the letter of the correct answer for each statement or question. Check your answers in the Answer Key.

1. What do you say for the *h* in a Spanish word?
   a. a very light *h* sound without a puff of air
   b. a soft *j* as in the English "jump"
   c. nothing

2. Except when it appears at the beginning of a word, the Spanish *y* has the same sound as the letter
   a. e
   b. i
   c. j

3. How many essential vowel sounds are there in Spanish?
   a. 5
   b. 10
   c. 20

4. In comparison with the vowels in English, the Spanish vowels are
   a. shorter
   b. longer
   c. higher in pitch

5. Which of these Spanish words contains the sound of *h* as in "hat"?
   a. ahora
   b. hijo
   c. guía

6. In Spanish, what letter makes the sound of the *y* in "yes"?
   a. k
   b. ll
   c. q

7. What is the difference between the *b* and the *v* in Spanish?
   a. The *b* is usually stronger than the *v*.
   b. The *b* is usually weaker than the *v*.
   c. There is no difference.

8. How do you pronounce *ü*, as in *bilingüe* ("bilingual")?
   a. like a soft *ph*
   b. like a *q*
   c. like a *w*

9. How do you pronounce the Spanish letter *d* when it comes between two vowels as in *nada*?
   a. like the *d* in "darling"
   b. like the *th* in "then"
   c. like the *th* in "breath"

10. How do you pronounce the *z* in Latin American Spanish?
    a. like the *s* in sun
    b. like the double *z* in "buzz"
    c. like a *ts*

Remember that the most important rule about accents is this: Everyone has an accent. There is no perfect way to speak any language. If you are understood and able to communicate, that is *¡lo importante* ("what is important")!

La buena educación: Show That You Are *bien educado(-a)*

How you speak and what you say are all part of *la buena educación,* "good upbringing," a very important trait in the eyes of Spaniards and Latin Americans. This is not related to schooling but to how you treat others. Usually the first impression of a person conveys this by his or her way of acting, dressing, and speaking. Personal hygiene and courtesy are of primary importance, from the look of the fingernails to table manners to the rituals of politeness.

The first rule of courtesy is to always greet everyone; acknowledge their presence. If you enter a bakery, for example, you greet the person there before placing your order. *Buenos días, señora. Buenas tardes, señor.* ("Good morning, ma'am. Good afternoon, sir.") Notice that *día* is masculine, so it's *Buenos días.* Spanish speakers are often astonished while visiting a home in the United States or Canada to see children pass by them without any greeting and even at times without saying anything to their own parents. This to the Spanish and Latin American mind is *mal educado.* The custom is that you show respect by greeting everyone. There are many words for greetings.

TOP TEN Ways of Greeting Someone, from Formal to Casual

1. **Buenos días.** Good morning. Good day. (somewhat formal and used until noon; open your mouth wide for endings)

2. **Buenas tardes.** Good afternoon. (somewhat formal; use this when it is still light out)

3. **Buenas noches.** Good night. Good evening. (use this when it is already dark)

4. **¿Cómo está usted?** (formal "you," singular) **¿Cómo están ustedes?** (formal "you," plural) How are you?

5. **¿Cómo le va?** (formal "you" for one person) **¿Cómo les va?** (formal "you" for more than one person) How are you doing? (slightly more casual than the above)

6. **Hola, ¿qué tal?** Hi, how's it going? (informal but not disrespectful and can be said anytime to anyone)

7. **¿Cómo te encuentras?** How are you doing? (literally, How do you find yourself?; somewhat casual, use with friends or acquaintances of your own age or with a child)

8. **¿Cómo estás, amigo(-a)?** How are you, pal? (for a friend, with *-o* ending for male and *-a* for female)

9. **¿Qui' ubo? ¿Quí' úbole?** How ya' doin'? What's up? (very casual, used in Mexico and other parts of Latin America for one or more friends)

10. **¿Qué tal, hombre? ¿Qué onda?** Hey, man, what's happenin'? (very casual slang expression for good friends who are *en la onda* or "on the sound wave"—i.e., "with it," like you!)

The advantage of greeting number 6, *Hola, ¿qué tal?*, is that you can use it with anyone without worrying about whether the "you" should be formal *usted* or informal *tú*, singular or plural. You can always add one or two of the other greetings because many people use two or three together, for example, *Hola, ¿qué tal? Buenos días.*

or *Hola, ¿qué tal? ¿Cómo están ustedes?* So the greeting is a good starting point while you collect your thoughts.

The expression "Good night" in English is usually a way of saying good-bye, not a greeting. In Spanish, *Buenas noches* is both: the common way of saying "Good evening" after the sun has gone down or one way of saying good-bye at night.

How to Say "You" in Spanish

In general it is best to use the formal *usted* for "you" until you are sure of what is expected, except when speaking to a child, when you generally use the *tú* form. Use *ustedes* when you are talking with more than one person. Later on you can always change from *usted* to the informal *tú* with a person you consider a real *amigo* or *amiga*, especially if you notice they are using *tú* with you. (See Appendix A for more discussion of this and for a description of the regional differences in this usage.) Notice that two abbreviations are very common for *usted* and *ustedes*. They are capitalized and have a period at the end to show they are abbreviations. They are all pronounced exactly the same, as *usted* or *ustedes*.

usted	Ud.	Vd.
ustedes	Uds.	Vds.

The abbreviation *Vds.* seems odd but it has a historical explanation because *usted* comes from the old-fashioned phrase *Vuestra merced* (Your Grace), which was used for the nobility. That is why *usted* patterns with the third-person verb forms and not the second: *Ud. es muy amable* (not *eres muy amable*). This was also true in English in colonial times: "Your Grace is [*not* are] very kind."

Greeting and Saying Good-Bye: *El toque, el besito, el abrazo*

The essential mark of courtesy in the Hispanic world is that you acknowledge the presence of someone else, and usually that involves not just words but also actions. This can mean being solicitous for their welfare and noticing if they need something. It also means that generally when greeting or saying good-bye people touch each other in various ways. If you see two men grabbing each other by the shoulders, embracing, and patting each other or two women kissing and hugging, you might think that they are siblings who were separated at birth. But, no! In fact, it's possible they had lunch together only a few hours earlier.

Although there are some variations in different regions, the following are the usual customs of the Spanish-speaking world regarding touching when a person is introduced to someone or happens to encounter a person he or she already knows.

 Ways People Interact When Meeting, Greeting, or Saying Good-Bye in Spanish

1. **beso en la mejilla** kiss on the cheek; usually it's up to the woman to come close and extend her cheek for a kiss from the man, which is usually so light as to almost just brush the cheek (unless there is a close bond of family or friendship). Between two women, either one can take the initiative, or at times they simply brush cheeks. No kiss between two men unless they are relatives or very good friends.

2. **beso en las dos mejillas** kiss on both cheeks; this occurs when two people haven't seen each other in quite some time or when they have been through difficult times. The same as above, but on both cheeks. (In Spain, this is the norm.)

3. **beso en la boca** kiss on the mouth; never! If someone does this to you during an introduction or casual encounter, he or she is trying to take advantage and should be pushed away and reprimanded with, *Un poco de respeto, ¡por favor!*

4. **beso en la mano** kiss on the hand; not very common. Sometimes a man will kiss a woman's hand as a gesture of gallantry, in imitation of older European ways. This may happen too if someone wishes to show great respect to an older person or someone in authority, such as a priest.

5. **besos para los niños** kisses for children; Spaniards and Latin Americans love children and they kiss and hug them a lot. Well-bred children usually offer their cheeks to adults and expect to be kissed, unless they are from the countryside, in which case they may be more reserved.

6. **dar la mano** to shake someone's hand; the men usually shake hands. A woman may also extend her hand rather than offer her cheek.

7. **abrazo** hug; men and/or women friends often hug each other when they meet or say good-bye.

8. **abrazo repetido** repeated hugs; really close men and/or women friends often hug each other several times if they want to show their affection and friendship.

9. **palmotearse** patting each other; men often pat each other on the shoulders or arms to show their affection.

10. **combinación de besito y abrazo** combination of little kiss and hug; these gestures of affection can be combined; it is certainly common to have a quick little kiss in addition to a hug between two good friends.

It's clear that in the Spanish-speaking world, people touch each other much more when they say hello and good-bye than they do in the United States and Canada (except for Quebec). There is nothing wrong or odd about this. In fact, many cultures have greetings that involve hugging and kissing as the Latinos do (without suffering negative consequences to their health). If you don't feel comfortable, though, you can always back away with an excuse such as *Perdón. Tengo un resfrío terrible.* ("Excuse me. I have a terrible cold.") No one will get upset because of this.

On the other hand, some people feel that northerners suffer more from depression not just from the colder climate, but because they don't receive much caressing or physical contact to show affection. So, consider giving the *besito, abrazo,* or *apretón de manos* (hand squeezing) a try and you might even find you like it!

The Doors of Courtesy

Many English-speaking people learn an old rhyme in childhood:

> *The doors of courtesy have two keys.*
> *One is "thank you" and the other is "please."*

These "keys" are important in Spanish-speaking cultures, too. Here are some variations on them. First of all, imagine that you are staying at a hotel and want to ask for the key to your room.

TOP FIVE Ways to Ask for a Key, from Casual to Formal

1. **¡La llave, porfa!** Key, please! (casual, slang)

2. **La llave, por favor.** The key, please.

3. **Favor de darme la llave.** Please give me the key.

4. **¿Podría usted darme la llave?** Could you give me the key?

5. **¿Me podría dar la llave, por favor?** Could you please give me the key? (very polite)

TOP TEN Ways to Say Thank You, from Simple to Very Grateful

1. **Gracias.** Thanks. Thank you.

2. **Muchas gracias.** Thank you very much.

3. **Muchas gracias, muy amable.** Thank you very much, very kind of you.

4. **Mil gracias.** Thanks very much. (Literally, A thousand thanks.)

5. **Muchísimas gracias.** Many thanks.

6. **Muchísimas gracias. Estoy muy agradecido(-a).** Thank you so very much. I am very grateful.

7. **Muchísimas gracias. Usted ha sido muy amable conmigo.** Thank you so very much. You have been very kind to me.

8. **Se lo agradezco muchísimo.** I am very, very grateful to you.

9. **Se lo agradezco infinitamente.** I am extremely grateful to you.

10. **Muchas gracias por su bondad. Estoy muy agradecido(-a).** Thank you so much for your kindness. I am very grateful.

The rituals for greeting people discussed earlier are also used when saying good-bye. Indeed, the expression "saying good-bye" seems woefully inadequate to translate the Spanish verb *despedirse*, which is closer to the old-fashioned English expression "to take leave," because the *despedida* involves actions as well as words (*toque, abrazo, besito*). Interestingly, Spanish good-byes are usually shorter than English ones. English speakers often seem to linger endlessly at the doorway, talking on and on, as though they need to generate the right climate of social warmth before leaving. In the Latino world, it's "We touch each other, then we go." Here are some words and phrases to use when you take leave of your Spanish-speaking friends, *cuando usted se despide de sus amigos.*

TOP TEN Ways of Saying Good-Bye (Taking Leave of Someone)

1. **Adiós.** Good-bye. (literally, to God; as in the English equivalent, which comes from the old phrase "God be wi' ye")

2. **Hasta luego.** See you later.

3. **Hasta la vista.** Until the next time we see each other. (Literally, Until sight.)

4. **Adiós, hasta la vista (hasta luego).** Good-bye, until the next time we see each other (see you later). (It's common to combine two or three of the above phrases.)

5. **Hasta pronto.** See you soon. (Literally, Until soon.)

6. **Hasta la próxima (vez).** Until the next time.

7. **Hasta la semana (el mes) que viene.** Until next week (month).

8. **Hasta el sábado que viene.** Until next Saturday.

9. **Nos vemos pronto.** We'll see each other soon.

10. **Me voy. ¡Chau!** I'm going. Bye! (*Chau* is from the Italian *ciao* and is used a lot in the Southern Cone. Sometimes the diminutive is added for affection and it becomes *¡Chaucito!*)

Cortesía y bien hablar, cien puertas te abrirán.
Courtesy and good speaking manners will open
a hundred doors for you.
—SPANISH PROVERB

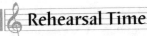 Rehearsal Time

La buena educación. What do you remember about *la buena edu-cación*? Circle the letter of the correct option for each statement or question. Check your answers in the Answer Key.

1. To be *bien educado(-a)*, you need to have
   a. received a good upbringing at home.
   b. graduated from a good university.
   c. traveled widely and learned a second language.

2. A good way to greet two friends you meet up with at the market is
   a. ¿Cómo le va?
   b. ¿Cómo te encuentras?
   c. Hola, ¿qué tal?

3. To say "good evening" after dark, you say
   a. Buenos días.
   b. Buenas tardes.
   c. Buenas noches.

4. What is the correct abbreviation of *ustedes*?
   a. Uds.
   b. Vds.
   c. either one of these

5. In Spain and Latin America the usual greeting between two women includes
   a. un beso en la boca.
   b. un beso en la mano.
   c. un beso en la mejilla.

6. To tell someone you are very grateful to them, you can say, *Estoy muy...*
   a. agradecido(-a).
   b. favorecido(-a).
   c. inclinado(-a).

7. ¿Cómo se dice *hugs* en español?
   a. abrazos
   b. besos
   c. toques

8. To say, "Until next week," you can say, *Hasta la semana...*
   a. luego.
   b. la vista.
   c. que viene.

Cómo iniciar una conversación: How to Start a Conversation with a Stranger

Before we say good-bye to this chapter, let's pull everything together and imagine that you are on a beach, in a park, in a museum, or at an outdoor café and you want to start up a conversation so you can try out the Spanish you have learned. The first thing to do is to get someone's attention. After that, you can present the statement or question you hope will launch a conversation. Remember that in general Latinos are known for being open, tolerant, and *simpáticos*.

TOP FIVE Ways to Begin Talking to a Stranger

1. **Perdone usted.** Excuse me. (a common way to start out, but you have to have eye contact)

2. **Oiga, señor (señorita, señora).** Excuse me (Please talk to me), sir (miss, ma'am). (This is a good thing to say in Spain or South America if you are not sure that the person sees you; *Oiga* is a polite subjunctive form meaning "Hear," but it can sound somewhat rude to Mexicans or Central Americans.)

3. **Disculpe, señor (señorita, señora).** Excuse me, sir, (miss, ma'am). (This is the best way to get someone's attention in Mexico or Central America.)

4. **Perdone la interrupción.** Excuse me for interrupting you.

5. **Buenos días. ¿Podría usted ayudarme?** Good day. Could you help me? ("Please" is not necessary because this is in the conditional, but you can always add *por favor*.)

After you have the person's attention, you then present a topic, which can be something you need, something you see, or the direct approach, a straightforward expression of interest in getting to know the other person.

TOP TEN Conversation Starters, from the Indirect to the Very Direct

1. **Perdone. ¿Sabe usted qué hora es?** Excuse me. Do you know what time it is?

2. **Oiga. (Disculpe.) ¿Sabría usted dónde está el correo (el museo de arte)?** Do you know where the post office (art

museum) is? (From this, you can start to talk about the letters you have to mail or the paintings you want to see.)

3. **Perdone la interrupción. Busco una tienda (farmacia). ¿Podría usted ayudarme?** Excuse me for interrupting you. I'm looking for a store (pharmacy). Could you help me? (To continue, talk about what you want to buy.)

4. **Oiga, ¿conoce usted el hotel Tres Marías? Estoy perdido(-a).** Excuse me. Do you know where the Tres Marías Hotel is? I'm lost. (Then you can expand on why you are lost or on where you come from and how different the streets are there.)

5. **¿Podría usted ayudarme? Busco un restaurante "bueno, bonito y barato".** Could you help me? I'm looking for a "good, lovely, and cheap" restaurant. (Mexicans call these the 3 *B*'s that you always look for in things. Try to start a conversation about food or restaurants.)

6. **Buenas tardes. Tengo una pregunta. ¿Dónde podría alquilar una bicicleta (patines)?** Good afternoon. I have a question. Where could I rent a bicycle (skates)?

7. **Perdone. ¿Podría usted decirme algo sobre este monumento (edificio)?** Excuse me. Could you tell me something about this monument (building)?

8. **Buenas tardes. ¡Qué bella vista!, ¿no?** Good afternoon. What a beautiful view, don't you think? (This is a direct attempt to start a conversation and depends on there being a lovely view in front of you, unless you opt for irony and say this in front of a place that is just the opposite. You will know right away if the other person is in the mood for chatting.)

9. **Buenas noches. Me llamo... ¿Cómo se llama usted?** Good evening. My name is . . . What is your name? (This very direct approach should be accompanied by a big smile, *una sonrisa muy grande*. You win or lose in the first few moments.)

10. **Hola, ¿qué tal? Soy de... ¿De dónde es usted?** Hi, how are you doing? I'm from . . . Where are you from? (As direct as they come, this approach gives you the advantage of being able to talk about your home country and wherever the other person comes from.)

Those Important Hesitation Words

When an English speaker doesn't know what to say next, he or she often stalls by making these sounds: "uh . . . uh . . . " or "um . . . um . . . " This is not usually done by Spanish speakers. In Spanish, people use hesitation words when they don't know what to say and need to think for a few moments.

TOP FIVE   Common Hesitation Words Used in Spanish in Place of "Uh" or "Um"

1. **este**

2. **bueno**

3. **pues**

4. **bien**

5. **pues bien**

So, for example, if you want to tell someone to meet you at a restaurant but can't immediately remember its name, you might say, *Nos vemos esta noche en... este... pues... Los pinos, en el restaurante Los pinos.* (We'll see each other tonight at the . . . uh . . . uh . . . Pines, the Pines Restaurant.) So don't be surprised if you hear these words sprinkled around in everyday conversations, and consider adopting one for your own use when you need to stall for time.

As the Spanish say, *Bien comenzado, medio acabado* or "Well begun, half done (halfway there)." So get up your courage and give Spanish conversation a try!

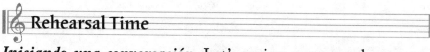

Rehearsal Time

Iniciando una conversación. Let's review some good conversational openers in Spanish. Read the following and fill in the missing word for each phrase. Check your answers against the Answer Key.

1. In Mexico, to get the attention of a woman who is a stranger, say _____, *señorita.*

2. In Spain to get the attention of a man who is not looking at you, you could say, _____, *señor.*

3. Using an indirect method to start a conversation, ask for information, such as where the post office is: *¿Sabría usted dónde está el _____?*

4. Alternatively, try to elicit an opinon about a visual cue, such as a lovely view: *¡Qué bella _____!, ¿no?*

5. Or, you can gamble everything on the direct approach and try to find out where the person is from: *Hola, ¿qué tal? Soy de... ¿De _____ es usted?*

Sonido y sentido

Active Listening . . . or
Hang in There!

Preview

1. What's the gesture for "Watch out!" among Spanish speakers?

2. How do they say "Ow!," "Oops!," or "Yuck!"?

3. What word can you use to call for help in an emergency?

4. What do *compa*, *bici*, and *compu* mean?

5. How about *ai*, *to'l*, and *'tons*?

6. What's the difference between *¿Está Gabriel en casa?* and *¿Está en casa Gabriel?*

7. What can you say when you don't (or do!) understand someone?

8. If you hear someone say, *¿Mande?*, what country is he or she from?

9. How do you ask about the meaning of a word in Spanish ("What does . . . mean?")?

10. How can you agree with someone or disagree without being disagreeable?

Sonido y sentido: "sound and sense." Sometimes it's hard to put the two together. But when it comes to understanding Spanish, you can develop a strategy: active listening.

For example, two English speakers sit down at a Mexican restaurant to order lunch. One asks the waiter, *¿Qué nos recomienda?*, a phrase he dug out of a travel book just before walking in. The waiter spews forth a long response, and our traveler *no entiende ni papa* ("doesn't understand beans"—literally, "not even a potato"). His inclination is to just give up and point to the menu. Fortunately, his companion hears one word that he thinks he understands: *pollo.* *¿Pollo?*, he asks hesitantly. The waiter, this time more slowly, repeats what he said the first time. Now the persistent companion seizes on another word: *arroz.* He's got it! What the waiter had said was: *Pues, les sugiero que prueben el arroz con pollo... hoy está sabrosísimo.* ("I suggest that you try the chicken with rice . . . it's delicious today.") Both diners enjoy the best thing being served at the moment.

Later the waiter comes back. He rattles off a long speech, none of which either of the English speakers understands. One of them, at a total loss, says *No comprendo.* His friend, once again concentrating hard, thinks: What is this guy probably saying? We've just eaten; now what is he asking us? He guesses that the list of incomprehensible things the waiter rattled off are dessert choices. He asks *¿Hay flan?* Bingo! The waiter brings them a delicious dessert (*flan* is a custard pudding).

There are many strategies that people use to communicate, but using background knowledge and paying attention to context clues are two of the most important. In this chapter you'll look at ways to make the most of what you've got: active listening.

¡Zas!, ¡Bah!, ¡Huácala!: Interjecciones y gestos

First, consider the obvious: nonverbal communication. Body language, gestures, and some common interjections can give crucial context clues to the meaning of a word or phrase. With a little background knowledge about these topics, you will be able to use active listening skills to boost your Spanish comprehension.

Understanding Body Language

In general, Hispanics may sit or stand closer to each other than English speakers do. They are more likely to touch—for instance, two women may sit very close to each other or walk arm-in-arm. Men may embrace or put their arms around each other's shoulders. Greetings and leave-takings may involve hugs, kisses, or hearty pats on the back. It's considered very rude to talk with one's back turned to someone; always turn around and say *Perdón* if you notice that you have turned your back on someone—for instance, at a social gathering.

However, some body language is the same in the Hispanic world as among English speakers. Many gestures, for example, are the same. Spanish speakers shrug their shoulders to indicate that they don't know something, and they hit the palm of the hand to the head to say "How silly!" or "I should have remembered!" They put one hand to the ear for "What?" and shake their heads "yes" or "no." (Shaking the head "no" may be accompanied by a gesture with the index finger pointed up and wagging back and forth; this reinforces the "no" and is likely to be used when something is prohibited—for example, don't walk on the lawn or don't touch that museum piece.) You may see them holding an index finger to the mouth to mean "Shhh!," as English speakers do, or putting the thumb and fingers in the shape of a mouth opening and closing several times to indicate "Blah, blah, blah!" They touch wood for luck, and they hold the thumb and index finger up in a circle to mean *¡Perfecto!*—all gestures that are used in the United States and Canada.

There are also gestures that are not used among English speakers:

TOP TEN Common Gestures and Their Meanings

1. **¡Ojo!** Pay attention! Look! (The index finger is held vertically under the eye, pointing toward the eye.)

2. **Más o menos.** Regular. Okay. (The hand is held palm down and tilted back and forth.)

3. **Dinero (o falta de dinero).** Money (or lack of money). (The thumb rubs against the index and middle fingers.)

4. **Un momento.** Just a minute. (The thumb and index finger are almost touching, indicating a small space between them.)

5. **Está loco(-a).** He's (She's) crazy. (The index finger is held to the temple and the hand is rotated.)

6. **¡Tacaño(-a)!** What a tightwad! How cheap! (The hand is touching the elbow.)

7. **¡Qué problema! ¡Dios mío!** What a problem! Oh, dear! That was close! Or **¡Cantidad!** A bunch! (The wrist is held out and the hand is shaken quickly; the hand is in a position as

though playing a guitar except that the elbow is in and the wrist is limp.)

8. **Vamos a comer.** Let's eat. (The fingers are touching the thumb and held to the mouth shaping a kiss; the elbow is down so the forearm is vertical.)

9. **Está para chuparse los dedos. ¡Qué rico!** How tasty! (Literally, It's to lick the fingers.) Delicious! (A bit similar to gesture 8; the person kisses the thumb and fingers together and then extends them as the hand moves away from the mouth.)

10. **La cuenta, por favor.** Check, please. (The person pretends to write with an imaginary pencil.)

If you watch Spanish-language movies, you will see these gestures, or you might ask a Hispanic friend to show them to you in person.

Sometimes a single sound can also carry a lot of meaning, with no words at all.

TOP TEN Sounds That Have Meaning

1. **¡Huy!** Wow! Ooh! Whoa! (unpleasant surprise) *¡Huy! ¡Qué fría está el agua!* Wow! How cold the water is! *¡Huy! ¡Qué araña más fea!* Whoa! What an ugly spider!

2. **¡Bah!** Whatever! Yeah, right! (disdain or skepticism) *¡Bah! Eso no me importa.* That doesn't matter to me. I don't care. *¡Bah! No te creo.* Yeah, right! I don't believe you.

3. **¿Eh?** Okay? (after a statement, similar to *¿de acuerdo?*) *Haz la tarea, ¿eh?* Do the job (task, homework), okay?

4. **¡Eh!** Hey! *¡Eh! Esas llaves son mías.* Hey! Those are my keys.

5. **¡Ay!** Oh! (pain, fear) *¡Ay, pero qué susto me dio!* Oh, what a scare it gave me! *¡Ay, qué dolor! Me golpeé.* Ow, that hurts (what pain)! I hit myself.

6. **¡Zas!** Presto! Zap! Bam! (indicating something is done or happens rapidly) *Ella iba caminando y ¡Zas! se tropezó con la silla.* She was walking along and Bam! she ran into the chair.

7. **¡Ups!** Oops! *¡Ups! Me equivoqué de habitación.* Oops! I have the wrong room. (I made a mistake with the room.)

8. **Hmm...** Yum . . . *Hmm... ¡qué sabroso está este pollo!* Yum . . . how delicious this chicken is!

9. **¡Huaca! ¡Huácala!** Yuck! (used in Mexico, Central America, Caribbean) *Esta comida no huele bien... ¡Huácala!* This food doesn't smell good . . . Yuck!

10. **¡Órale!** All right! Okay! (used in Mexico to accept an invitation or encourage someone to do something) *¿Quieres bailar? —¡Órale!* Do you want to dance? —All right! *¿Le pregunto a esa chica si quiere bailar conmigo? —¡Órale, pues!* Shall I ask that girl if she wants to dance with me? —Go for it!

There are some other special expressions like the preceding one that are also used in Mexico. *¡Úhule!* ("Yikes!") usually indicates a put-down; it's used in Mexico and parts of Central America. For example: *¿Qué te dijo? ¿Mentiroso? ¡Úhule!* ("What did he say to you? Liar? Yikes!") The expression *¡Ándale!* means "Right! That's it!" *¿Cómo va la rumba? ¿Así? —¡Ándale!* ("How does the rumba go? Like this?" "That's it! Way to go!") Finally, in Mexico, Central America, and parts of Colombia you will hear *¡Híjole!* used to express surprise, meaning something like "Wow!," "Darn!," or "Holy smoke!" For example, *¿Sabes que Graciela sale para Europa mañana? —¡Híjole! Debo llamarla.* ("Do you know that Graciela is leaving for Europe tomorrow?" "Wow! I should call her."), or *¡Híjole! Se me olvidó el cumpleaños de mi mamá.* ("Holy smoke! I forgot my mom's birthday.")

Here are some very common interjections that consist of just one word:

TOP TEN Very Useful One-Word Interjections

1. **¡Lástima!** Too bad!

2. **¡Suerte!** Good luck!

3. **¡Cuidado!** Be careful!

4. **¡Tranquilo!** Calm down! (*Tranquila* would be used if you are talking to a girl or woman.)

5. **¡Ánimo!** Hang in there! Buck up!

6. **¡Caramba!** Wow!

7. **¡Socorro!** Help!

8. **¡Oiga!** (*usted* form) **¡Oye!** (*tú* form) Listen! Hey! (used to get someone's attention)

9. **¡Basta!** That's enough!

10. **¡Hombre!** Wow! Man! (used when addressing women as well as men)

The first two of these one-word interjections can be preceded by *¡Qué... !*: *¡Qué lástima! ¡Qué suerte! ¡Qué... !* often means "What . . . !" or "How . . . !" It can precede nouns or adjectives to form interjections.

TOP TEN Interjections with *¡Qué... !*

¡Qué... ! + noun (person, place, thing, or feeling)

1. **¡Qué alegría!** How happy I am! (Literally, What happiness!)

2. **¡Qué barbaridad!** Jeez! How awful! Good grief! (Literally, What barbarity!)

3. **¡Qué gusto!** What a pleasure!

4. **¡Qué mala suerte!** What bad luck!

5. **¡Qué molestia!** What a pain! (Or, in colloquial Spanish: *¡Qué lata!* [literally, What a tin can!])

6. **¡Qué tonterías!** What nonsense!

¡Qué... ! + adjective (descriptive word)

7. **¡Qué bonita!** How pretty (she or it is)!

8. **¡Qué inteligente!** How intelligent (he or she is)!

9. **¡Qué simpáticos!** How nice (they are)!

10. **¡Qué ridículo!** How ridiculous!

The descriptive word has to agree with the person or thing described, masculine or feminine, singular or plural.

Rehearsal Time

¿Qué dice usted? What Spanish interjection can you use in each of these situations? Check your answers in the Answer Key.

1. Your friend is just about to walk out in front of an oncoming car.

2. Someone tries to steal your wallet and you want help.

3. You stub your toe and are in pain.

4. The tour driver gets upset because someone is late; you try to calm him down.

5. You want to tell the tour guide that you think the park (*el parque*) he is pointing out is very pretty.

¡Lógico! Circle the letter of the logical response. Check your answers in the Answer Key.

1. ¿Has oído las noticias? Fernando y Olivia se van a divorciar.
   a. ¡Socorro!
   b. ¡Qué molestia!
   c. ¡Caramba!

2. Después de una semana, no he podido encontrar un apartamento aquí.
   a. ¡Oiga!
   b. ¡Ánimo!
   c. ¡Qué alegría!

3. Perdí el avión a Madrid y no hay otro hasta mañana.
   a. ¡Qué lástima!
   b. ¡Qué gusto!
   c. ¡Qué tonterías!

4. Esa carne no sirve... mejor no la comes.
   a. ¡Hmm!
   b. ¡Zas!
   c. ¡Huácala!

Agarrando la onda

There are a variety of techniques that you can train yourself to use to become an active listener and *agarrar la onda* ("catch the sound wave" or "get with it"). Here are a few of them:

Listening for Stressed Words

Without thinking about it, you stress the important words in anything you say in English. Try reading any passage out loud and you'll see that the important words have more stress, or emphasis, in speech. In fact, if you listen to a conversation or paragraph read aloud and take notes, you'll find that your notes look like a telegram. Look at these examples in English; the stressed words are in capital letters.

WAITER: What would you like to ORDER?
CUSTOMER: TWO CHICKEN TACOS and a BEER.
WAITER: Do you want RICE and BEANS?
CUSTOMER: YES, please. And could you bring me a FORK?

The same thing happens in Spanish:

MESERO: ¿Qué desea PEDIR?
CLIENTE: DOS TACOS de POLLO y una CERVEZA.
MESERO: ¿Quiere ARROZ y FRIJOLES?
CLIENTE: Sí, por favor. Y ¿me podría traer un TENEDOR?

You don't need to understand every word in a sentence. If you resign yourself to not understanding everything and focus on the stressed words, you can often get the gist. *¡No se dé por vencido(-a)!* "Don't give up!"

Understanding Tone of Voice

Sometimes tone of voice is very important. Someone's words may be perfectly polite, but their tone of voice may be unfriendly. For instance, if you touch the fruit or vegetables at the marketplace, a vendor may say *¿En qué le puedo servir?* ("How can I help you?") but with a tone of voice that implies that any idiot would know better than to fondle the produce. Pay attention to a person's tone of voice and remember that it can say more than his or her words.

Understanding Missing Words

Sometimes there are words that are understood but that are missing in a sentence. Of course, the obvious example for English speakers is when a subject pronoun is missing because the verb form tells who the subject is: *[Nosotros] Somos de Lima.* ("We're from Lima.") Here are some other examples:

> *Esteban... ¿aquí?* Esteban . . . [is] here?
> *Todo eso... tonterías.* All of that . . . [is] nonsense.
> *Ese chico debe esperar; tan impaciente...* That boy should wait; [he's] so impatient . . .
> *Esto para ti.* This [is] for you.
> *Me dio un susto...* It gave me [such] a [terrible] fright . . .
> *Sí, un pedazo de pan; con tal de comer algo...* Yes, a piece of bread; just [so I can] eat something . . .
> *Ni idea.* [I have] No idea.
> *¡[Estoy] Listo!* [I'm] Ready! (A girl or woman would say *¡Lista!*)

Well, you get the picture. Sometimes if a message sounds incomplete, it may be! Try to fill in the understood words based on the context.

Understanding Reductions and Linking

In English there are many words that you "reduce" or cut down, leaving letters or syllables unpronounced. Sometimes there are elisions, or linking, when two syllables are run together and pronounced as one. Here's a conversation that you might hear in American English:

CUSTOMER: Ya got my shirts ready?
CLERK: I dunno. Lemme check. Whatcher last name?
CUSTOMER: Romero.
CLERK: . . . I don't see'em. I'll haveta look in the back. Doya wanna wait?
CUSTOMER: Well, I don't have a lotta time, but I gotta do some errands anyway, so I'll come back later. Cudja havem ready by five?

The same kind of thing happens in Spanish. Here are some of the most common examples:

TOP TEN Common Reductions or Linkings

1. **n'a (nada)** *Eso no tiene n'a que ver conmigo.* That has nothing to do with me.

2. **p'a (para); p'al (para el)** *Vamos p'a San José.* Let's go to San Jose. *Fernando fue pa'l mercado.* Fernando went to the market(place).

3. **'tá, 'tás, 'tán, (está, estás, están)** ¿*'Tá seguro?* Are you sure? *'Tás loca.* You're crazy. ¿*Qué 'tán esperando?* What are you waiting for?

4. **de'pué' (después)** ¿*Qué pasó de'pué'?* What happened afterward?

5. **'ora (ahora)** *'Ora, ¿qué hacemos?* Now what should we do?

6. **'tons (entonces)** *'Tons, ¿pa' qué compran tantas cosas?* So why are they buying so many things?

7. **ai (allí)** *Ai 'tá Paco.* There's Paco.

8. **'on', 'onde (donde, dónde); pa'onde (para donde, para dónde)** *¿'Ón' 'tá tu hermano?* Where's your brother? *No sé 'onde 'tá.* I don't know where he is. *¿Pa'ónde vas?* Where are you going?

9. **p'a'lante, d'a'lante (para adelante, de adelante); p'atrás, d'atrás (para atrás, de atrás)** *Hay que echar p'a'lante.* You have to move forward, keep plugging. *El asiento d'a'lante está ocupado.* The front seat is occupied. *No mires p'atrás.* Don't look back. *Ponlo en el asiento d'atrás.* Put it in the back seat.

10. **to'l (todo el)** *Pienso en ella to'l tiempo.* I think about her all the time.

¿Qué 'seso?: Linking with Vowels

Be aware that when a word ends with a vowel and the following word begins with that vowel, the words are often pronounced as one.

TOP FIVE Examples of Linking with Vowels

1. **¿Qué 'seso? (¿Qué es eso?)** What's that?

2. **¿Susana? Está con l'abogada (la abogada).** Susana? She's with the lawyer.

3. **Ella es mayor d'edad (de edad).** She's an adult—not a minor.

4. **No lo sabía yo hast'ahora (hasta ahora).** I didn't know (it) until now.

5. **Desde'l (Desde el) día que la vi la amo.** Since the day I saw her, I've loved her.

Linking also occurs with words that start with a silent *h*.

¿Adónde vas, m'ijo (mi hijo)? Where are you going, son?
¿Qué vas'acer? (¿Qué vas a hacer?) What are you going to do?
S'iciera (Si hiciera) buen tiempo, podrías ir a nadar. If it were good weather, you could go swimming.

Understanding Shortened Words or Expressions

Many words or expressions are customarily shortened in informal speech. For example:

¿Este regalo es para mí? Chasgracias (Muchas gracias). This present is for me? Thank you.
Cómprame un helado, mamá, porfa (por favor). Buy me an ice cream cone, Mom, please.
¿Éste es tu hermano? Chogusto (Mucho gusto). This is your brother? Glad to meet you.
Necesito ir a la cocina. Conper (Con permiso). I need to go to the kitchen. Excuse me.

There are many nouns that are shortened. Can you guess what the following might be? Answers are at the bottom of page 51.

TOP TEN Short Forms of Nouns

1. **la tele**

2. **la bici**

3. **la compu**

4. **el (la) profe**

5. **la migra**

6. **la depre**

7. **las mate**

8. **el (la) cole**

9. **el compa**

10. **la peli**

Other short forms you may hear include:

seño(ra)	ma'am
abue(lo), abue(la)	grandpa, grandma
el super(mercado)	supermarket
la u or **la uni(versidad)**	university
la moto(cicleta)	motorcycle
el finde (semana)	weekend

Answers: 1. **la televisión** television (also, *el tele* for *el televisor*, the set); 2. **la bicicleta** bicycle; 3. **la computadora** computer; 4. **el (la) profesor(a)** teacher, professor; 5. **la migración** Immigration, INS (in the United States); 6. **la depresión** depression; 7. **las matemáticas** mathematics; 8. **el (la) colega** colleague, pal; 9. **el compadre** close male friend and often godfather of one's child (Latin America); 10. **la película** movie

el dire(ctor) or **la dire(ctora)**   principal, director (school)
el insti(tuto)   high school (Spain)

In Mexico and Central America, you'll hear *el refri(gerador)* or *la refri(geradora)* for "fridge" and *'mano* or *'mana* for *hermano* or *hermana*, used in the sense of "close friend." *Hola, 'mano, ¿qué tal?*

Understanding Word Order

Word order in Spanish is very flexible, as you probably know. Look at these examples:

¿Está Gabriel en casa?
¿Gabriel está en casa?
¿Está en casa Gabriel?

All of these sentences mean the same thing: Is Gabriel home? The subject can go before or after the verb. Similarly, intonation plays a role. The voice goes down in declarative statements, and it goes up at the end of a question, just as in English:

Ya están aquí los invitados. The guests are here already. (voice goes down at the end)

¿Ya están aquí los invitados? Are the guests here already? (voice goes up at the end)

Los invitados ya están aquí. The guests are here already. (voice goes down at the end)

¿Los invitados ya están aquí? The guests are here already? (voice goes up at the end)

Look at the following sentences. What do they mean? Pay attention to the verb forms and try to determine the subjects. The answers are at the bottom of page 53.

1. *A mí nadie me habla así.*

2. *Con tanto trabajo que hacer, no tengo tiempo.*

3. *Más amable que Marcela no hay nadie.*

4. *Muy cansado parece tu hermano.*

5. *Un apartamento en el centro queremos alquilar.*

6. *¿Ariel? Al aeropuerto no llegó. No sé dónde está.*

🎼 Rehearsal Time

Atajos. (Shortcuts.) Sometimes shortened forms of words are used in Spanish, just as in English. What do the *italicized* words in the following short conversations mean? Check your answers in the Answer Key.

A: Vamos al (1) *super*. Necesito comprar leche.
B: Está bien. (2) *Abue*, ¿quiere ir con nosotros?

A: Vi en la (3) *tele* que los (4) *profes* de la (5) *uni* están en huelga ("on strike").
B: No me digas. Es la tercera vez este año.

A: Voy a la tienda para comprar un monitor para mi (6) *compu*.
B: ¿Vas en tu (7) *moto*?
A: No, en carro. Felipe me va a llevar.

Answers: 1. No one talks to me that way. 2. With so much work to do, I don't have time. 3. There's no one nicer than Marcela. 4. Your brother looks very tired. 5. We want to rent an apartment downtown. 6. Ariel? He didn't arrive at the airport. I don't know where he is.

A: Oye, (8) *compa*, recibiste los papeles de la (9) *migra*?
B: Sí. ¿Me ayudas a completarlos?
A: Cómo no, hoy mismo si quieres.
B: (10) *Chasgracias*.

A: Federico salió ahora en (11) *bici*... ¿para dónde va?
B: Creo que va al (12) *insti*. Tiene una cita con la (13) *dire*.

A: Begoña, ¿quieres ir a ver una (14) *peli*?
B: No, no me siento bien, mamá. Tengo una (15) *depre*.
A: Vamos, m'ija, (16) *porfa*. Quiero ver el nuevo film de
   Almodóvar.

¿Cómo? Más despacio... Ah, sí, ¡claro!

Active listeners know how to let other people know when they need
help, when they just aren't following. You do this in your own language all the time, like when you ask Uncle Henry to start over
from the beginning because you haven't followed his directions to
his new house, or when Mom mumbles something about an apple
pie, or when the dentist tells you in blitzkrieg style what he's going
to do that isn't going to hurt a bit. Here are some ways to get clarification in Spanish.

TOP FIVE Ways to Tell Someone You're Not Following or to
Slow Down

1. **¿Cómo?** What?

2. **No comprendo. (No entiendo.)** I don't understand.

3. **¿Qué dijo (dijiste)? ¿Qué decía(s)?** What did you say? What were you saying?

4. **¿Qué quiere decir la palabra... ?** What does the word . . . mean?

5. **Más despacio, por favor.** Slower, please.

In Mexico, you will hear the very common *¿Mande?* (from the verb *mandar*, meaning "to order") used for "What?"

If you think you understood but need clarification, just restate what you think you heard with a "confirmation tag" like *¿verdad?*, *¿no?*, and so forth: *Así que nos vamos a ver en el café Margarita, ¿verdad?/¿no?/¿no es cierto?* ("So we'll see each other at the Café Margarita, right?/isn't that so?/isn't that true?")

Or you can ask for repetition or clarification: *¿Podría repetir lo que dijo? No entendí...* ("Could you repeat what you said? I didn't understand . . . ") *¿Es decir que nos vamos a reunir a las once?* ("That's to say that we're going to meet at eleven?")

Finally, there's the wonderful informal expression *¿Y eso?* (literally, "And that?") meaning "What does that mean?" or "What's up with that?" For instance, someone makes a comment that baffles you or they are wearing something odd or they are carrying something that seems out of place, you say *¿Y eso?*.

As with any language, listening is a key to good relationships with other people. People want to talk about their problems, and they like to have someone to voice their opinions to. Try to show that you are listening and that you understand. When possible or appropriate, respond using a person's name—no one gets tired of hearing his or her own name! On the next page are some ways to show that you are tuned in to the person who is speaking to you.

TOP TEN Ways to Show Enthusiasm (and That You Understand)

1. **¿De veras?** Really?

2. **¡No me diga!** (*usted* form) **¡No me digas!** (*tú* form) Really? (Literally, You don't say!)

3. **¿En serio?** Seriously?

4. **¡Qué interesante (horrible, maravilloso, etcétera)!** How interesting (horrible, marvelous, etc.)!

5. **¿Y después? ¿Y entonces?** And after that? And then?

6. **¿Qué pasó después?** What happened after that?

7. **Sí, entiendo.** Yes, I understand.

8. **Sí, claro, cómo no.** Yes, sure, of course.

9. **¿Hace cuánto tiempo pasó eso?** How long ago did that happen?

10. **Y ¿qué hacía(s) mientras pasaba eso?** And what were you doing while that was going on?

When having a discussion, if you agree with what is said, it's good to say so, to reinforce what the other person is saying and indicate that you follow.

TOP TEN Ways to Agree

1. **Sí, ¡cómo no!** Yes, of course!

2. **Claro.** Sure.

3. **Exacto.** Exactly.

4. **Por supuesto.** Of course.

5. **Eso es.** That's it.

6. **Cierto. Correcto.** Right. Correct.

7. **Vale.** (Spain) **Vaya. Vaya pues.** Great, agreed, understood. (used in Mexico, Central America, and Caribbean; sometimes reduced to *Va' pues*)

8. **Sí, es verdad.** Yes, it's true.

9. **Estoy de acuerdo.** I agree.

10. **Como quiera.** (*usted* form) **Como quieras.** (*tú* form) As you like. Whatever you want. (used when a suggestion is made)

It's been said that no one can ever really "win" an argument—making other people feel that their ideas or opinions are inferior may just make them cling to them more stubbornly. It's sometimes more practical to let the other person think your ideas are his or her own by saying things like *Como tú bien sabes...* ("As you well know . . .") or *Estoy seguro(-a) que estamos de acuerdo de que...* ("I'm sure that we agree that . . ."). However, you may run across some things about which you really want to express your dissatisfaction and firmly make it clear that you do not agree. In addition to making some of the preceding expressions negative (*No, no es verdad/cierto* or *No estoy de acuerdo*), here are some ways to do that:

TOP TEN Ways to Disagree or Express Disbelief

1. **Estoy de acuerdo en parte, pero...** I partly agree, but . . .

2. **Pues, sí, hasta cierto punto, pero por otra parte...** Well, yes, up to a point, but on the other hand . . .

3. **Bueno, eso depende.** Well, that depends.

4. **Al contrario...** On the contrary . . .

5. **¡Qué va! ¡Vamos!** Oh, come on!

6. **Increíble. Imposible. No puede ser.** Incredible. Impossible. It can't be.

7. **¡Qué tonterías!** What nonsense!

8. **¡Qué ridículo!** How ridiculous!

9. **¡De ninguna manera!** No way! (used when some kind of action is proposed)

10. **Para nada.** No way. (colloquial)

De ninguna manera is normally used when you disagree about doing something: *¿Vamos a la fiesta de Tupperware? —¡De ninguna manera!* ("Shall we go to the Tupperware party?" "No way!")

Other colloquial ways to say this are: *¡Ni a la fuerza!* (literally, "Not even by force!"). *¡Ni loco(-a)!* (literally, "Not even crazy!"). *¡Ni a palos!* (literally, "Not even because of blows!").

Para nada is used in cases like: *¿No tienes ganas de ir? —Para nada.* ("You don't want to go?" "No way.") *¿Te gusta el pescado con chocolate? —Para nada.* ("Do you like fish with chocolate?" "No way.")

If you are not sure if the person you are talking to is serious, you can say *¿Habla(s) en broma? ¿Está(s) bromeando?* ("Are you joking?") or *¿Habla(s) en serio?* ("Are you serious?").

Some Final Tips

Take advantage of whatever situations are available to listen and speak to people in Spanish. Listen to songs. Listen to the radio. Watch TV. Speak to as many people as possible when you have an opportunity—in stores, in restaurants, waiting for the bus, anywhere that you find Spanish-speaking people in your community or while traveling. Learn ways to start a conversation. For example, you can say: *Disculpe. ¿Hay un buen restaurante cerca de aquí?* ("Excuse me. Is there a good restaurant nearby?") *¿Sabría usted qué hora es?* ("Would you know what time it is?") *¿Tiene usted la hora?* ("Do you have the time?")

On a bus, you can ask about your stop; for instance, *¿Está lejos el museo de arte moderno?* ("Is the modern art museum far away?") In a store, you can make a comment about the merchandise or the prices; for example, *¡Qué caro ese televisor!* ("How expensive that TV set is!") While waiting you can ask about how long another person has waited: *¿Hace mucho que está aquí?* ("Have you been here long?")

Speak slowly if you need to, but speak! Don't be afraid to make mistakes. Through active listening and speaking Spanish, you will soon develop confidence as your skills improve. Remember the Spanish saying: *Hablando se entiende la gente* ("By talking, people understand each other").

Rehearsal Time

Lo mismo es Chana que Juana. (It's six to one and half a dozen to the other.) There are many ways to say the same thing. Can you think of a Spanish word or phrase that has the same meaning as the *italicized* word(s)? There is more than one possible answer. Check your answers in the Answer Key.

A: ¿Conoces a Alejandro?

B: Sí, (1) *cómo no.*

A: Su esposa se llama Pilar, ¿no?

B: (2) *Correcto.*

A: A las nueve en el teatro, así quedamos. No veo la hora de salir.

B: ¿Cómo? (3) *No comprendo.* ¿No nos vamos a ver en el restaurante a las siete?

A: ¿Quieres bailar la macarena, Juanita?

B: (4) *¡Ni loca!*

A: Hoy iba caminando por la avenida principal y vi a un señor con una llama en plena calle...

B: (5) *¿Y entonces?*

A: Me dicen que sacaste la lotería, Carmen.

B: ¿La lotería? (6) *¿Hablas en broma?* (7) *¡Qué tonterías!*

Situaciones. What could you say in Spanish in these situations? There may be more than one possible answer. Check your answers in the Answer Key.

1. Your friend is talking a mile a minute. Tell her you don't understand and ask her to slow down: *No* _____. *Más* _____, *por favor.*

2. A good friend asks you if you want to see a movie later. You say, "Yes, whatever you want": *Sí, como* _____.

3. Someone tells you all Canadians and Americans are rich. Disagree with him politely.

4. A lady tells you a long story about her famous grandfather. Say "Really? How interesting!"

5. Your Spanish friend tells you about a *tapa*. Ask her what the word *tapa* means. *¿Qué... ?* (She will tell you that it's an appetizer in Spain.)

TUNE-UP
3

¡*Buen provecho!*

Eating and Drinking:
Not Just Tacos and Margaritas!

1. What are *tapas*? *Moros y cristianos?*

2. Why are many names of foods in Spanish from Arabic?

3. How do you say you can't eat or don't want spicy food?

4. What's a good way to make a toast to a friend or an acquaintance?

5. How do you call the waiter in a restaurant?

6. How do you get the special meal of the day?

7. What do you say if you want to order a draft beer? The house red wine?

8. If the waitress doesn't bring you the check right away, is that bad service from her point of view?

9. How do you compliment your hostess on a delicious meal?

10. If someone says to you *Me importa un pepino* or asks about your *media naranja*, what do they mean?

When people north of the Rio Grande think of a menu in Spanish, chances are they're thinking of Mexican food. Almost everyone knows what a taco, an enchilada, or a burrito is, thanks in part to TV ads featuring breakfast burritos or hyperactive chihuahuas barking *Yo quiero Taco Bell*. But in *los Estados Unidos de México*, there are thirty-one different states, each with its own cuisine, and this is only a small sampling of the many delectable food choices available. Spanish can be the key that opens the doors to exquisite banquet halls, which are different in each Hispanic country. And those in the know are proclaiming that Spain's *nueva cocina* is the best in Europe, replacing France's *nouvelle cuisine*. According to many American chefs and a cover article in *The Wine Spectator* in the summer of 2003, Spain is "the new source of Europe's most exciting wine and food."

An important thing to remember: While Mexican food can be very spicy, Spaniards and most Latin Americans do not eat spicy food regularly.

Las comidas y los sabores: ¡Ahúa!

English-speaking visitors to Spain may find their stomachs in shock the first few days as they try to adjust to radically different meal-times. Breakfast (*el desayuno*) is very light, possibly just coffee and bread or hot chocolate and *churros* (long fritters dipped in the chocolate). The main meal of the day is *la comida*: because Spain has a warm climate, this large noon meal was traditionally followed by the *siesta*, so that people could rest during the hottest part of the day. (The word *siesta* comes from the word meaning "sixth" in Latin; it was the sixth hour of a day that began at 6:00 A.M.—i.e., noon.) Shops were closed for about three hours in the afternoon. Nowadays in most big cities, this custom has had to be abandoned to avoid four rush hours. Still, *la comida* is a very large meal. Then in the early evening, people have *tapas* ("snacks") to tide them over until *la cena* ("supper"), a lighter meal that may begin at 9:00 or even 10:00 P.M. Going out to a movie after dinner at 11:00 P.M. requires major adjustment for many visitors.

These customs were altered somewhat in Hispanic America, but even so breakfast is usually very light, the main meal is at lunchtime, and dinner is often late. In Mexico or Central America, breakfast might be *pan dulce* (a sweet, dry bread) and coffee. In many countries there is a mid-morning snack (a *tentempié*, something to keep you "on your feet," *tente en pie*); in Colombia, for instance, this might be *arepas* ("thick corn tortillas"), sometimes accompanied by other things, such as *menudo* ("tripe soup"). The big meal of the day is *el almuerzo* (lunch). (In Mexico, as in Spain, it's called *la comida*; a light supper in Mexico may be called *la merienda*, which means "snack" in most countries.) Even a business lunch may last for several hours, beginning with small talk and food, switching to conversation about art, national events, or whatever after eating and turning to business matters only at the end. Don't go to dinner before 6:00 P.M. anywhere or you'll probably find the restaurant empty. In most of the Southern Cone, people have tea in the late afternoon and eat dinner at 8:00 or 9:00 P.M. In Chile, to have late-afternoon tea is *tomar once*, which some say came from the fact that the word *aguardiente* ("brandy") has eleven letters: *tomar once* may have been a euphemism for those who substituted brandy for tea. Notice that *tomar* is used for liquids, including *tomar la sopa* and *tomar el desayuno* (because breakfast is mainly a beverage).

People in Spanish-speaking countries enjoy meals together in general and mealtime is usually important for family time. Very often meals involve relatives beyond the nuclear family, particularly on Sundays. There is much less of a tendency to snack or eat at all hours than there is in many American and Canadian households.

What's in a Name?

When the Moors conquered Spain in the Middle Ages, they introduced their system of irrigation and agriculture to the Iberian Peninsula. Many names of foods in Spanish come from Arabic words; for instance, words that start with *al-* (which means "the" in Arabic), like *albaricoque* ("apricot"), *albóndiga* ("meatball"), *alcaparra* ("caper"), *almíbar* ("syrup"), or *alcohol*. Here are some other examples.

TOP TEN Food Words from Arabic

1. **el aceite** oil

2. **la aceituna** olive

3. **el arroz** rice

4. **el atún** tuna

5. **el azúcar** sugar

6. **el café** coffee

7. **el limón** lemon *or* lime

8. **la naranja** orange

9. **la sandía** watermelon

10. **la zanahoria** carrot

Others include: *el azafrán* ("saffron"), *la berenjena* ("eggplant"), *el fideo* ("noodle"), *el sorbete* ("sherbet"), *el tamarindo* ("tamarind fruit"), and *la toronja* ("grapefruit").

Centuries later, when the Spanish arrived in the New World, they encountered American foods. In Mexico they found Emperor Montezuma drinking fifty cups of chocolate a day—but he wouldn't have had sugar in it. It was a bitter, frothy drink prepared in a *jícara*, a native gourd. In Peru they found potatoes of every size, shape, and color. New varieties of beans (such as black, lima, and pinto) were abundant, as were squashes and, in tropical areas, a dazzling array of fruits. They tasted turkey (*el pavo*) for the first time. (In Mexico and Central America, it's called *guajolote*, from the Nahuatl Indian word *huexolotl*.) Here are some foods and the names of the indigenous languages that the words in Spanish came from.

TOP TEN Food Words from Native American Languages

1. **la papaya** papaya (Carib)

2. **el maíz** corn (Taino)

3. **el tomate** tomato (Nahuatl)

4. **el chocolate** chocolate (Nahuatl)

5. **la vainilla** vanilla (*tlilxocitl* en Nahuatl)

6. **el chile** chili (Nahuatl)

7. **el aguacate** avocado (Nahuatl)

8. **la patata** potato (Taino, used in Spain)

9. **la tapioca** tapioca (Tupi)

10. **la yuca** cassava (Carib)

Other Spanish food words that are derived from Native American languages include: *el maní* ("peanut," from Taino, used in the Caribbean and most of South America); *el cacahuate* ("peanut," from Nahuatl, used in Mexico and parts of Central America); *la mandioca* ("cassava," a starchy tuber, from Tupi), and *el zapallo* ("squash," from Quechua).

La papa ("potato") also comes from Quechua. In most of Latin America and Spain, the verb *papear* ("to potato") is colloquial for "to eat," and in Mexico, the Caribbean, Colombia, and Chile *la papa* refers to food in general. (In Peru, it's *el papeo*.) The potato was very important to the indigenous Americans who cultivated it.

How do you talk about your likes and dislikes where food is concerned? Here are some useful phrases.

TOP FIVE Ways to Talk About Food Preferences

1. **Me gusta la comida picante, pero mi novio prefiere la comida suave.** I like spicy food, but my boyfriend prefers bland food.

2. **Este café es muy amargo; le falta azúcar.** This coffee is very bitter; it needs sugar.

3. **Se me antoja algo dulce, quizás un helado de chocolate o un arroz con leche.** I feel like (eating) something sweet, maybe chocolate ice cream or rice pudding. (in Spain: *Me apetece algo dulce...*)

4. **Esta limonada es muy ácida.** This lemonade is very sour.

5. **Este bistec está bien cocido; las papas fritas están muy saladas.** This steak is well-done; the french fries are very salty. (In Spain and some other places, it's more common to say *bien hecho* for "well done"; "rare" is usually *poco cocido* or *poco hecho*. You may also hear *jugoso* for "rare" or *a punto* for "medium.")

For the adventurous, there are many wonderful places to find local specialties other than in *el café, la cafetería,* or *el restaurante.*

TOP TEN Places to Eat or Drink

1. **el mercado** open-air market, which will usually have not only fresh fruits, vegetables, and cheese but also many local specialties; the *mercado* is often a good place for an inexpensive meal

2. **la pensión** boarding house that serves meals; *pensión completa* refers to a plan in which you stay at the *pensión* and take your meals there

3. **el parador** in Spain, government-run hotel with a restaurant that serves typical local dishes; *paradores* are often in castles, monasteries, and so on, and usually are rather expensive

4. **la fonda, la posada o la hostería** inn that serves food and often specializes in typical regional dishes

5. **la parrilla** place where grilled meats are served; this may also be called a *churrasquería,* from the Brazilian word *churrasco* (barbecue)

6. **el salón de té** tearoom that serves food, especially important in the Southern Cone

7. **la chifa** in Ecuador, Peru, and northern Chile, Chinese restaurant that features *taillarines* ("noodles") with vegetables and meat, as well as other Asian dishes

8. **la hacienda (la estancia)** in Mexico, ranch that has been transformed into a restaurant, often with gardens and mariachi musicians; in Argentina, the *estancias* are similar (minus the mariachis) and usually specialize in barbecued meat

9. **el bar** usually a small restaurant in Latin America that serves food and drinks; it can also be a bar but that's not the normal meaning; *el club* or *el nightclub* may be used for "bar"

10. **la cantina** bar traditionally for men in Mexico, Colombia, and Argentina, although this is changing and women also go to *cantinas* now; food is also served in a *cantina*

TOP FIVE Special Places for Those Special Foods

1. **la panadería** bakery that may serve coffee or other drinks as well as *pan* ("bread") and sweets

2. **la chocolatería** chocolate shop or stand

3. **la taquería** place in Mexico or Central America that serves *tacos*

4. **la juguería** place that sells *jugos* ("fruit juices")

5. **la pastelería** a shop that serves cake or other sweets and drinks

Rehearsal Time

La lógica de la comida. (Food logic.) Choose the logical response. Check your answers in the Answer Key.

1. ¡Huy! Este café es muy amargo. ¿Me das un poco de...
   a. sal
   b. azúcar
   c. limón

2. Soy vegetariano, así que no como...
   a. carne
   b. frutas
   c. vegetales

3. Necesito un vaso de agua, por favor. Estos chiles rellenos son un poco...
   a. suaves
   b. jugosos
   c. picantes

4. Se me antoja algo dulce, quizás un...
   a. taco de pollo
   b. helado de chocolate
   c. aguacate

5. Tengo ganas de tomar un jugo de mango. ¿Qué tal si vamos a una...
   a. juguería
   b. cantina
   c. pensión

6. ¿El bistec? Lo quiero bien hecho, bien...
   a. ácido
   b. dulce
   c. cocido

Come y bebe, que la vida es breve: las bebidas

Come y bebe, que la vida es breve ("Eat and drink, for life is short")
is an old Spanish saying. Spain is famous for the excellent wines they
produce and for *jerez* (the origin of our word "sherry"), which
comes from the town *Jerez de la Frontera*. Red wine is referred to
as *vino tinto*, rosé is *rosado*, and white is, of course, *blanco*. A dry
wine is *seco* and a sweet wine is *dulce*. *La sangría*, now a party drink
in the United States and Canada, is a mixture of wine, soda, sometimes a bit of brandy, and oranges and lemons or limes. In Spain
you can also savor *horchata*, a sweet nonalcoholic beverage made
from barley or rice and almonds. Of course, these drinks were
brought by Spaniards to the Americas. Chile and Argentina, for
instance, also produce world-class wines. In pretty much all of
Latin America you can find *sangría* or *horchata*.

Chocolate has been important in Mexico since prehispanic
times. A Mexican saying about how to keep a friend advises having
cuentas claras ("accounts clear" or in order; that is, no debt) and *chocolate espeso* ("thick chocolate," not watered down): *Cuentas claras,
chocolate espeso, amistades largas*. Another famous Mexican expression about chocolate you may know from the title of the movie
Como agua para chocolate (*Like Water for Chocolate*), which means
seething with anger or passion, like boiled water ready to be poured
over ground chocolate. A lesser-known but very traditional nonalcoholic drink in Mexico and Central America is *atole*, a thick corn
beverage sweetened and often flavored with almonds, chocolate, or
other local ingredients.

Another drink that predates the Spanish in Mexico is *pulque*, a
kind of frothy ale that is actually high in vitamins and proteins and
was the main alcoholic drink in Mexico before the conquest. *Pulque*
comes from the maguey or century plant, the same plant used to
make *tequila*, which is the main ingredient of a *margarita* (along
with lemon juice and Cointreau). Mexico is also known for its
Kahlua, a coffee-flavored liqueur, and for *mezcal* and the little worm
(*el gusanito*) contained in it.

La cerveza ("beer") is found pretty much everywhere in the Hispanic world. In Latin America, a draft beer is *una cerveza de barril*; in Spain, you can order *una caña*. In many places, light-colored beers are called *rubias* ("blonds"); in Mexico and parts of Central America, they are also known as *chelas* (a slang word meaning "blonds"). Dark beers are often called *negras* or *maltas* ("malt beers").

In Andean countries, you can try *chicha*, a fermented corn libation of indigenous origin. Peru and Chile are known for *pisco*, a white grape brandy that is used in *pisco* sours (with lemon juice, egg white, and sugar). Peru is also known for *Inka Cola*, a sugary soda pop that tastes like bubble gum. In Chile, you can try *mote con huesillo*, nonalcoholic peach nectar with barley kernels, or a *guindado*, a fermented alcoholic drink with brandy, cinnamon, and cloves.

La Juguería: Tutti-Frutti

One of the most delightful Latin American experiences is the *juguería*. You can get *jugo de naranja* or *fresa* ("orange" or "strawberry juice"), but there is a rich assortment of other fruits as well; all of the following are from the Americas except the mango, the watermelon, and the tamarind.

TOP TEN Delicious Fruit Drinks

1. **el maracuyá** passion fruit

2. **la guanábana** custard apple, soursop

3. **el mango** mango

4. **la papaya** papaya

5. **la guayaba** guava (from an Arawak word)

6. **la piña** pineapple

7. **el mamey** (from a Taino word), **el zapote** (from a Nahuatl word) marmalade plum

8. **la mora** blackberry

9. **la sandía** watermelon

10. **el tamarindo** tamarind

On menus in restaurants, these drinks may be called *batidos* or *licuados* and in that case probably will contain water or milk. You may be asked *¿Con agua o con leche?*

Is Coffee Your Cup of Tea?

Many Hispanic countries are famous for their coffees, which can be ordered in a variety of ways: *café negro*, *café con leche* (with a lot of milk), and *expreso*. In large towns or cities you can find cappuccinos. If you want decaf, ask for *café descafeinado*, although it may be hard to find. In Colombia, people call the very strong, thick coffee that is normally served *tinto*; try one and you'll be amazed to realize that the average Colombian downs many *tintos* a day. In Spain, Cuba, and the Southern Cone *expreso* with a bit of milk is called *un cortado*; *un carajillo* is coffee with brandy. In general, there is a saying about how Hispanics like their *café*:

Caliente hot
Amargo bitter
Fuerte strong, and
Espeso thick

If you prefer tea (*el té*) to coffee and want herbal tea, ask for *té de hierbas* or *una infusión* (*de hierbas*); common ones are *manzanilla* ("camomile") or *hierbabuena* ("wild mint"). In Colombia these are commonly known as *aromáticas*, and in Chile as *agüitas*. If you want tea with a large jolt of caffeine, try *yerba mate* in the Southern Cone; it traditionally is drunk in a gourd (*mate*) with a *bombilla*, a metal straw that filters out the tea leaves. Sipping *yerba mate* in a decorated gourd, it's easy to imagine oneself back in time among the *gauchos* ("cowboys"), who adopted this indigenous custom.

Water, Water . . . It's Not Everywhere

People used to having a glass of ice water with their meals may have to learn to adapt to customs in other countries. In restaurants, there probably will not be any drinking water on the table; if you don't want *agua mineral* ("mineral water"), which will cost a bit of money, you can ask for *agua común*. Of course, this might depend on what country you are in and what kind of restaurant it is because there are still areas where bottled water is essential to avoid *mal de turista*. If this is a problem, don't forget to specify *sin hielo* ("without ice") or ask if the ice is *de agua pura*. (Also, ask if the fruit drink you are thinking of ordering contains water.) If you do order *agua mineral*, you may be asked if you would like it *con gas* ("carbonated") or *sin gas*.

TOP TEN Ways to Order a Beverage

1. **Para empezar, una botella de vino rosado.** To begin with, a bottle of rosé wine.

2. **El vino tinto de la casa.** The house red wine.

3. **Quisiera algo sin alcohol. ¿Qué gaseosas (sodas, refrescos) tiene?** I'd like something nonalcoholic. What soft drinks do you have?

4. **Una botella de agua mineral con gas.** A bottle of carbonated mineral water.

5. **Un café con leche y un café negro.** A coffee with milk and a black coffee.

6. **Me trae un café descafeinado, por favor.** Bring me a decaf coffee, please. (Literally, this would be *traígame* but it's just as common to hear *me trae*, a simpler construction.)

7. **Un té de hierbas. (Una infusión.)** Herbal tea.

8. **Me gustaría probar el jugo de guanábana.** I'd like to try the custard apple juice.

9. **Para mí, un jugo de mango y piña.** For me, a mango and pineapple juice.

10. **Una rubia de barril.** A draft light beer.

If you go out to *tomar una copa* (have an alcoholic drink), here are some ways to make a toast:

TOP FIVE Ways to Make a Toast

1. **¡Salud!** Cheers! To your health! (also, in Mexico, *¡Salucitas!*)

2. **¡Salud, dinero y amor (y el tiempo para gozarlos)!** Health, money, and love (and the time to enjoy them)!

3. **¡Chin, chin!** Cheers! (imitating the sound of glass clinking, used in Spain and parts of Latin America)

4. **¡Fondo blanco!** Bottoms up! (literally, White bottom [of glass]!; used in most of Latin America)

5. **¡Para los (las) que amamos!** For those whom we love!

A toast accompanied by gestures is *¡Arriba, abajo, al centro y p'adentro!* (literally, "Up, down, to the center, and inside!"), something like "Down the hatch!" The glass is held out upward, downward, to the center, and then to the mouth. Sometimes this is just said as *¡Al centro y p'adentro!*

Rehearsal Time

Todo sobre las bebidas. (All about beverages.) Complete these sentences about various kinds of drinks in Spanish, choosing from the words listed on the right. Check your answers in the Answer Key.

1. Un brindis muy común es «Salud, dinero y _____.»

   descafeinado

2. Una infusión es un té de _____.

   amor

3. El vino de color rojo se llama vino _____.

   jugos

4. El café sin cafeína es el café _____.

   hierbas

5. Se puede pedir agua mineral sin gas o _____.

   tinto

6. La cerveza de color amarilla se llama cerveza _____.

   gaseosa

7. En una juguería se puede tomar _____.

   con gas

8. Otra palabra para soda es _____.

   rubia

En el restaurante

In a restaurant in Spain or Latin America, you will probably be served several courses. First are the *entradas* or *entremeses* ("appetizers"; these are also called *antojitos* in Mexico). Soup may follow, and then come the *platos fuertes* or *platos principales* (the "main dishes")—meat, poultry, or fish with potatoes, rice, salad, or vegetables. Finally comes the *postre* ("dessert"), which might be fruit, cheese, *flan* (custard made from eggs and sweetened condensed milk with caramelized sugar), *arroz con leche* ("rice pudding"), ice cream, or other sweets. Coffee is sometimes ordered with dessert and sometimes afterward; a cordial or liqueur may follow that.

TOP TEN Things a Waiter May Say to You

1. **¿Cuántas personas son?** How many are in your party?

2. **¿Una mesa para dos?** A table for two?

3. **¿Qué se les ofrece?** What can I offer you? Or, in Spain, **¿Qué les pongo?** What shall I serve (put before) you?

4. **¿Qué gustan tomar?** What do you want to drink?

5. **¿Desean pedir ahora?** Do you want to order now?

6. **¿Qué les traigo para empezar?** What shall I bring you to begin with?

7. **Permítanme recomendarles el arroz con pollo.** Allow me to recommend the chicken with rice (to you).

8. **¿Les gustaría probar la especialidad de la casa?** Would you like to try the house specialty?

9. **¿Qué gustan de postre?** What do you want for dessert?

10. **No, no aceptamos tarjetas de crédito.** No, we don't accept credit cards.

TOP TEN Things You May Say to a Waiter

1. **Somos cinco. Tenemos una reservación.** There are five of us. We have a reservation.

2. **¡Señor! ¡Señorita!** Sir! Miss!

3. **¿Qué nos recomienda?** What do you recommend?

4. **¿Cuál es la especialidad de la casa?** What's the house specialty?

5. **¿De qué es la sopa del día?** What's the soup of the day?

6. **Necesito un menú y la lista de vinos.** I need a menu and the wine list.

7. **¿Me trae un tenedor, por favor?** Will you bring me a fork, please?

8. **Nos faltan servilletas. (Nos faltan los cubiertos.)** We need napkins. (We need silverware.)

9. **Esto no es lo que pedí.** This is not what I ordered.

10. **La cuenta, por favor.** Check, please.

Don't say *¡Camarero(-a)!* or *¡Mesero(-a)!* or *¡Mozo(-a)!* to call a waiter or waitress. The most polite thing to say is *¡Por favor!, Señor!,* or *¡Señorita!* In Mexico or Colombia you might hear the term *¡Joven!* even if the waiter is sixty years old. Another tip: If you order salad, don't specify a dressing because usually it will come with a house dressing.

If you take advantage of fixed-price meals or specialties, your food may be considerably less expensive. In most places, you can ask for *el menú del día*, a full meal at a fixed price. In Mexico and many parts of South America, this is called *la comida corrida* (in

Colombia it is called *la comida corriente*). In Chile it's also known as *la colación*. Of course, you can also make sure to get domestic wines or beers, which are often much less expensive than imported ones. And don't be afraid to ask questions about the bill.

TOP FIVE   Questions That Can Save You Money

1. **¿Cuáles son los vinos de la casa?** What are the house wines?

2. **¿Es una cerveza doméstica o importada?** Is it a domestic or imported beer?

3. **¿Cuál es el menú del día? ¿Cuál es la comida corrida?** What's the special meal of the day?

4. **¿Está incluida la propina? (¿Está incluido el servicio?)** Is the tip (service) included?

5. **No entiendo. ¿Para qué son estos 200 pesos?** I don't understand. What are these 200 pesos for?

In most of the Hispanic world, you have to ask for the check rather than waiting for it to be brought to you. This is politeness on the part of the waiter or waitress, who does not want to rush you, but it is sometimes mistaken for bad service by English speakers. In many places, the tip is included, but, if not, you can leave 15 percent or so for service. Separate checks are not made everywhere, but you can say *Quisiéramos pagar por separado* ("We'd like to pay separately") and see what the response is. When people each pay their own bill or "go dutch," Mexicans say they are *saliendo a la americana*, but in the Southern Cone, Peru, and Bolivia this is known as *saliendo a la inglesa*. In some countries, the bill is jokingly referred to as *la dolorosa* ("the painful one"). (In Spain, the expression *hacer un sinpa* refers to leaving without paying—*sin pagar*—the check, avoiding "the painful one" entirely.)

If you are in Argentina or Uruguay and you see the sign *tenedor libre* ("free fork," meaning all you can eat), you may have found a real deal, especially if you are very hungry.

 Rehearsal Time

¿Qué nos recomienda? Are you restaurant savvy? Answer the questions for each situation and check your answers in the Answer Key.

1. You're in a restaurant and you want to get the waiter's attention. How do you address him?

2. You see the word *entrada* on the menu. What does it mean? What's another word with the same meaning?

3. You're in Spain and the waiter says to you, *¿Qué le pongo?* What does he want to know?

4. You hear someone at a neighboring table ask for *la comida corrida*. What does he want? What's another expression for this?

5. How do you ask for the soup of the day? The house specialty?

6. You're in Argentina and you see the sign *Tenedor libre*. Does that mean they're giving away forks?

7. What are two questions that can save you money in a restaurant?

¡Mi casa es tu casa!

When you are invited to dinner in a home in the Hispanic world, you may want to take flowers, wine, or a gift, as you would in the

United States or Canada. You don't need to arrive exactly on time; people will expect you to be a bit late (but not so late that dinner would be held up). Latin hospitality is renowned, and greetings of welcome are especially warm.

TOP FIVE Things Your Host or Hostess May Say to Welcome You

1. **¡Bienvenido(-a)! Mi casa es tu casa.** Welcome! My house is your house. (Notice that *Bienvenido* has to agree with the person being welcomed; if there are two people, it would be *Bienvenidos* unless they are both female, in which case it would be *Bienvenidas*.)

2. **Gracias por venir.** Thanks for coming.

3. **Estás en tu casa.** Make yourself at home. (Literally, You're in your home.)

4. **Me alegro de verte. Qué gusto de verte.** I'm happy to see you. What a pleasure to see you.

5. **La casa es chica; el corazón grande.** The house is small; the heart [is] large. (used in Southern Cone, Mexico)

As elsewhere, a meal in someone's home may be formal or informal. An informal meal might even be potluck. In Mexico, if someone invites you to a *cena formal* and says *Es de traje*, know that it doesn't mean you are to wear a suit (*traje*); it means you are supposed to bring something—for instance, *Traje la ensalada* ("I brought the salad"), typical Mexican use of ironic humor with a play on words.

Latins enjoy food, but a meal is much more than the food on the table. Conversation is usually lively, and people enjoy each other's company while eating. While Americans might get up immediately after the meal and move on to other activities, Hispanics have the delightful custom of the *sobremesa*. People sit at the table after a meal and chat. Sharing company and conversation is just as important as sharing food, and the *sobremesa* must surely aid digestion. When someone eats and runs, others tease him or her by saying, *Comida hecha, amistad deshecha* ("Meal done/finished, friendship undone/finished").

In Mexico, your host or hostess may prepare a *botana*, a plate of hors d'oeuvres such as cheese, salsa or guacamole dip, olives, carrots or celery, *tortillas* (flat cakes made of corn or wheat), *nopales* (the fruit of the *tuna* or prickly pear cactus, high in vitamins and minerals), or *chicharrones* ("fried pork skins"). These appetizers (called *antojitos* in Mexico) can be enough to constitute an entire meal. In Mexico and Central America, *frijoles* ("beans") are almost always served with the *platos fuertes*. A Salvadoran child at a dinner in the United States featuring *arroz con pollo* once asked, *¿Pero dónde están los frijoles?*, to the laughter of all present.

In some places, such as Mexico, it's considered polite to leave a small amount of food on one's plate (just a bite) to show that the host or hostess has given you the right amount of food (you're not going hungry). Similarly, people often do not take the last portion of food from a serving dish; this is called *la de la vergüenza* ("the one of shame") in Spain and the Dominican Republic because no one dares to take it.

TOP TEN Dinnertime Expressions

1. **La comida está servida. Siéntense, por favor.** Dinner is served. Sit down, please.

2. **¡Un brindis! Quisiera hacer un brindis.** A toast! I'd like to make a toast.

3. **Brindemos por el cocinero (la cocinera).** A toast to the cook. (Literally, Let's make a toast to the cook.)

4. **Buen provecho.** Bon appétit. Enjoy your meal.

5. **Favor de pasarme el pan. Pásame el pan, por favor.** Please pass the bread.

6. **La sopa está caliente. ¿Te la puedo servir?** The soup is hot. May I serve you (it)?

7. **Sírvate el arroz, por favor.** Help yourself to the rice, please.

8. **¿Quieres más ensalada?** Do you want more salad?

9. **Solamente un poquito.** Just a little bit.

10. **Una porción pequeña.** A small portion (of a dish that is cut in pieces, like a roast or a cake).

TOP TEN Things You May Say to Your Host or Hostess

1. **¡Qué rico! (¡Qué sabroso! ¡Qué delicioso!)** How delicious!

2. **¡Qué delicia!** How delectable! (Literally, What a delicacy!; used in Mexico, Chile, Peru, Argentina)

3. **La comida estuvo excelente. Estuvo riquísimo todo.** The meal was excellent. Everything was very delicious.

4. **Este pastel está para chuparse los dedos.** This cake or tart is very tasty. (literally, to lick one's fingers, finger-licking good; colloquial)

5. **Estoy satisfecho(-a), gracias.** I'm full, thank you.

6. **Ya se hizo tarde. Debo irme. (Debemos irnos.)** It's gotten late. I should go. (We should go.)

7. **Muchas gracias por la invitación. Gracias por invitarme.** Thank you for the invitation. Thank you for inviting me.

8. **Fue una tarde muy agradable.** It was a very pleasant evening.

9. **Lo pasamos muy bien.** We had a great time.

10. **Lo pasamos de maravilla.** We had a wonderful time.

Your host(ess) will probably ask you to stay longer: *¿No puedes quedarte? ¿Ya te vas? ¿Tan temprano?* ("Can't you stay? Are you going already? So early?") This is polite and often expected—it doesn't mean you should feel obligated to stay longer. You may also hear *Espero que no sea la última vez que venga* ("I hope this isn't the last time you come" or "Please come again"). Remember, however, that in most Latin countries people are night owls, and parties often last a long time. If you are tired, just say that you have things to do the next day: *Mañana tengo que madrugar/trabajar/salir para...* ("Tomorrow I have to get up early/work/leave for . . .") *Lo siento, pero ya me tengo que retirar.* ("Sorry, but I have to leave now.")

🎼 Rehearsal Time

La invitación. You go to the house of your friend Tomás for dinner. What do you say to him during the evening? In some cases, there is an English cue to help, but in any case there is more than one possible answer. Check the Answer Key for some suggestions if you need help.

Tomás: Bienvenido(-a). Mi casa es tu casa.
Usted: Muchas gracias. (1) _____. (Say you're happy to see him.)
Tomás: Adelante. (Come in.)

Tomás: La comida está lista. Siéntate, por favor.

Usted: (2) _____. (Propose a toast to the cook, Tomás.)

Tomás: ¡Salud! Sírvate el arroz.

Usted: Gracias. (3) _____. (Say "Bon appétit!")

Tomás: Pásame el pan, por favor.

Usted: Hmmm, esta carne está (4) _____.

Tomás: Gracias. ¿Quieres más?

Usted: Bueno, sí, pero solamente un (5) _____.

Tomás: ¿Otra porción del pastel?

Usted: No, gracias, estoy (6) _____. Ya se hizo tarde. Debo irme.

Tomás: ¿Tan temprano?

Usted: Sí, tengo que (7) _____. Gracias por (8) _____.

Tomás: Pues, gracias por venir.

Usted: (9) _____. (Say that you had a very pleasant evening.)

Entre las gentes, hay mil gustos diferentes

There is a saying that *Entre las gentes, hay mil gustos diferentes* ("Among groups of people, there are a thousand different tastes/predilections"), and certainly each Hispanic country and region has its own special foods. Here are ten well-known dishes.

TOP TEN Specialties from Spain or Latin America

1. **(la) paella** dish that may contain fish or shellfish, chicken, meat, or vegetables, but that always contains rice, olive oil, and saffron; the original *paella* was cooked over a fire in the open air

2. **(el) gazpacho** cold tomato soup (a common dish in Spain during the hot summer months)

3. **(el) lechón asado** suckling pig

4. **(los) moros y cristianos** rice and black beans (literally, Moors and Christians)

5. **(el) ceviche** sliced fish marinated in lime juice with garlic, salt, pepper, chilies, onion, and cilantro

6. **(las) empanadas** turnovers with meat, fish, eggs, onions, olives, raisins, or whatever regional ingredients are desired, in a dough made of flour, oil, milk, water, and salt; they're usually baked (*al horno*)

7. **(los) tamales** corn dough placed on corn husks or banana leaves, topped with a filling (normally meat, beans, or cheese), rolled, and steamed; in Andean regions, corn tamales are called *humitas*

8. **(la) ropa vieja** dish made from shredded meat (shredded like "old clothes"—hence the name), onions, and other condiments

9. **(el) sancocho** stew with several meats or fish, yucca, plantain, corn, vegetables (Caribbean and northern South America)

10. **(la) parrillada** barbecued meat usually including *chorizos* ("sausages"), *morcillas* ("blood sausages"), *costillas* ("ribs"), *filetes* or *bifes* ("steaks"), *riñones* ("kidneys"), and/or *hígados* ("livers"), often accompanied by a sauce called *chimichurri* (South America); very similar is *churrasco* (this name came originally from Brazil)

Variety, the Spice of Life: Regional Cuisines

Spain is one of the world's largest olive-oil producers, helpful in raising good cholesterol and lowering bad. Many things are cooked in it, including the famous Spanish *tortilla*, which is a potato omelette (not the flat corn bread in Mexico or Central America). Spain is also known for *jamón serrano* (cured ham from the *sierra*, "mountains"), *gambas a la plancha* ("grilled shrimp"), and *alioli* (a garlic mayonnaise sauce). But most famous of all are the *tapas* ("appetizers"), which are many and varied. Some tapas bars specialize in just one thing—for instance, *mejillones* ("mussels"); to ask for a serving or portion of *tapas*, ask for *una ración*. Foods from Spain such as *paella*, *gazpacho*, and *lechón asado* are found all over the Spanish-speaking world.

TOP FIVE Foods with Different Names in Spain

1. **el jugo** (juice) is called **el zumo**

2. **el cacahuate** (peanut) is called **el cacahuete**

3. **los camarones** (shrimp) are called **las gambas**

4. **el durazno** (peach) is called **el melocotón**

5. **la toronja** (grapefruit) is called **el pomelo**

Note also that *la torta* means "cake" in Spain and parts of South America, but it means "sandwich" in Mexico; *el pastel* is used for "cake" in Mexico and Central America. Finally, in Spain a *taco* is not something to eat, it's a swear word!

In the United States and Canada, it's easy to find restaurants that specialize in Mexican, Puerto Rican, or Cuban dishes because there are many citizens and residents originally from these areas. Here are a few of their most common dishes.

Mexico

(el) guacamole dip made of avocado, tomato, onion, garlic, and lime or lemon juice, often served with *totopos* ("chips")

(los) frijoles refritos beans that have been cooked and then refried

(la) quesadilla tortilla and melted cheese

(los) chiles en nogada peppers stuffed with meat, onions, raisins, etc. in a cream sauce with walnuts and pomegranates

(el) pozole soup with hominy and pork

Cuba

(el) picadillo ground beef with onion, tomato, bell pepper, olives, raisins

(la) yuca con mojo boiled cassava with garlic and sour orange sauce

(el) sofrito tomato sauce that serves as the basis for many stews and other dishes in many Caribbean areas; it can contain cilantro, green peppers, onion, garlic, capers, and oil

(el) adobo seasoning in many Caribbean areas that contains garlic and onion powder, black pepper, and oregano

Puerto Rico

(los) tostones fried green plantain slices

(las) frituras fritters served as appetizers

(el) mofongo mashed fried green plantain rolled and often stuffed with meat or vegetables

(los) pasteles dumplings made from taro root, potato, and/or unripe bananas and then stuffed with meat or seafood

Like Cuba and Puerto Rico, the nearby Dominican Republic is famous for dishes containing black beans, rice, plantains, and cassava, and is especially known for *sancocho* (a stew with meat or fish, vegetables, and plantains). The word *barbacoa* ("barbecue") in Spanish came from a Taino word; Spanish explorers found native Caribbeans on the island of Hispaniola (now the Dominican Republic and Haiti) preparing fish over a wood fire, just as they do today on the beach or in fancy restaurants.

In El Salvador, people enjoy *pupusas*, fried corn tortillas stuffed with meat, cheese, and/or beans. Nicaragua is associated with *tres leches*, sponge cake with milk syrup and meringue, and *tajadas*, plaintain chips. Costa Rica is known for its *gallo pinto* (rice and bean mixture that is eaten pretty much around the clock, even for breakfast) and for *casado* ("married man"), a dish with rice, beans, meat or fish, and salad.

Moving down to South America, there are a vast number of national dishes. Following are a few of them. Some of these are eaten in more than one country, of course.

Colombia

(las) arepas thick corn tortillas
(el) ajiaco chicken, potato, and corn soup

Venezuela

(el) mondongo tripe with corn, potatoes, and vegetables in bouillon
(el) pabellón shredded meat, rice, beans, and fried green plantain
(el) pasticho a pasta dish like lasagna

Ecuador

(los) llapingachos fried mashed potato and cheese pancakes
(el) locro stew or soup with potatoes, corn, avocado, or cheese topping

(el) seco stew usually made of meat with rice
(las) tostadas de maíz fried corn pancakes

Peru

(la) mazamorra sweet corn pudding
(el) lomo saltado chopped steak with onions, potatoes, rice, tomatoes
(las) papas a la huancaína potatoes in a rich white sauce

Bolivia

(el) chuño freeze-dried potatoes
(las) salteñas turnovers similar to *empanadas*

Chile

(el) pastel de choclo meat and vegetable casserole with corn topping
(el) curanto fish, shellfish, chicken, pork, lamb, beef, and potato stew
(la) paila marina fish chowder
(el) chupe de locos abalone stew
kuchen pastries, often with fruit (from the German word and influence of German settlers in Chile)

Argentina

(los) ñoquis gnocchi, one of many Italian pasta dishes available in Argentina
(la) milanesa breaded steak
(el) bife a caballo steak with two fried eggs and french fries
(el) puchero dish with beef, sausage, chicken, tomatoes, corn, onions, and vegetables

Uruguay

(el) chivito steak, cheese, and BLT sandwich
(el) pancho hot dog

Paraguay

(el) locro corn-based stew
(la) sopa paraguaya corn bread with onion and cheese

In the Southern Cone, beans are usually called *porotos*, not *frijoles*; *la toronja* ("grapefruit") is known as *el pomelo* (as it is in Spain); *la fresa* ("strawberry") is known as *la frutilla*, and *el aguacate* ("avocado") is *la palta*.

Y, a la postre...

To end this discussion of food and drink, here *a la postre* ("for dessert"—literally, "at the end") are ten common expressions containing names of foods in Spanish and their literal translations. Try to get the gist of the following sentences; then match them with the appropriate idiomatic English meanings that follow (*a* to *j*). The answers are at the bottom of page 94.

TOP TEN Common Expressions with Names of Foods or Drinks

1. **Eres como arroz blanco; te veo hasta en la sopa.** You're like white rice; I see you even in the soup.

2. **Marisa se cree la última Coca-Cola en el desierto.** Marisa thinks she's the last Coca-Cola in the desert.

3. **Hay que decir al pan *pan* y al vino *vino*.** You have to call bread *bread* and wine *wine*.

4. **Me importa un pepino.** It matters a cucumber to me.

5. **Mi profesor de historia no es ni chicha ni limonada.** My history teacher is neither corn liquor nor lemonade.

6. **Felipe es tan fresco como una lechuga.** Felipe is as fresh as a head of lettuce.

7. **¿Dónde está tu media naranja?** Where's your orange half?

8. **Miguelito es más bueno que el pan.** Miguelito is better than bread.

9. **Su jefe lo mandó a freír espárragos.** His boss told him to go fry asparagus.

10. **De ese libro no entendí ni papa.** I didn't understand even a potato about that book.

---

a. Miguelito is as good as gold.
b. My history teacher is mediocre, insipid.
c. I didn't understand beans about that book.
d. His boss told him to go jump in the lake.
e. Marisa is stuck-up.
f. Felipe is very fresh (sassy or forward). (This can also mean "cool as a cucumber.")
g. Where's your better half?
h. I don't give a darn.
i. You seem to pop up everywhere.
j. You have to call a spade a spade, tell it like it is.

Rehearsal Time

La verdad sobre las comidas. (The truth about foods.) What do you remember about typical Hispanic foods? Answer **V** for *verdad* or **F** for *falso*. Check your answers in the Answer Key.

1. La paella siempre contiene arroz.

2. El gazpacho es una sopa fría.

3. El lechón asado es un postre.

4. Un plato de arroz y frijoles negros se llama moros y cristianos.

5. El ceviche normalmente contiene carne de vaca.

6. A los vegetarianos les encantan las parrilladas.

Answers: 1. i, 2. e, 3. j, 4. h, 5. b, 6. f, 7. g, 8. a, 9. d, 10. c

Amor, pasión y aventura

The Fine Arts of Love and Romance

Preview

1. How do you say "darling" or "sweetheart" in Spanish?

2. What are "green stories"?

3. How have lovers in Spain traditionally used the book called *Rimas*?

4. What do you say when you want to ask someone to go out with you?

5. How do you accept or decline an invitation?

6. Why do young couples like *boleros*?

7. What are the two different meanings of the word *salsa*?

8. What are the three *F*'s that Mexican women look for in a husband?

9. What does it mean to "throw flowers" at someone?

10. What Spanish word means "love at first sight"?

Spanish Is the Lovin' Tongue

Spanish is the lovin' tongue,
Sweet as evening, bright as day.
Was a gal I learned it from
Way down by Sonora Way.

Oh, I don't look much like a lover,
Still, I say her love words over
Evenings when I'm all alone . . .
¡Mi amor, mi corazón!

One of the many versions of the old cowboy song "Spanish Is the Lovin' Tongue," these words express a widely held stereotype of the Spanish language: that it is somehow more sensual and expressive, more personal and intimate, than English. As is the case with many (but not all) stereotypes, there is *un granito de verdad* ("a grain of truth") in this idea, and that is partly why Spanish and Latin American songs are becoming more and more popular all over the world. The following section explains some of the historic and grammatical reasons for these ideas.

Most people agree that it is easier to use English for giving directions or explaining how to assemble something because you can be more concise and it's faster to *ir al grano* (literally, "go to the grain," or "get to the point"). But for poetry and song, for spirituality or seduction, for describing people or analyzing feelings, Spanish has certain advantages in its power of expression.

Una lengua melodiosa y seductora

One reason for the expressive power of Spanish is its seductive "music," the soft mellifluous sounds that seem to caress the tongue. This is a quality Spanish shares to some extent with French, Italian, Portuguese, Catalan, and Romanian. All these languages have a common origin: they began from the everyday speech of the Roman soldiers who conquered much of Europe during the first millennium and imposed the discipline of the Roman Empire. They left behind a rough Latin that was gradually altered and shaped by the influence of local dialects, as well as regional tastes and preferences, resulting in the modern European languages that we call today the romance languages (meaning "derived from the Romans"). Many people think that the term "romance languages" refers to the romantic aura of love and sexual attraction projected by the cultures where these languages are spoken, and no wonder! The word "romance" actually contains this meaning as well because many traditions of courtly love were developed over the centuries in these languages through songs, ballads, poems, stories, and the earliest examples of the novel. The sounds of these languages are intimately tied to passionate expressions of love and desire.

Read with an affectionate tone the following terms of endearment and the sentences that follow them. These are examples of words used by lovers throughout the Spanish-speaking world. Listen to the sweetness of the sounds as they roll off your tongue, play-act a love scene in your mind (role playing is a good way to imprint phrases in your memory), and try to capture the seductive power and "music" of Spanish.

TOP TEN Names to Call Your Honey (Male or Female) and Examples of "Sweet Nothings"

1. **alma mía, mi alma** (literally, [my] soul) *Ven acá, alma mía.* Come here, darling.

2. **amor, mi amor, amor de mi vida** (literally, [my] love, love of my life) *No tengas pena, mi amor.* Don't feel embarrassed (upset), my love.

3. **amorcito, mi amorcito, mi amorciano** (literally, [my] little love, my Martian love) *Amorcito, dame un abrazo.* Sweetie, give me a hug.

4. **ángel, mi ángel, ángel de mi vida** (literally, [my] angel, angel of my life) *Dame un besito, mi ángel.* Give me a little kiss, angel.

5. **cariño, mi cariño** (literally, [my] affection or caress) *Y ahora, unos besotes, cariño.* And now, some smooches, dearest.

6. **cielo, mi cielo, cielo mío** (literally, [my] heaven or sky) *Cielo mío, no te enojes.* Honey, don't get angry.

7. **corazón, mi corazón** (literally, [my] heart) *¿Quieres dar una vuelta, mi corazón?* Do you want to go for a spin (a walk, a drive), sweetheart?

8. **luz de mi vida, luz de mis ojos** (literally, light of my life, light of my eyes) *Vamos a tomar una copa, luz de mi vida.* Let's have a drink, light of my life.

9. **mi pichón, pichoncito** (literally, my turtledove, little turledove) *Vamos a bailar, pichoncito.* Let's dance, little turtle-dove.

10. **tesoro, mi tesorito, tesoro de mi vida** (literally, treasure, my little treasure, treasure of my life) *Y ahora, tesorito, ¡vamos a hacer el amor!* And now, my treasure, let's make love!

As you can see, the diminutive endings such as *-ito* or *-cito* are often used in Spanish terms of endearment, adding the suggestion of smallness and affection. But in the fifth example, an augmentative ending, *-ote*, is used to suggest large size and a bit of humor with the idea of *besotes*, "big sloppy kisses." Some of these terms have exact equivalents in the two languages, such as *mi amor*, "my love," but most of them don't. "Honey" is a common endearment in English, but no one calls their lover *miel de abeja* in Spanish, just as *cielo* is often used in Spanish but no English speaker says, "I love you, my sky (or my heaven)!"

While these are common endearments for lovers, some of them are used at times in other situations. Men, particularly those in Venezuela, Colombia, the Carribbean islands, and parts of Mexico and Central America, often use terms like *mi amor* or *mi reina* ("my queen") when dealing with any woman they consider attractive, regardless of age or circumstance. This can happen when being served in a store or office or restaurant. Nowadays, some women do the same thing in a humorous or ironic way when dealing with men. This form of speaking, which is almost a kind of *coqueteo* ("flirtation"), is sometimes called *el trato criollo* ("the Creole treatment") and it is not meant to offend or to be taken too seriously.

TOP TEN Names to Call Your Darling

1. **chato(-a)** pug-nosed, small nosed; while a "Roman" or aquiline nose is thought of as distinguished, a small nose is considered cute

2. **flaco(-a)** skinny one; generally used in an affectionate way for someone thin

3. **gordo(-a), gordito(-a)** fat or plump one, little chubby one; this is not an insult—being a bit fat or chubby is often considered attractive (healthy, perhaps because there's more to love)

4. **lindo(-a) precioso(-a)** precious beauty

5. **mamacita, papacito, mami, papi** little mama, little father, mommy, daddy; these do not imply that the person you say them to is older than you, and in fact they are said even to children

6. **mi dueño(-a)** my owner or my master, my mistress

7. **mi rey, mi reina** my king, my queen

8. **m'ijo (mi hijo), m'ija (mi hija)** my son, my daughter; they are also used for a good friend who is about the same age as you or younger

9. **muñeco(-a)** doll

10. **querido(-a)** dear; this is used to express affection and also, of course, at the beginning of letters or postcards: *Querido David*, *Querida María*, or *Queridos amigos*

Nicknames, especially ones referring to personal physical characteristics, are often used in Spanish-speaking societies; not only the most common ones, like *gordo*, *flaco*, and *chato*, but others that are more inventive and elaborate. (These can be used for anyone, not just sweethearts.) Another term common in many places for "darling" or "dear" is *negro(-a)*, *negrito(-a)* ("little black one"), which may seem odd to English speakers because it is used to refer to people of all skin colors, but it is very common and affectionate.

♪ Rehearsal Time

Palabras dulces. (Sweet words.) Match the literal meanings to the terms of endearment you can say to your honey in Spanish. Check your answers in the Answer Key.

1. the word for affection
2. light of my eyes
3. little treasure
4. my queen
5. love of my life
6. little mama
7. daddy
8. dear
9. small-nosed one
10. my master

a. amor de mi vida
b. amorcito
c. cariño
d. chato(-a)
e. cielo mío
f. corazón
g. luz de mis ojos
h. mamacita
i. mi dueño
j. mi reina
k. papi
l. pichoncito
m. querido(-a)
n. tesorito

Poesía sin puritanismo

Besides its seductive music, Spanish is more passionate and sensual than English in other ways. Partly this is due to its lack of the Puritan influence that imbued English with a strong burden of guilt and shame many centuries ago. Even though customs have changed radically, traces of this shame and evasion remain in the language and its way of viewing sex and romance. For example, in English people call sexual jokes, stories, and thoughts "dirty," refer to an extramarital relationship as an "affair," and to the product of such a union as an "illegitimate child." In contrast to these terms relating sex to filth, business, and illegality, the Spanish equivalents refer to the color green, adventure, and nature.

TOP FIVE Shameless Spanish Terms Relating to Sex

1. **una aventura** an adventure (affair); a love relationship outside of marriage

2. **un hijo natural** a natural child (illegitimate child); a child born from an extramarital relationship

3. **historias verdes** green stories (dirty stories); humorous stories about sex

4. **chistes verdes** green jokes (dirty jokes); jokes about sex

5. **un viejo verde** a green old man (dirty old man); an old man who still thinks about sex

One of the great vehicles for passion is poetry, which holds an exalted place in all Spanish-speaking cultures. In his autobiography, *Vivir para contarlo (Living to Tell the Tale)*, the world-famous Colombian novelist Gabriel García Márquez talks about the passion that he and his friends felt for poetry during their teens and twenties, how they would furtively scribble their own poems, rush to bookstores to read the newest poetry from abroad, and ardently follow the most revered poets of the day the way many adolescents today follow the lives of rock stars. The young men in his group were even more passionate about poetry than they were about *fútbol* ("soccer"), a sport that also inflamed them. They in no way felt that poetry was for sissies or only for girls. In Latin America and Spain, poets have traditionally been greatly respected by the general public, and their governments have frequently awarded them jobs or diplomatic posts. Often their poems deal with political and social issues of the day, but their most popular and transcendent theme is, of course, love.

Young men traditionally use poetry in their efforts to *enamorar* ("win over") the young women who have become the objects of their hearts' desire. In a recent open letter on the Internet, New York dramatist Ariel Dorfman (most famous for his play *Death and the Maiden*) recalls growing up in Chile, memorizing lines from the love sonnets of the great Nobel Prize–winning poet Pablo Neruda, and quoting them to a ravishing young lady. (Unfortunately, she merely looked disdainfully at him and suggested he would do better to quote Neruda's *«Una canción desesperada»* ["A Desperate Song"]!) The short verses of the most famous of all the romantic poets of Spain, Gustavo Adolfo Bécquer (1863–1888), have also been traditionally used by Latin lovers. His book of *Rimas* illustrates the many shades of love as it begins to bloom, grows, bursts forth, then falters and fades through the varying moments of a relationship. Indeed, there is a *rima* for almost every nuance of a lover's feelings. One of the favorites for young men to quote, generally while lifting a glass of wine and looking deeply into the eyes of a young woman, is the one that follows. Read it aloud slowly and try to hear its soft lyrical sounds.

Rima XIII

Por una mirada, un mundo,
por una sonrisa, un cielo,

por un beso... yo no sé

¡Qué te diera por un beso!

Rhyme XII

In exchange for a look, a world,
in exchange for a smile,
   a heaven,
in exchange for a kiss . . .
I don't know
what I could ever give you
for a kiss!

     —GUSTAVO ADOLFO BÉCQUER

The speaker simply expresses his total admiration and desire in a humble and pleading way. Some *galanes* ("suitors," young men interested in romance) say this is very effective, especially with *gringas* who are not used to this kind of treatment from *gringo* men, reputed to be much more *seco* ("dry," matter-of-fact) than Latinos. There is an endless number of poets and styles to choose from and every country has its poet-heroes.

On a more intense and openly erotic note, you have the works of the Nicaraguan Rubén Darío (1867–1916), one of the classic love poets of Latin America. Read the verses that follow to feel the passionate power of his poetry.

Que el amor no admite cuerdas reflexiones

For Love Does Not Permit Sane Thinking

**Señora, amor es violento,
y cuando nos transfigura
nos enciende el pensamiento
la locura.**

Lady, love is violent
and when it transforms us
our thoughts are inflamed
by madness.

**No pidas paz a
mis brazos
que a los tuyos tienen
presos:
Son de guerra mis abrazos
y son de incendio mis besos;
y sería vano intento
el tornar mi mente obscura
si me enciende el
pensamiento
la locura.**

Don't beg for peace from
my arms
that have imprisoned yours:

For my embraces are of war
and my kisses are of fire;
and it would be a vain attempt
to turn my mind to darkness
if my thoughts are inflamed

by madness.

Of course, of the many types of love, one of the most intense is the spiritual longing of human beings for God. Spanish is also the language of the great mystic writers of the sixteenth century, Teresa de Ávila and San Juan de la Cruz, whose impassioned works have thrilled and inspired people from many cultures. Although they deal with spiritual themes, this poetry, too, is ripe with sensuality. In one of his most famous poems, San Juan de la Cruz describes the quest of the soul for God in erotic detail, with the soul portrayed as a young country girl running through fields of flowers in a passionate search for the *Amado* ("Beloved"), who is God. Read the verses in which she finally finds and joins with him:

Cántico espiritual

**En la interior bodega
de mi Amado bebí, y
cuando salía
por toda aquella vega
ya cosa no sabía**

**y el ganado perdí que
antes seguía.
Allí me dio
su pecho,
allí me enseñó ciencia
muy sabrosa
y yo le di de hecho
a mí sin dejar cosa,
allí le prometí de ser
su Esposa.**

Spiritual Song

In the inner wine cellar
of my Beloved I drank, and
    when I left
all through that whole meadow
I could no longer recognize
    a thing

and I lost the cattle I had been
    tending.
There he pulled me to his
    chest,
there he taught me a most
    delicious science
and I gave him completely
myself, without holding back,
there I promised him to be
his wife.

This and two other poems of San Juan, *«La noche oscura del alma»* ("The Dark Night of the Soul") and *«Llama de amor viva»* ("Flame of Living Love") are universal classics in the literature of mysticism that at the same time present vivid images of sensual love.

Getting Started: How to Invite Someone to Go Out with You

Whether it be sublime or down-to-earth, every relationship must have a beginning. Perhaps someone has caught your eye and you would like to get to know him or her better. It may be simply to have company at the dinner table or it could be the start of a beautiful friendship. In English we typically say, "Would you like to go out for coffee (or for a drink)?" In Spanish it's more common to say: *¿Quisieras (Quisiera usted) dar una vuelta?* ("Would you like to go for a walk [or ride]?") The same word *vuelta* can be used to refer to either walk or ride (as well as the word *paseo*).

But there are many other ways to invite someone out. Here are some of them.

TOP TEN Examples of How to Invite Someone Out

1. **Hace mucho ruido aquí. Mejor nos vamos a otra parte, ¿no?** It's really noisy here. It would be better to go somewhere else, don't you think?

2. **Hay una buena película en el cine. ¿Podríamos verla esta noche, tú (usted) y yo?** There's a good film at the movie theater. Could we go and see it tonight, you and I?

3. **¿Por qué no vamos al museo de arte? Dicen que es muy interesante.** Why don't we go to the art museum? They say it's very interesting.

4. **Voy a la plaza. ¿Te (Le) importaría acompañarme?** I'm going to the square. Would you mind coming along with me?

5. **Tengo que comprar un regalo. ¿Quisieras acompañarme? (¿Quisiera usted acompañarme?)** I have to buy a present. Would you like to accompany me?

6. **Podríamos cenar juntos, ¿qué te (le) parece?** We could have supper together, what do you think?

7. **¿Y si fuéramos a tomar una copa ahora?** What if we were to go out for a drink now?

8. **Quiero tomar la lección de tango del hotel, pero no tengo pareja. ¿Te (Le) interesaría?** I want to take the tango lesson at the hotel but don't have a partner. Would you be interested?

9. **¿Te (Le) gustaría ir al parque conmigo?** Would you like to go to the park with me?

10. **¿Qué tal si damos una vuelta?** How about if we go out for a walk (or ride)?

One thing to remember with invitations is that in most parts of the Spanish-speaking world it is understood that the one who invites, pays. On the other hand, if a group of people are sitting around together and decide to go out to eat, that is different. In that case, usually everyone pays his or her own bill.

There are many different ways to accept or decline an invitation. Here are some of them.

TOP TEN Ways to Accept an Invitation, from the Mildly Indifferent to the Openly Enthusiastic

1. **Bueno, está bien.** Sure, all right.

2. **Pues, sí. De acuerdo.** Well, yes. O.K.

3. **¿Por qué no?** Why not?

4. **Buena idea. Vamos, pues.** Good idea. Let's go, then.

5. **Sí, estaría encantado(-a).** Yes, I'd be delighted.

6. **Claro que sí, gracias.** But of course, thank you.

7. **Sí, me encantaría.** Yes, I'd love to.

8. **¡Cómo no! Con mucho gusto.** Of course! With pleasure.

9. **¡Qué idea más linda! Gracias por la invitación.** What a wonderful idea! Thanks for the invitation.

10. **¡Fantástico! ¡Con muchísimo gusto!** Fantastic! With great pleasure!

TOP FIVE Ways to Decline an Invitation When You Really Do Not Want to Go

1. **No puedo. Tengo mucho que hacer.** I can't. I have a lot to do.

2. **Gracias, pero es imposible.** Thanks, but it's impossible.

3. **No, gracias. No es posible.** No, thanks. It's not possible.

4. **Estoy muy ocupado(-a). No puedo ir.** I'm very busy. I can't go.

5. **No, no puedo, gracias. No tengo mucho tiempo.** No, I can't, thanks. I don't have much time.

TOP FIVE Ways to Decline an Invitation When You Really *Do* Want to Go but Can't

1. **¡Qué lástima! Realmente me encantaría, pero no me es posible hoy.** What a shame! I really would love to, but it's not possible for me today.

2. **Muchas gracias por la invitación. Tengo otros planes, pero ¿por qué no lo hacemos otro día?** Thank you very much for the invitation. I have other plans, but why don't we do it another time?

3. **Desgraciadamente, no puedo hoy. ¿Tal vez mañana?** Unfortunately, I can't today. Maybe tomorrow?

4. **¡Qué lástima! Tengo un compromiso esta tarde (noche). ¿Quizás en otra oportunidad?** What a pity! I have an engagement this afternoon (tonight). Perhaps some other time?

5. **Ay, ¡cómo me gustaría! No es posible mañana, pero pasado mañana estoy libre.** Oh, how I would like to! It isn't possible tomorrow, but the day after tomorrow I'm free.

Rehearsal Time

La pasión en palabras y poesía. (Passion in words and poetry.) Complete the sentences with the appropriate missing word from the list that follows. Check your answers in the Answer Key.

1. An extramarital affair (love relationship) is called in Spanish *una* _____.

   aventura

2. A dirty joke (one about sex) is called *un chiste* _____.

   beso

3. An illegitimate child (born outside of wedlock) is *un hijo* _____.

   bodega

4. The verb that means "to make (someone) fall in love with you" is _____.

   enamorar

5. In one of his famous *rimas*, the great love poet of Spain, Gustavo Adolfo Bécquer, says that he

doesn't know what he could possibly give *por un*
_____.   locura

6. Rubén Darío, the famous romantic poet from
Nicaragua, describes love as a violent force that
inflames our thoughts *con* _____.   natural

7. The Spanish mystical poet San Juan de la Cruz
speaks of drinking from the Beloved in the
interior _____.   verde

Invitaciones. Choose the correct word to complete the sentences.

1. Hace mucho _____ aquí. Mejor nos vamos a otra parte,
¿no?
   a. taco
   b. ruido
   c. dinero

2. Tengo que comprar un regalo. ¿Quisieras _____?
   a. manejarla
   b. acompañarme
   c. investigarlo

3. ¿Y si fuéramos a tomar una _____ ahora?
   a. bolsa
   b. copa
   c. manzana

4. ¿Qué tal si nos _____ una vuelta?
   a. damos
   b. encontramos
   c. traemos

5. Bueno, _____ bien.
   a. es
   b. está
   c. hace

6. Sí, estaría _____.
   a. enajenado(-a)
   b. encantado(-a)
   c. enamorado(-a)

7. ¡Qué idea _____ linda! Gracias por la invitación.
   a. más
   b. menos
   c. muy

8. No puedo. Tengo mucho que _____.
   a. buscar
   b. comprender
   c. hacer

9. Desgraciadamente, no puedo hoy. ¿Tal vez _____?
   a. ayer
   b. tarde
   c. mañana

10. ¡Qué lástima! Tengo un _____ esta tarde. ¿Quizás en otra oportunidad?
    a. compromiso
    b. gusto
    c. edificio

Música y amores

You only have to think of the many romantic songs in Spanish that are so popular today to realize that the tradition of love poetry lives on. Each region of the Spanish-speaking world has its own rhythm and song traditions, and many of them are dedicated to the theme of love. In contrast to parties in the United States and Canada, which usually revolve around eating, drinking, and talking (with perhaps a bit of background music), most parties and gatherings in Spain and Latin America wind up with singing, dancing, and/or playing music. Many of the song lyrics are more explicitly erotic than most songs in English, but not in a vulgar way. In the song «*Burbujas de amor*» ("Love Bubbles") by the Dominican singer-songwriter Juan Luis Guerra, a lover imagines himself as a fish swimming down into the sweet waters and lush net of his beloved and then on into other suggestive places.

There are many types of songs that deal mainly with love and passion and sensual rhythms that are used for dancing. Here are some of them:

TOP TEN Romantic Musical Traditions of Spain and Latin America

1. **la música andina** the haunting music of the Andes mountains; *Conjuntos* ("groups") from northern Argentina, Bolivia, Chile, Ecuador, and Peru play lilting melodies and lively dances with a strong indigenous influence, using guitars and special instruments like *la zampoña* (a pan pipe made from reeds), *la quena* (a reed flute), *el charango* (a stringed instrument made from an armadillo shell), and various kinds of *tambores* ("drums")

2. **los boleros** slow romantic songs that couples dance to at the end of the evening, *muy apretados* ("tightly pressed together")

3. **la cumbia** a catchy Colombian rhythm, generally accompanied by spicy lyrics; it is not too hard for *gringos* to dance to, because a simple swaying movement right on the beat does the trick.

4. **la música de los mariachi** the universally popular Mexican love tunes sung in melodic harmonies and occasional falsettos by trios and larger groups with guitars, horns, and drums; the lyrics are often very *halagadoras* ("flattering") and aimed at softening the will of a beautiful woman.

5. **el merengue** a Caribbean rhythm born in the rural areas of the Dominican Republic providing the background beat for heartfelt and often witty lyrics about the yearning for love and, in some cases, social justice

6. **las rancheras** country music songs in waltz tempo from the North of Mexico, with common themes like *la mujer ingrata* ("the unresponsive woman") or the loneliness and longing of a man far away from his *amada* ("beloved") or his *pueblo natal* ("home town") or state, for example, Guanajuato, Jalisco, etc., sung to the accompaniment of guitars, horns, and sometimes drums

7. **la salsa** the most famous of Latino rhythms, *salsa* is an amalgam of Cuban and Puerto Rican dance tempos with jazz from the United States; the name comes from the word for hot chili sauce (*salsa picante*). It's usually hard for *gringos* to dance *salsa* because the steps are done counter-tempo or off the beat.

8. **el flamenco** the best known of the many musical traditions of Spain, the Gypsy music of Andalucía, the southernmost province; dancers in elaborate costumes perform a complicated *zapateo* ("tap dance") with sensual movements, often responding in speed and intensity to the *palmadas* ("hand clapping") of the viewing public. Usually this spectacle includes guitars and the *cante jondo* ("deep-throat song") of yearning and anguish. The best performers are said to be *gitanos* ("Gypsies") especially those who have *ángel* (a mysterious quality that cannot be defined). Many of the *ritmos del flamenco* (such as *sevillanas*) are played in *los clubes nocturnos* ("nightclubs") of Madrid and other big cities where couples dance to them all night long.

9. **el son de Cuba** music that originated from ancient rituals of the Afro-Cuban religion called *santería* (somewhat similar to the better-known voodoo of Haiti); it has influenced *salsa* and

other modern rhythms and continues to be sung and danced today.

10. **el tango** an intensely emotional dance and song tradition said to have appeared simultaneously in the ports of Buenos Aires, Argentina, and Montevideo, Uruguay, toward the end of the nineteenth century; the syncopated melodies are played in 2/4 or 4/4 time by *violines* and a special type of accordion, called the *bandoleón*, along with plaintive lyrics about love, longing, social injustice, and the anguish of life. Dramatically attired dancers execute intricate steps and sensual poses in perfect unison. The choreographer Juan Carlos Copes describes it like this: *«El tango es un corazón y cuatro piernas»* ("The tango is one heart and four legs").

Rehearsal Time

Ritmos revueltos. (Scrambled rhythms.) Unscramble the letters and write the names in Spanish of some different types of Latin music next to their descriptions. Check your answers in the Answer Key.

1. Cuban music with an ancient religious origin: **nos**

   _____

2. A catchy rhythm from Colombia: **bucima** _____

3. Mexican country music from the north: **chanarer**

   _____

4. The sad and sensual song and dance from Argentina and Uruguay: **gonat** _____

5. A Cuban-Puerto Rican hybrid beat with influences from U.S. jazz, danced in nightclubs around the world: **lassa**

   _____

6. The sensual dance and song tradition of southern Spain:
   encolamf _____

Buscando al príncipe azul

There's a popular saying in Spanish: *El hombre y el oso, cuanto más feo, más hermoso.* ("For a man or a bear, the uglier [he is], the more handsome [he seems].") This would sound strange to most young girls in the English-speaking world. When they think from time to time about meeting their prince charming they generally imagine a man who is "tall, dark, and handsome." But Mexican girls say that their *príncipe azul* (literally, "blue prince") should have the 3 *F*'s; that is, he must be *fuerte, feo y formal* ("strong, ugly, and serious")! A little further south in Argentina, Chile, and Uruguay, the saying goes that the ideal man should be *feo, peludo y hediondo* ("ugly, hairy, and stinky").

What could possibly motivate young women to want men like this? Different cultures have norms and ideals that seem surprising to people from other places, but sometimes there are explanations beneath the surface. One Mexican girl explained why she favors the 3 *F*'s in this way: "If I marry a handsome man, he is less likely to be faithful to me, so that is why I would like one who is *feo* ('ugly'). It's important for him to be *fuerte* ('strong') so he can earn good money and protect his family, and, most essential of all, he should be *formal* ('serious and proper'), not just some *sinvergüenza que no vale un bledo* ('useless bum who isn't worth a piece of pigweed')." Of course, this description doesn't explain the ideal of masculinity in the Southern Cone as *peludo y hediondo* ("hairy and stinky"). Perhaps this is the old-fashioned view of a very heterosexual male who does not care too much about his appearance, one so full of male hormones that he will be guaranteed to produce lots of children!

Whatever your ideal may be, most people look for that one right person, a soul mate or life companion. Here are some ways to refer to him or her in Spanish:

TOP FIVE Ways to Describe Your Soul Mate

1. **la horma de tu zapato** the wooden model of your shoe; a perfect fit, what makes you feel good and comfortable. *Es la horma de mi zapato.* He (She) is just what I was looking for.

2. **tu ídolo** your idol or ideal, referring to your adored one, most admired person, or dream lover. *Alejandro dice que Jennifer López es su ídolo.* Alexander says that Jennifer López is his idol.

3. **tu media naranja** your orange half, the person who makes you feel complete, your better half; perhaps the closest way of saying "soul mate." *Conocí a mi media naranja en el gimnasio.* I met my soul mate (husband, wife, companion) at the gym.

4. **tu peoresnada** your worse-is-nothing or better-than-nothing; ironic or humorous way of referring to your lover or mate. *Amalia fue a la fiesta sin su peoresnada.* Amalia went to the party without her current boyfriend.

5. **tu príncipe azul, la mujer de tus sueños** your prince charming, the woman of your dreams. *Muchos jóvenes buscan su príncipe azul o la mujer de sus sueños en el Internet.* Lots of young people look for their prince charming or the woman of their dreams on the Internet.

Rehearsal Time

Buscando el amor. (Looking for love.) Circle the Spanish word or phrase that best fits each definition. Check your answers in the Answer Key.

1. A young girl's image of the perfect man to marry
   a. cuanto oso
   b. príncipe azul
   c. sinvergüenza

2. The important trait of being serious and hardworking
   a. formal
   b. fuerte
   c. hermoso

3. My soul mate or better half
   a. mi media naranja
   b. mi otra mitad
   c. la respuesta a mi pregunta

4. Someone I worship and admire, even if he or she might be unattainable
   a. la santa de mi iglesia
   b. mi diseño
   c. mi ídolo

5. My current boyfriend or girlfriend who is better than nothing
   a. mi sinisueño
   b. mi peoresnada
   c. mi cuadro roto

El arte de enamorar or Whatever Happened to the Latin Lover?

Curiously, there is no verb in modern English to express *enamorar*, the active Spanish verb meaning "to make someone fall in love with you." Of course, there used to be verbs for that in Renaissance times, in the days of courtly love when one spoke about "wooing" or trying to "enamor" someone. It seems this gallant masculine behavior has fallen out of favor in the English-speaking world, but not so in Spanish-speaking cultures where the tradition is alive and well. Young Mexican women may look for the 3 *F*'s when seeking a *buen partido* ("good match for marriage"), but most of them enjoy romantic overtures too. They simply don't trust them. Perhaps that is why some Latino women say they find gringo men less passionate and exciting but more trustworthy. Conversely, *gringas* often fall head over heels for the Latino guys because no one has ever tried to *enamorar* or *conquistar* ("win") them before.

TOP FIVE Techniques of Latin Lovers to *enamorar* a Woman

1. **echarle flores, hacer cumplidos** to throw flowers at her: in fact, *echar flores* is an idiom that means the same as *hacer cumplidos*, "to compliment," or *elogiar*, "to praise" someone. Man or woman, flattery is a sure way to a person's heart.

2. **hacerle ojitos, coquetear** to make "little eyes" at her, to flirt; *el coqueteo* ("flirting") often involves looking deeply into someone's eyes, reciting poetry, giving little gifts or flowers, or just remembering someone's preferences.

3. **llevarle serenata** to give her a serenade; the ultimate expression of romantic love, the young man brings a professional group, or some of his friends with guitars and other instruments, to his sweetheart's house to wake her up in the morning or lull her to sleep in the evening with romantic songs beneath her window.

4. **el besuqueo y los abrazotes** smooching and squeezing; the timing must be right for this, but usually the first steps are light *toques* ("touches") on the arm or elbow to help her up the steps or to guide her away from a puddle. The progress is made *poco a poco* ("little by little") because, as the old proverb counsels, *La mujer y la guitarra—con la mano.*

5. **el cachondeo** making out (literally, horning around); this of course leads to various things like *la cama* ("bed"), *una aventura* ("a love affair"), or *el matrimonio* ("marriage").

The Art of Flattering Compliments: *piropos, contrapiropos,* and Plain Old *cumplidos*

In Spanish-speaking cultures, boys begin at an early age to talk about women, analyze how they think, and discuss strategies about how to *conquistar* ("win") them. Women from English-speaking cultures, regardless of their age, notice a difference when they enter a room or walk down the street simply because men look at them more, usually provoking a reaction from the women. A pretty young Mexican girl visiting in Boston once broke down in tears after her first day, complaining to her sister, *«¡Ya no tengo pegue! No me miran los gringos.»* ("I don't have sex appeal anymore! The gringos don't look at me.") Her sister, who had lived in the United States for awhile, consoled her by telling her not to worry because the gringos don't look at anybody. Once she returned home, she'd receive plenty of attention again.

Spanish and Latin American men are known for their *piropos* ("flattering compliments" to women, flirtatious remarks). Of course, as is typical in Spanish, a language rich in specific verbs, there is a verb for this: *piropear*. It is especially common to hear these *piropos* in the street where men gather to gaze at the women walking by and throw out their comments to the general public ear.

Such street compliments are not appreciated by all women, but in many places they been developed into something approaching a high art, often mixing poetry, humor, and word play to please their target and delight the passersby. In these days of increasing equality, some women throw out *piropos* or make *contrapiropos* (smart comebacks or "put-downs") to turn the tables on their spontaneous admirers.

TOP TEN Examples of Mexican *piropos*, from Simple to Humorous and Artful

1. **¡Qué piernón!** What a pair of legs! (Literally, What a big leg!)

2. **¡Qué curvas y yo sin freno!** What curves and me with no brakes!

3. **¡Qué bombón y yo con diabetes!** What candy and me with diabetes!

4. **Si como lo mueves, lo bates... ¡qué rico chocolate!** If you mix it the way you move it, what tasty chocolate!

5. **Mamacita, si así son las vías, ¿cómo estará la estación?** Babe, if the railroad tracks are like that, what will the station be like?

6. **Eres tan dulce... que con sólo mirarte engordo.** You're so sweet that from just looking at you I get fat.

7. **Estás como Paco... ¡como pa'-co-merte, guapérrima!** You are like Paco... like gonna' eat you up, gorgeous! (This includes a play on words, *paco-merte*—the nickname Paco and the sound of *pa' comerte* [*para comerte*, to eat you up].)

8. **Me gusta el mar, me gusta la brisa, pero más me gusta tu bella sonrisa.** I like the sea, I like the breeze, but I like your beautiful smile more.

9. **Tengo frío, tengo calor. Tengo todo, menos tu amor.** I'm cold, I'm hot. I have everything, except your love. (This loses

in translation because to say "I'm cold, I'm hot" in Spanish you use the verb *tener* [to have (cold, heat)] so the idea of having everything except your love comes across better.)

10. **Tu madre debió ser pastelera pues una niña como tú no la hace cualquiera.** Your mother must have been a pastry chef because a girl like you can't be created by just anyone.

Though not as common as street compliments from men, the *piropos* and *contrapiropos* from women can be just as spicy and inventive. Here's a sampling, once again from Mexico:

TOP FIVE Examples of How Mexican Women Talk Back: *piropos* and *contrapiropos,* from Provocative to Humorous to Disdainful

1. **Si quieres ser doctor, estudia medicina. Si quieres ser mi novio, espérame en la esquina.** If you want to be a doctor, study medicine. If you want to be my boyfriend, wait for me on the corner. (provocative)

2. **Cuando pasé por tu casa, me lanzaste una flor. Pero, la próxima vez, sin maceta, ¡por favor!** When I passed by your house, you threw me a flower. But the next time I go by, without a flowerpot, please! (humorous) (There is a play on words in this comeback, because *lanzar una flor* has the double meaning of giving a compliment or literally throwing a flower.)

3. **Soy mexicana de nacimiento y respeto mi bandera. Los besos de mis labios no se los doy a cualquiera.** I'm a native-born Mexican woman and I respect my flag. Kisses from my lips I don't give to just any old guy. (ambiguous) (This

doesn't express encouragement, but doesn't completely close the door, either.)

4. **Tus besos piden ansias. Tus brazos piden amor. ¡Pero tu cochino pescuezo sólo pide agua y jabón!** Your kisses are asking for yearning. Your arms are asking for love. But your filthy neck is only asking for water and soap! (disdainful)

5. **Cuando pases por mi lado, no te quites el sombrero. Porque a hombres como tú, ¡los tiro al basurero!** When you pass by me, don't take off your hat. Because (I take) men like you and throw them in the garbage can! (totally insulting)

Even if you aren't a Latin lover, you may want to *echar una flor* or *hacer un cumplido* ("give a compliment") now and then. Here's a chance to practice some in both the *usted* and the *tú* forms.

TOP FIVE Trusty Compliments You Can Give, from Subtle to Very Direct

1. **Usted sabe mucho sobre las computadoras, señor Montes.** You know a lot about computers, Mr. Montes. In the *tú* form: *Sabes mucho sobre las computadoras, Miguel.* (familiar)

2. **Le queda muy bien ese color, señorita Domínguez.** That color is very good on you, Miss Domínguez. In the *tú* form: *Te queda muy bien ese color, Sofía.* (familiar)

3. **Me encanta su voz, señor Jiménez.** Your voice fascinates me, Mr. Jiménez. In the *tú* form: *Me encanta tu voz, Iván.* (familiar)

4. **¿Sabe usted que me cae muy bien, señorita Rubio?** Do you know that I like you a lot, Miss Rubio? In the *tú* form: *¿Sabes que me caes superbien, Teresa?* (familiar)

5. **En realidad, ¡usted es muy buena gente, señor Juárez!** Actually, you are a really nice guy, Mr. Juárez! In the *tú* form: *En realidad, ¡eres muy buena gente!* (familiar)

Do We *enamorar* Ourselves?

In English, you "fall in love." It's as though something quite outside of your control just happens, as if the Grand Canyon opened up in front of you and you somehow managed to fall in. In Spanish, *nos enamoramos de alguien*: "we make ourselves fall in love with someone," like an illusion that starts inside of us until we find someone to project it on. So we must switch our minds to the Spanish way of thinking when we use the verb *enamorarse de* to talk about "falling in love with" ("enamoring ourselves of") someone. Practice this with the following "love story."

TOP FIVE Sad Steps in a Love Quadrangle, from a Female Point of View

1. **Yo me enamoré de ti.** I fell in love with you.

2. **Tú te enamoraste de ella.** You fell in love with her.

3. **Ella se enamoró de él.** She fell in love with him.

4. **Él se enamoró de mí.** He fell in love with me.

5. **¡Pero yo me desenamoré de todos!** But I fell out of love with everyone!

You can fall out of love, too, and that is what the reflexive verb *desenamorarse* means in the above sentence. Another example: *Ahora él está desenamorándose de ella*. ("Now he is falling out of love with her.")

However you say it, no one can explain the process of love, whether it is "love at first sight," called *el flechazo* in Spanish ("the arrow wound," referring to a blow from Cupid's arrow) or a slow process that happens *paulatinamente* ("gradually"). Here are some Spanish proverbs with ideas about that mysterious thing called love:

TOP FIVE Proverbs About Love

1. **Adonde el corazón se inclina, el pie camina.** To the place where the heart is inclined, the foot walks.

2. **Cada oveja con su pareja.** Every sheep with its partner.

3. **El amor y el interés se fueron al campo un día. Pudo más el interés que el amor que se tenía.** Love and self-interest went off to battle one day. Self-interest won out and love went away.

4. **Cuando el hambre entra por la puerta, el amor sale por la ventana.** When hunger enters the door, love goes out the window.

5. **Contigo pan y cebolla.** With you, bread and onions. (I will stay with you even if we are poor.)

Rehearsal Time

Piropos and *contrapiropos.* How well do you understand the Mexican street compliments and comebacks from the Top Ten *piropos* and the Top Five *contrapiropos*? Look back at these lists and put the correct number from them next to each description. Check your answers in the Answer Key.

1. A flattering poem to a woman's smile.

2. The comical comeback by a woman to a man who has "thrown her a flower."

3. A compliment using the metaphor of a car driving down a winding street.

4. An artful poem to a woman, suggesting she is a very special creation, thanks to her mother.

5. The simple expression of admiration for a woman's shapely legs.

El vocabulario del amor: sinónimos. Match the words on the left to their correct synonyms or definitions. Check your answers in the Answer Key.

1. el flechazo   a. conquistar

2. el charango   b. la horma de tu zapato

3. echar flores   c. el amor a primera vista

4. enamorar   d. el hombre ideal

5. el flamenco   e. guitarra hecha del caparazón del armadillo

6. hacer ojitos   f. música del sur de España

7. historias verdes   g. cuentos sobre temas sexuales

8. el príncipe azul   h. coquetear

9. tu media naranja   i. hacer cumplidos

El vocabulario del amor: antónimos. Match the words on the left to their antonyms, words with very different or opposite meanings. Check your answers in the Answer Key.

1. peludo   a. hermoso

2. violento   b. sin pelo (calvo)

3. casarse   c. tranquilo, suave

4. chato(-a)   d. persona de nariz prominente

5. enamorarse   e. sinvergüenza

6. feo   f. perfumado

7. gordo   g. desenamorarse

8. hediondo   h. equilibrio mental

9. hombre formal   i. divorciarse

10. locura   j. flaco

El amor es el único camino que no tiene final.
Love is the only road that has no end.
—Eduardo Palomo, a popular Mexican
actor who died suddenly from a
stroke at the age of 41 in November
2003, leaving behind his much
beloved wife and children and
an adoring public

TUNE-UP
5

¡Viajar es vivir!

Traveling the Many Worlds of Spanish-Speaking Cultures

1. How many countries have Spanish as an official language?

2. Who was the first European to drink a cup of hot chocolate?

3. Where is the world's highest waterfall?

4. What is the biggest mistake you can make when trying to speak Spanish?

5. When buying tickets, what difference is there between *boletos* and *entradas*?

6. Where do you go for a haircut and how do you ask for directions to get there?

7. What do you say to find out if it's safe to drink the tap water?

8. At a hotel, how do you ask for a private bathroom or for air conditioning?

9. What do you say if there's no hot water or it's too noisy?

10. What happens during *la Tomatina* in Spain and *la Diablada* in Bolivia?

It is sometimes said, *Viajar es vivir* ("To travel is to live") because the experience of entering into a different environment and culture stimulates the senses with its novelty and excitement. This is especially true in the Spanish-speaking world because of its great diversity (*la gran diversidad*), the rich variety of foods, dress, physical appearance, customs, and landscapes that extends over four continents. This unique blending of cultures began over 500 years ago when Spain—a country that had already been a melting pot for millennia—collided with the native societies of the New World. That is why some visitors today view Latin America as "Europe with a Latin twist." With the introduction of African elements to Latin America shortly afterward, this melting pot became even richer and more diverse with new foods, music, and other linguistic and cultural influences.

Una vista panorámica del mundo hispano

Paradoxically, underlying this diversity is another remarkable aspect of the Spanish-speaking world: its amazing unity, *la asombrosa unidad*. Whether you are hiking in the Andes among descendants of the Incas, listening to tango music in a bar in Buenos Aires, or bargaining for silver jewelry in Mexico City's *mercado de artesanías*, you will perceive the similarity: one major language, one dominant religion, and even the same basic urban plan in almost every city and town.

Although a number of regional languages are spoken in Spain itself and native languages thrive in many parts of Latin America, the presence of Spanish, *el español* (also called *el castellano*), is everywhere. The same is true for the customs, practices, and monuments of the Catholic religion. And despite minor variations, every *ciudad* or *pueblo* has its central square, called *la plaza central, el centro*, or, in Mexico, *el zócalo*. This is the heart of the city or town, often graced with a park, surrounded by impressive old buildings (barring the repeated onslaught of past earthquakes), and nearly always filled with people who come to *dar una vuelta* or *dar un paseo* ("take a stroll"), to see and be seen.

This surprising unity is one reason that you often hear people say in Spanish: *¡El mundo es un pañuelo!*, a phrase that literally means "The world is a handkerchief!" but more or less translates as, "Isn't it a small world!"

Finding Your Way Around the Spanish-Speaking World

This unity in diversity means that you can travel to many unique destinations in the far-flung corners of the globe and still communicate in Spanish. You can find almost anything your heart desires in one of these places. True, there are regional differences in the way the language is spoken (see Tune-Up 9), but these are not so great as to cause many problems. Spanish is the official language of twenty-one countries. Here is a quick look at them.

España, la «madre patria»

Since Neolithic times (twenty thousand years ago), when humans left their handprints in the *cuevas de Altamira* ("Altamira Caves"), Spain has been a crossroads of cultures. Iberians, Visigoths, Romans, Moors—all have left their traces in buildings and artifacts. From sophisticated cities like Barcelona or Madrid to beach resorts like San Sebastián in the north or Marbella in the south, Spain has something for every taste: medieval walled towns full of castles and monasteries, cathedrals shimmering in silver and gold, paintings by world-famous artists like El Greco, Velásquez, and Goya. The unique architecture blending Christian and Islamic elements is especially evident in Andalucía, the exotic region in the south that stood as the last stronghold of *los moros* ("the Moors"), who invaded from North Africa in 711 and remained for more than 700 years, until they were finally beaten back by the Christians during the *Reconquista* ("Reconquest"). Sevilla, Córdoba, and Granada are the three jewels of the region, cosmopolitan urban centers with ancient churches, mosques, palaces, parks, and monuments exquisitely preserved.

México, nuestro vecino (Neighbor) de América del Norte

Mexico has more people than any other Spanish-speaking country. Its warm climate, stunning colonial and indigenous structures, and breathtaking natural wonders make it a popular tourist destination. Beach resorts such as Acapulco, Puerto Vallarta, and Mazatlán on the Pacific Ocean are especially inviting to tourists; Cancún on the Yucatán Peninsula not only offers lovely beach resorts but is close to fascinating ruins of the ancient Mayans. Farther south in the interior is *la Ciudad de México* ("Mexico City"), also called *el D. F.* (short for *Distrito Federal*, the "federal district," because, as the capital, it does not belong to any of the thirty-one states). It was built over the ruins of the ancient Aztec capital of Tenochtitlán, where Emperor Moctezuma invited the Spanish conquistador Hernán Cortés to a cup of hot chocolate (the first ever tasted by a European) in 1518. Today's Mexico City is a dynamic place filled with museums, art galleries, stores, restaurants, markets, and fascinating Aztec ruins. Tourists may visit the nearby site of a much earlier, pre-Aztec culture and climb the unforgettable *Pirámides del Sol y de la Luna* ("Pyramids of the Sun and Moon"). Ruins of equally ancient cultures abound in many parts of the nation, as do colonial cities such as Guanajuato, a United Nations world-heritage site carved into the side of a cliff near silver mines that have been operating since the sixteenth century.

Estados Unidos (EE.UU.) (U.S.A.) y partes de Canadá

Although English is the only official language of the United States, Spanish is heard in many places, especially in the southwest, Florida, and large cities like Los Angeles, Chicago, and New York. People of Spanish-speaking origin now form the largest minority group, over 12 percent of the population, with the highest number being of Mexican background, but with representation from all the Spanish-speaking countries. Many consider this to be poetic justice because historically Spaniards did a lot of the exploration and settling of what is now the United States, as you can tell by a glance at the names on a map: *Colorado* ("Red"), *Nevada* ("Snowfall"), *Santa Fe* ("Holy Faith"), *Sangre de Cristo* ("Blood of Christ") Mountains, *Amarillo* ("Yellow"), *Sacramento* ("sacrament"), or *San Diego* ("Saint James"). Canada is a bilingual country with both English and French as official languages, but the number of Spanish-speaking immigrants has increased greatly in the last few decades, especially in some of its larger cities like Montreal, Toronto, Vancouver, Calgary, and Edmonton.

Tres islas del Caribe: Cuba, República Dominicana y Puerto Rico

These three island nations are blessed with a delightful climate, majestic palm trees, and a Latin beat. Cuba has been ruled for almost fifty years by Fidel Castro, who still claims to enforce a type of communism, but tourists have a great time there swimming, fishing, and dancing while freely disposing of their capital. The Dominican Republic attracts many visitors, too, especially to its beautiful beaches for swimming, surfing, sailing, and excellent windsurfing. Puerto Rico is officially an *estado libre asociado* (literally, a "free associated state"), a title usually translated as "commonwealth partner" of the United States. This means that Puerto Ricans move freely to and from the mainland; also, many institutions, like the health and education systems, are similar. Tourists flock to Puerto Rico to hike in the lush interior or swim and snorkel at the beach resorts.

América Central, desde el norte hacia el sur (from North to South): Guatemala, El Salvador, Honduras, Nicaragua, Costa Rica, Panamá

These six warm countries were described by Chilean poet Pablo Neruda as «*la dulce cintura de América*» ("the sweet waistline of America") because they occupy the narrow band of land connecting North and South America. This means they have a lot of coastline on two oceans, lush vegetation, and a great diversity of sweet fruits and tropical flora and fauna. Highlights for tourists include the intriguing ruins of ancient Mayan cities such as Tikal in Guatemala and Copán in Honduras, the incomparable *Bosque Nubloso de Montecristo* ("Montecristo Cloud Forest") in the north of El Salvador (with many rare species of plants and animals), the picturesque colonial city of Granada in Nicaragua, the natural *baños termales* ("thermal baths") near the faithfully erupting fireworks of *el Volcán Arenal* ("Arenal Volcano") in Costa Rica, and Panama's *Museo Interoceánico* ("Interoceanic Museum") and *Jardines Botánicos* ("Botanical Gardens").

El norte de Sudamérica: Venezuela, Colombia, Ecuador

Venezuela is an oil-rich Caribbean country with sparkling white-sand beaches, warm crystal waters, and tropical sunshine all year long. It has a sophisticated, cosmopolitan capital, Caracas; sections of broad open plains; tropical Amazon jungles; the world's highest waterfall, *el Salto Ángel*; and the largest number of avian species of any nation on the planet, making it a paradise for birdwatchers.

Colombia has several important cities: on the Caribbean coast, there are Barranquilla and Cartagena, a beautiful old city with historic ramparts and the *Castillo de San Felipe de Barajas*, considered a masterpiece of seventeenth-century engineering. Medellín, Manizales and Cali are in the mountains as well as the capital, Bogotá, which boasts many artistic treasures including pre-Columbian gold artifacts in its *Museo del Oro* ("Gold Museum"), modern paintings in the *Donación Botero*, and precious gems in the *Mercado de las Esmeraldas* ("Emerald Market").

The capital of Ecuador is Quito, an architectural gem of the Spanish colonial period often described as the most beautiful of all Latin American cities, with its stately churches, monasteries, and museums. The city is surrounded by volcanoes, some of which are still active; every day its newspapers publish a volcano report alongside the weather report. Twenty-six kilometers away is a monument marking the exact location of the equator (*ecuador*), with a museum for tourists including displays about the many indigenous communities of the nation.

El corazón central (Heartland) *de Sudamérica: Perú, Bolivia, Paraguay*

Lima, the capital of Peru, offers a combination of attractive modern architecture and magnificent colonial neighborhoods. Also in Peru you can see the awe-inspiring ancient Incan city of Machu Picchu, with its breathtaking views; the mysterious *Nazca Lines*, giant figures traced in the sand of the desert; and the *Reserva Nacional de Paracas*, with its golden beaches and millions of birds.

Bolivia boasts the highest-altitude capital in the world, La Paz, built inside the crater of a prehistoric volcano, at over 12,000 feet; in La Paz you can see fascinating places such as the *Museo de los Metales Preciosos* ("Museum of Precious Metals") and the *Mercado de los Brujos* ("Wizards' Market"). Many travelers choose to visit the legendary *Lago de Titicaca* ("Lake Titicaca"), with its butterfly-winged boats, and the nearby pre-Columbian ruins of Tiwanaku, an ancient site of immense stone carvings and a fabled irrigation system, built by the Aymará civilization over a thousand years ago.

In Asunción, the capital of Paraguay, tourists can tour the *Casa Vida* ("Life House"), an authentic colonial mansion that is now a museum, the *Jardín Botánico* ("Botanical Garden"), and the *Museo del Barro* ("Museum of Clay"). Other points of interest are the city of Itaguá, famous for the intricate Paraguayan lace called *ñandutí*, and Itapú, the largest hydroelectric station in the world; from this point you can cross *el Puente de la Amistad* and arrive at one of the planet's most beautiful natural wonders, the *Cataratas de Iguazú* ("Iguazú Falls").

El Cono Sur (The Southern Cone): *Chile, Uruguay, Argentina*

The long, skinny nation of Chile stretches from the Atacama Desert in the north (the driest spot on earth and site of many archaeological discoveries, including the oldest mummies ever found) to the cold, wet tundra of Punta Arenas in the south. The country lies between sea and mountains, the Pacific Ocean on the west and the Andes to the east, so it is not surprising that it is famous for the variety of its seafood. It offers tourists a wealth of diverse climates and opportunities for amusement: sightseeing and shopping in the large, busy city of Santiago; horseback riding in the mountains; wine-tasting in the central valleys, where the best-tasting wines of Latin America are bottled; hiking in the rolling green hills in the south; or boating along the coast.

Uruguay, a small country to the south of Brazil, has a charming capital city, Montevideo, that looks quite European with its lovely old buildings, bookshops, boutiques, and tango bars. (It shares the passion for tango with its larger neighbor Argentina.) The nearby beaches of Punta del Este are a popular vacation spot during the summer season (which is the winter season in the Northern Hemisphere). The natural *baños termales* ("hot springs") in the north are a tourist attraction all year-round.

Next door, Argentina's famous capital, Buenos Aires, is bustling, stylish, and cosmopolitan. Sometimes called *el París de Latinoamérica*, it is famous for its museums, art galleries, the renowned *Teatro Colón*, parks, tango bars, and a marvelous variety of restaurants, particularly those specializing in *la parrillada* ("grilled meats"). The picturesque neighborhood of La Boca offers handicrafts, spontaneous tango, and a bohemian atmosphere. Away from the capital and to the north is the beautiful old city of Salta in a dry, mountainous landscape where wild llamas graze by the roadside and the mineral-rich soil reflects many colors. In the south is Bariloche, where you can ski in the winter and swim in the summer, surrounded by a landscape that recalls Switzerland. And in the far south, at the seeming end of the earth, you can visit the wild parks of Patagonia and witness the calving of immense glaciers.

África: Guinea Ecuatorial (Ecuatorial Guinea) *y otras regiones*

Only this one small country in Africa, situated on the west coast below Cameroon, has Spanish as its official language. First under French control, then Spanish, it gained independence in the 1960s. The capital is Malabo and the native language Bibi is also widely spoken. Spanish is spoken in other parts of the continent as a second language, especially in the north.

Islas para todos los gustos (Islands for Everyone's Taste)

There are other islands where Spanish is spoken, besides the ones mentioned above, and they are quite diverse. Spain's *las Canarias* ("the Canary Islands") provide a wonderful vacation spot with warm and sunny beaches and fancy resorts. Ecuador's *las Galápagos* are famous for the giant *tortugas* ("turtles") and other exotic species that played a role in inspiring Darwin's theory of evolution. Chile's *Isla de Pascua* ("Easter Island") is quite mysterious, with its huge heads carved of stone facing the sea, left by some unknown culture long ago. Venezuela's *Isla Margarita* is a paradise of warm waters and lovely sand beaches. Who knows? One of these just might be *la isla de tus sueños* ("the island of your dreams").

Rehearsal Time

Historia y geografía. (History and geography.) How much do you know about the history and geography of the Spanish-speaking world? Circle the letter of the correct option for each statement. Check your answers in the Answer Key.

1. If you go to the *zócalo* in a Mexican city, you are going to:
   a. a musical theater
   b. a public square
   c. an outdoor café

2. Spanish is the official language of how many countries?
   a. 11
   b. 21
   c. 31

3. For about how many years did the Moors rule some parts of Spain?
   a. 100
   b. 400
   c. 700

4. The visitor who wants to see impressive pre-Aztec ruins near Mexico City can go to:
   a. las Pirámides del Sol y de la Luna
   b. Guanajuato
   c. la península de Yucatán

5. Which Caribbean island has a special association with the United States that allows its citizens to enter and leave without a visa?
   a. Cuba
   b. the Dominican Republic
   c. Puerto Rico

6. How many separate Spanish-speaking nations form Central America?
   a. four
   b. six
   c. eight

7. The world's highest waterfall, *el Salto Ángel*, is in:
   a. Colombia
   b. Ecuador
   c. Venezuela

8. The highest-altitude capital in the world is:
   a. Asunción, Paraguay
   b. La Paz, Bolivia
   c. Lima, Perú

9. The most ancient mummies in the world (three times older than those of Egypt) come from
   a. Atacama, Chile
   b. Bariloche, Argentina
   c. Montevideo, Uruguay

10. Where did Darwin observe strange varieties of plants and animals that played a role in inspiring his theory of evolution?
    a. las Galápagos, Ecuador
    b. Guinea Ecuatorial
    c. Isla de Pascua

De viaje

Wherever you decide to go, leave shyness at home and speak Spanish when you have the chance. It's better to make a few mistakes (which usually will not impede communication) than not to be heard at all. *El error más grande es no decir nada.* ("The biggest mistake is to say nothing.") Remember that, in general, Latinos are sociable, curious about people, and enjoy interacting with others. They are also tolerant about the way foreigners speak their language and eager to try to understand.

Of course, you may find that people listen courteously to your request in Spanish and then respond in English. Don't be offended by this as they like to practice their language skills too and may think that this is the best way to make you feel comfortable. Chat for a while in English and then go back to trying out your Spanish. You might find that they welcome returning to good old *castellano* (*español*) and will give you the chance to practice more. Let's look at some ways to put together sentences that will be useful during your travels. First of all, the most important verbs.

TOP FIVE Good Starters for Expressing Your Needs and Wishes

1. **Busco (Buscamos)...** I am looking for (We are looking for) . . .

2. **Necesito (Necesitamos)...** I need (We need) . . .

3. **Quiero (Queremos)...** I want (We want) . . .

4. **Quisiera (Quisiéramos)...** I would like (We would like) . . .

5. **Me gustaría (Nos gustaría)...** I would like (We would like) . . .

TOP TEN Things You Might Want After Arriving in a New Place:
busco (necesito)...

1. **hospedaje, un buen hotel, una pensión** lodging, a good hotel, a family-run boarding house. A *pensión* is similar to a B & B (bed and breakfast); it is usually cheaper than a hotel and often provides one or more meals for an additional fee. It may not offer a private bath.

2. **un restaurante, un café, un cibercafé** a restaurant, a café, a cybercafé (where you can plug into the Internet or check your e-mail)

3. **una farmacia** a drugstore, pharmacy; this is a place to buy medicines and drugs but does not usually have clothing, food, toys, or odds and ends as many North American drugstores do

4. **los baños, aseos, sanitarios públicos** public restrooms; in Spain, *aseos* is the most common word

5. **un banco** a bank; notice that this word also means *bench*. There are also businesses that change money, often at a slightly higher rate, called *casas de cambio*.

6. **un guía bilingüe, un guía que sepa inglés** a bilingual guide, a guide who knows English; use *un* for a male and *una* for a female. If it makes no difference which, then use *un*. *Una guía* also means "guidebook"; *la guía de teléfonos* refers to the telephone book.

7. **boletos (billetes) o entradas** tickets; these are called *billetes* in Spain and *boletos* in most other places. However, when you are talking about tickets for admission (to a dance, movie, museum, etc.), use *entradas*.

8. **un traje de baño, toallas, jabón, pasta dentífrica** a bathing suit, towels, soap, toothpaste

9. **un plano de la ciudad** a map of the city; notice that *mapa* is the usual word for "map," but it's used more for a map of the country, province, or state (*un mapa del país, de la provincia, del estado*). To buy these you go to *una librería*, a bookstore.

10. **unas botellas de agua potable** some bottles of drinking water

---

TOP TEN Things to Do After You've Settled In: *quisiera (me gustaría)...*

1. **alquilar un bote (un auto, una camioneta, una moto)** rent a boat (a car, a van, a motorscooter); in Mexico it is common to say *arrendar* or *rentar*

2. **comprar comida (ropa, recuerdos, pinturas)** buy food (clothing, souvenirs, paintings)

3. **hacer una excursión a las montañas (a la selva, a una ciudad colonial)** take a trip to the mountains (to the jungle, to a colonial city)

4. **ir al teatro (a un museo, a una hacienda)** go to the theater (to a museum, to a ranch)

5. **hacer un paseo a caballo (a un volcán, a una ciudad colonial)** go for an outing on horseback (to a volcano, to a colonial city)

6. **nadar en el mar (en una piscina, en un río)** swim in the sea (in a swimming pool, in a river)

7. **pescar en el océano (en un lago, en un río)** fish in the ocean (in a lake, in a river)

8. **tomar clases de baile (buceo, esnórquel, español, tango)** take dance (scuba, snorkeling, Spanish, tango) classes

9. **ver bailes tradicionales (un espectáculo, un pueblo típico [sin mucho turismo])** see traditional dances (a show, an authentic or typical town [without much tourism])

10. **visitar un sitio histórico (unas ruinas antiguas, una ciudad colonial, un lugar exótico)** visit a historic site (some ancient ruins, a colonial city, an exotic place)

TOP TEN Key Places for the Traveler in Any City or Town: *busco (necesito)...*

1. **una agencia de viajes** a travel agency; the place to buy *boletos (billetes)*

2. **el correo** the post office; the place to buy *estampillas* (stamps, often called *timbres* in Mexico and *sellos* in Spain)

3. **la embajada/el consulado de Estados Unidos (Canadá)** the embassy/consulate of the United States (Canada)

4. **la estación de trenes (la terminal de buses, el aeropuerto)** the train station (the bus terminal, the airport); in Mexico you may hear *la terminal* used for trains as well as buses

5. **el hospital** the hospital

6. **una lavandería (tintorería, zapatería)** a laundry (dry cleaners, shoe store)

7. **el mercado** the market; a good place to buy handicrafts, food (like fruit, vegetables, cheese), and sometimes many other things at good prices

8. **una peluquería (para hombres, para mujeres), un salón de belleza, una estética** a barber shop or hairdresser (for men, for women), beauty parlor, spa shop

9. **la plaza central** the main square; this is often a beautiful park surrounded by old buildings like *la catedral* ("cathedral") and *el municipio* ("city hall")

10. **una tienda de comestibles (de ropa, de recuerdos)** a grocery store (clothing store, souvenir shop)

Even the most seasoned travelers need to ask for directions from time to time. There are those moments when you might feel *más perdido(-a) que una cucaracha en un baile de gallinas* ("more lost than a cockroach at a hen's ball"), as the old saying goes. When that happens, here are some ways to ask for directions, beginning from the specific (when you know the name of where you want to go) to the general (when you have only a vague idea). Remember that to catch the attention of someone passing by you may have to start out with an attention-getting word such as: *¡Oiga!*, a polite way of saying, "Stop and listen to me!" This word works well in Spain and many parts of Latin America, but in Mexico and Central America, it may seem too direct. In these countries it is better to use the extremely polite form: *¡Disculpe!*, which literally means "Forgive (me)!" (If talking to more than one person, use, *¡Oigan!*, *¡Disculpen!*) One word of caution, though, is to remember that in some places people may answer out of politeness even if they are not sure of the answer. If you detect uncertainty, check with someone else.

TOP FIVE Ways to Ask for Directions, from Specific to General

1. **¡Oiga! (¡Disculpe!) ¿Dónde está el hotel La Perla (el restaurante Don Pedro)?** Excuse me! Where is the La Perla Hotel (Don Pedro restaurant)?

2. **¡Oigan! (¡Disculpen!) La terminal de autobuses (El Banco Central)... ¿está cerca de aquí?** Excuse me (plural, to more than one person)! The bus station (Central Bank) . . . is it nearby?

3. **¡Oiga (Disculpe), señor (señorita, señora)! ¿Cómo llego a la plaza central (al zócalo)?** Excuse me, sir (miss, ma'am)! How do I get to the main square? (The usual word is *plaza* but it is often called *el zócalo* in Mexico.)

4. **Perdone. ¿Hay alguna agencia de viajes (escuela de español) cerca de aquí?** Excuse me. Is there a travel agency (Spanish school) nearby?

5. **Perdonen, señores (señoritas). ¿Dónde hay un albergue (una casa de cambio)?** Excuse me, gentlemen (ladies). Where is there a hostel (money exchange)?

Rehearsal Time

¿Qué busca usted? Match the places below to the appropriate situations. Check your answers in the Answer Key.

1. Your clothes are all dirty and you are leaving for another city tomorrow.

   a. una agencia de viajes

2. The hotel you are staying at costs *un ojo de la cara* (literally, "an eye

from your face"—i.e., an arm and
a leg) and you want something
cheaper.   b. un banco

3. You would like to make arrange-
ments to go on a tour of the
region.   c. los servicios públicos

4. You have a headache and need
aspirin.   d. el correo

5. You are sick of eating out all the
time and want to buy some fruit
and cheese.   e. una farmacia

6. It's high time you sent some post-
cards to your friends back home.   f. una lavandería

7. You are having a bad hair day and
realize you need a trim.   g. el mercado

8. After starting out the day with
three cups of coffee, you feel an
urgent need.   h. una peluquería

9. You need to buy a map.   i. una pensión

10. All your local currency is gone.   j. una librería

¿Qué necesita hacer? Match the phrases below to the appropriate
situations to show what you need to do. Check your answers in the
Answer Key.

1. You are staying in an interesting   a. comprar un traje de
city but keep getting lost.   baño

2. You want to find out about some
ancient ruins and can't under-
stand the signs in Spanish.   b. alquilar un bote

3. Your passport is missing!

4. It's very hot and you want to swim but have nothing to wear.

5. You want to attend a concert next Friday.

6. You and your friends are planning an all-day hike up to the top of a volcano and will need to take food.

7. People say the lake is full of fish and you want to go fishing.

c. buscar un(a) guía bilingüe

d. ir a la embajada

e. comprar unas entradas

f. encontrar una tienda de comestibles

g. comprar un plano de la ciudad

El viajero experto/The Savvy Traveler: Practical Tips for Travelers

La seguridad ("safety") and *la cortesía* ("courtesy") are important watchwords for traveling. Spain and Latin America are high-context cultures in which what you say is only one part of the message that you express to people. The manner in which you say something, the way you dress and move, your manners, and your attitude are all very important. (See the section *La buena educación* in Chapter 1.) Remember that it is polite to greet someone before asking for help or service, even in a store or business.

Staying on the Safe Side

While you want to dress well and make a good impression, it's best to leave the gold jewelry and Rolex at home and to take special care of your computer and expensive camera so that you don't become a target for a robbery. Many countries have had recent downturns in their economies that have caused an increase in theft. Here are some useful phrases relating to safety.

TOP TEN Useful Phrases for Safety and Courtesy

1. **¿Se puede tomar el agua de la llave?** Can one drink the water from the tap (spigot)? This is the most common way of saying this, but there are some regional variations: *el agua del grifo* (Spain), *el agua de la canilla* (Argentina and Uruguay), *el agua del caño* (Peru).

2. **¿Hay mucho peligro en la calle? ¿Se puede caminar tranquilamente por aquí?** Is there a lot of danger in the street? Can one walk safely around here? If people look uneasy when you ask this, you may want to consider taking a taxi.

3. **¿Dónde puedo conseguir un taxi seguro?** Where can I get a safe taxi? In many places there is no danger in simply hailing a taxi, but if you are not sure, it's better to have someone from your hotel or restaurant call a taxi for you. In some airports and train or bus stations there are *taxis controlados* ("controlled taxis"); you go to a window, explain where you want to go, and are then issued a ticket to bring out to the taxi stand.

4. **¿Cuánto me cobra para ir a... ?** How much would you charge me to go to . . . ? Before getting into a taxi, it's a good idea to ask about the fare; if the price seems high, try again with a different taxi and compare. You might want to write the name or *dirección* ("address") of your destination on a piece of paper to give to the driver.

5. **¿Me permitiría sacar una foto de los niños (de usted, de la casa)?** Would you allow me to take a photo of the children (of you, of the house?) Be careful to greet people and ask permission before taking photos of people or their belongings.

6. **¿Hay una caja fuerte donde pueda dejar algunas cosas?** Is there a safe where I could leave some things?

7. **¿Dónde se puede hacer una llamada telefónica?** Where can one make a phone call?

8. **¿Cuánto se cobra por hacer una llamada telefónica local (de larga distancia)?** How much do you charge for a local (long-distance) phone call?

9. **¿Cuál es la tasa de cambio del dólar de Estados Unidos (Canadá)?** What is the rate of exchange for the U.S. (Canadian) dollar? Ask first to avoid problems later.

10. **¿Qué se hace en caso de un terremoto (de temblores)?** What does one do in case of an earthquake (tremors)? Like San Francisco, there are many places in Latin America where people are used to the earth moving.

Avoiding Misunderstandings (*malentendidos*)

There are some small differences in the way things are calculated, written, arranged, or said in Spanish-speaking cultures in contrast with North America. For example, on calendars the week begins on Monday, so the day farthest to the left is *lunes* and not *domingo* ("Sunday") as on English-language calendars. It isn't that their way is better or worse than ours; it's just different.

TOP TEN Things to Know to Avoid *malentendidos*

1. **El espectáculo empieza a las veinte y treinta.** The show starts at 8:30 P.M. (literally, at twenty and thirty). It's common in some places to use the twenty-four-hour clock, as they do in the military, especially for events. The abbreviations A.M.

and P.M. are used in Mexico and some other places in writing, but not in spoken Spanish, so say *a las nueve de la mañana* for "at 9:00 A.M." and *a las nueve de la noche* for "at 9:00 P.M."

2. **La dirección es Avenida Flores 684.** The address is 684 Flores Avenue. The street (*calle*) or avenue comes first and the number next in Spanish, just the reverse of English usage. Notice that *dirección* is a false cognate that means "address." To say "direction," as in "We are going in the wrong direction," use *sentido*: *Vamos en sentido contrario.*

3. **Es un cheque de $7.001,85.** It's a check for seven thousand and one dollars and eighty-five cents. In many places, the *punto* ("period") and the *coma* ("comma") are used in the opposite way from English usage: the period separates the thousands from the hundreds (for example, *8.000 metros* for "8,000 meters") and the comma is used as a decimal point. In Mexico, however, the usage is the same as in Canada and the United States.

4. **Perdone, hay un error. La cuenta es de mil pesos, no de siete mil pesos.** Excuse me, there is a mistake. The bill comes to one thousand pesos, not seven thousand pesos. Many people from the United States and Canada mistake the number 1 for a 7 because the 1 is often written with a long line on top, but in Spanish-speaking countries the 7 can be distinguished by the horizontal line running through it: 7.

5. **3/11/06.** Is this March 11 or November 3? In the United States, it would be March 11, but in Spanish-speaking countries it would be *el 3 de noviembre* ("November 3"). If you are writing a date, it's a good idea to write out the month for the sake of clarity.

6. **¿Estamos en el primer piso o en la planta baja?** Are we on the second floor or the first floor? In Spain and most of Latin America, the *planta baja* is the one you enter on from the

street, the ground floor. The *primer piso* (literally, first floor) is one flight up from that, the equivalent of what is called the second floor in the United States and Canada.

7. **Vamos a reunirnos en la recepción.** We will meet at the registration desk. This is a common place for meeting in a hotel. A Spanish equivalent of the English word *lobby* doesn't exist, but some people use *entrada* ("entrance"), the French word *foyer*, the English "lobby" or, in certain places, *vestíbulo*.

8. **¿A cuántos kilómetros estamos del pueblo?** How many kilometers are we away from town? Notice that the metric system is used (as is common in most countries of the world other than the United States)—for example, milk is sold by the liter and the temperature is given in Centigrade rather than Fahrenheit, 33° being a hot day. Canadians are accustomed to this, but will find that sizes for shoes and clothing are different from what they are used to. (See Tune-Up 6.)

9. **Somos (Mis amigos son) de Estados Unidos.** We (My friends) are from the United States. It's better to express U.S. nationality this way and avoid the terms *americanos* or *norteamericanos*. Many people consider everyone from the Americas—North, South, and Central—as *americanos*. You can also use the word *estadounidense* for people from the United States: *Somos estadounidenses.*

10. **Camine usted cuatro cuadras (manzanas, calles) y doble a la derecha.** Walk four blocks and turn right. In Spain the word for "blocks" is *manzanas* (the same as the word for "apples"), but in most places it is *cuadras*, and, in a few, *calles*. In Costa Rica, however, people usually give directions in meters (which are roughly equivalent to U.S. yards): for example, *Camine 400 metros.*

In the Hotel

Because Spanish, like English, is a language rich in vocabulary, there are many synonyms. Here are some you might hear in hotels.

TOP FIVE Pairs of Synonyms Commonly Used in Hotels

1. **el ascensor / el elevador** elevator

2. **el cuarto / la habitación** room

3. **las maletas / las valijas** suitcases; **el equipaje** luggage

4. **la alberca** (Mexico) / **la piscina / la pileta** (Southern Cone) swimming pool

5. **las facilidades / los servicios** facilities

Your main communication in a hotel is usually with the person at the *recepción* ("main desk"). Here are some things you may want to say to him or her.

TOP TEN Handy Phrases to Say to a Hotel Desk Clerk *(el/la recepcionista)*

1. **¿Tienen habitaciones libres para esta noche?** Do you have rooms available for tonight?

2. **Quiero (Queremos) una habitación con cama sencilla (doble) y con baño privado.** I (We) would like a room with a single (double) bed and with a private bathroom.

3. **Queremos una habitación con aire acondicionado (con balcón, con televisor, con vista al mar).** We want a room with air conditioning (with a balcony, with a television, with a view of the ocean).

4. **Tengo una habitación reservada a nombre de...** I have a room reserved under the name . . .

5. **¿Me podría despertar a las seis de la mañana?** Could you wake me at six in the morning?

6. **¿Dónde se encuentra el ascensor (el gimnasio, el restaurante, la piscina, la estética, el estacionamiento) del hotel?** Where can I find the hotel elevator (gym, restaurant, swimming pool, spa, parking)?

7. **¿Tienen servicio de guardería?** Do you have child-care service?

8. **¿Quién me podría ayudar con mis maletas?** Who can help me with my suitcases?

9. **¿A qué hora tenemos que dejar la habitación?** What time do we have to check out (leave the room)?

10. **¿Me (Nos) puede pedir un taxi?** Can you call a taxi for me (us)?

Things That Happen . . . *(cosas que pasan...)*

From time to time things go wrong. As the Spanish say: *Cosas que pasan... ¡hasta en las mejores familias!* ("Things that happen . . . even in the best of families!") In most Spanish-speaking countries, people are more indirect than they are in the United States or even in Canada (where they are more indirect than their neighbors to the south). They will try their best to avoid conflicts and enable everyone to save face. Therefore, you often achieve more if you do not appear hot under the collar or imply an accusation. You are more likely to get quick results by expressing a problem in an impersonal and objective way rather than by phrasing it as a complaint. *Tengo un problema (urgente). ¿Podría usted ayudarme?*

TOP TEN Typical Problems

1. **No encuentro mi llave.** I can't find my key.

2. **Necesito un médico, por favor.** I need a doctor, please.

3. **Estoy perdido(-a). (Estamos perdidos[-as].)** I am lost. (We are lost.)

4. **Tuve (Tuvimos) mucho frío anoche.** I was (We were) very cold last night.

5. **Hace mucho calor en la habitación.** It's very hot in my (our) room.

6. **No hay agua caliente y me gustaría bañarme (tomar una ducha, ducharme).** There's no hot water and I would like to take a bath (take a shower, shower).

7. **Anoche hubo mucho ruido en la calle (en el pasillo).** Last night there was a lot of noise in the street (in the hallway).

8. **Tengo hambre y los restaurantes están cerrados.** I'm hungry and the restaurants are closed.

9. **Mi computadora (cartera) ha desaparecido.** My computer (wallet) has disappeared.

10. **No encuentro mis documentos (joyas).** I can't find my documents (jewelry).

If there is a serious problem and the desk clerk does not seem helpful, ask to speak to the manager: *Quisiera hablar con el (la) gerente, por favor.* ("I would like to speak with the manager, please.") In some places, you might want to make a report to the police (*la policía*) if you suspect a robbery (*un robo*), but this is not always wise. It's a good idea to ask the advice of someone who seems trustworthy, perhaps the manager of your hotel.

Rehearsal Time

El viajero experto. Are you a savvy traveler when you journey through Spanish-speaking lands? Complete the sentences with the missing words. Check your answers in the Answer Key.

1. You want to find out if the water is safe to drink and so you ask, *¿Se puede tomar el agua de la _____ ?*

2. To negotiate for a taxi to go downtown, you ask the driver, *¿Cuánto me _____ usted para ir al centro?*

3. To find out someone's address, you say, *¿Cuál es su _____ ?*

4. In Spain and most of Latin America the first floor in a hotel is up one flight of stairs and the ground floor is called *la planta _____ .*

5. To inquire what the check-out time is, you ask, *¿A qué hora tenemos que _____ la habitación?*

6. You've lost your key so you go to the desk clerk and say, *No encuentro mi _____ .*

7. There was a lot of noise during the night in the hallway of your hotel, so you complain about it: *Anoche hubo mucho* _____ *en el pasillo.*

8. If you do not get a good response, you ask to speak to the manager: *Quisiera hablar con el (la)* _____, *por favor.*

Fiestas y festivales

There are many wonderful festivals in Spain and Latin America that include music, dancing, eating, drinking, parades, costumes, and interesting local traditions. You may want to time your trip to coincide with one of these. Feast days of local patron saints, music festivals (like Cuba's international jazz festival in Havana), harvest celebrations (like Argentina's *Festival de la Vendimia* or wine fest in Mendoza), and historic holidays abound. The tradition of *Carnaval*, the spring holiday that occurs right before *Cuaresma* ("Lent," the Catholic season of fasting and penance that precedes Easter), is celebrated in many places; it is similar to *Mardi Gras* in New Orleans. In the United States many Mexican-Americans celebrate *el cinco de mayo* on May 5 each year, a good time to see typical Mexican foods, music, and dancing. Check with a guidebook or travel agent for the time and place of celebrations in the countries in which you will be traveling. Following is a small sampling of some of the many delightful and unusual celebrations that occur every year.

TOP TEN Unique Festivals You May Consider Attending

1. **Cabarete Alegría, República Dominicana** Joy Cabaret, Dominican Republic. Every weekend during the month of February Dominicans celebrate with mountain-bike races,

contests for sand-castle building, kite-flying competitions, and, finally, at the end of February with the *Encuentro Classic*, the Classic Meet, an international windsurfing show in which top performers of this sport defy the waves and winds of the hurricane season.

2. **El Día de los Muertos, México** The Day of the Dead, Mexico. Throughout the Hispanic world, November 1 is a day of remembrance for deceased relatives when families traditionally get together and go to the cemetery to decorate graves. In Mexico, it is celebrated with great fervor and pageantry with a variety of customs: eating sweet bread called *pan de muerto* (often decorated with the design of bones) and skull-shaped candies of sugar or chocolate called *calaveras* ("skulls"), singing humorous songs that insult or defy the Grim Reaper (*La Calaca*), building beautiful altars with *ofrendas* ("offerings") of food and drink for the dead souls who will return to earth, and, in some places, by going to the graves of relatives to eat and drink near them, often carrying *velas* ("candles"). The picturesque island town of Pátzcuaro in the state of Michoacán is especially well-known for the beauty of this celebration.

3. **La Diablada de Oruro, Bolivia** The Devil Dance of Oruro, Bolivia. Oruro is a mining town high in the Andes; every year its inhabitants perform the famous Devil Dance for a whole week during *Carnaval* in the spring. They dress up in colorful masks and costumes as devils, angels, toads, snakes, conquistadors, Incan princesses, and saints and enact an ancient Andean myth sacred to their Incan and Aymara ancestors. The story unfolds in numerous episodes that mix together native and Christian elements. Vigorous and acrobatic dances portray the hard-fought battles, which are mostly won by the devils, but on the last day the *Virgen del Socavón* ("Blessed Lady of the Mine Pit") helps the angels to a final victory. Unique and exuberant, this traditional week of dance draws observers from many parts of the world; they come to watch and then

lift a toast, afterward pouring their drink on the ground in honor of the *Pachamama* ("Earth goddess").

4. **La Feria Popular de San José, Costa Rica** The People's Fair of San José, Costa Rica. This begins on *Navidad*, December 25, in the capital and lasts until New Year. People come from all over for *el Tope*, the horse parade and the colorful carnaval with rides and games, but most of all for the twice-daily enactment of *corridas de toros a la tica* ("bullfights, Costa Rican style"), or as the locals say, *Todos contra el toro* ("Everybody against the bull"). Anyone can participate, including women. They all face off against one bull at a time in the middle of a huge ring and try their best to avoid the charging animal, provoking gasps and laughter from the spectators for an hour or two. The bull is not killed but every year one or two of the amateur bullfighters suffer severe injuries. The celebration ends each evening with clowns, food, and fireworks.

5. **Festival de San Juan Bautista, Puerto Rico** The Festival of Saint John the Baptist, Puerto Rico. This festival takes place in the capital city of San Juan on the feast day of its patron saint, June 24, with a mixture of religious and secular features to celebrate the spring solstice. Rhythmic music, dancing, prayers, fanciful costumes, and an elaborate parade combine to create an atmosphere of revelry. The culminating moment comes near midnight when the entire parade and all participants slowly enter the sea, in this way bringing the spirits of good luck into their lives.

6. **Inti Raymi, Perú** Sun Festival, Peru. The name of this solstice celebration is in Quechua, the language of the Incas, which is still spoken in many areas today. It takes place on June 24 in the ruins of the stone fortress called Sacsahuamán near the Andean city of Cuzco (which means "navel of the world"), the high-altitude capital of the ancient Incan Empire. There are spectacular dances, costumes, and parades by descendants

of the Incas, who perform ancient rites in honor of their ancestors.

7. **La fiesta de San Fermín** (also called **los sanfermines**), **España.** Saint Fermín Festival, Spain. On July 6 in the northern Spanish city of Pamplona, one of the most famous of all festivals begins with the explosion of a rocket: *el encierro* ("the running of the bulls"). The party lasts for several days with eating, dancing, and carousing, but the high point comes when the bulls are let loose in the streets to bring them to their new paddock. As they move along a prescribed course, daredevils (mostly young men) leap out in front to try to outrun them. Predictably from time to time people are wounded or killed, but this does not happen often enough to put an end to the festival or diminish the general atmosphere of revelry and abandon.

8. **La Semana Criolla, Uruguay** Creole Week, Uruguay. This is a week of fun and traditional pastimes with some activities similar to those of a rodeo. The *gaucho* is the romantic figure of the Uruguayan and Argentine cowboy who herded cows and sheep in centuries past. Celebrations include lamb and beef barbecues, taming of horses, demonstrations of riding and cattle roping, folk music, and performances of the stately *pericón* dance by men and women in elegant costumes who trade flirtatious insults in rhyme as they pace the intricate steps. Of course, there is also drinking of the traditional bitter *yerba mate* tea through a silver straw called a *bombilla*.

9. **Semana Santa en Sevilla, España** Holy Week in Seville, Spain. The week before Easter, the fabled city of Sevilla in the south of Spain is completely transformed into a backdrop for the reenactment of the passion and death of Jesus Christ. Statues and religious objects are carried through the streets, and there is mournful music as processions of *penitentes* ("penitents"), some of them dressed in traditional costume, file

through. The climax is the arrival of Easter, with ceremonies in the many elegant and elaborate old churches, followed by feasting, joyful music, and dance.

10. **La Tomatina, España** The Tomato Festival, Spain. This notorious festivity is rather new, but since its inception it has drawn a lot of onlookers each year to the small town of Buñol in Valencia on the last Wednesday of August. On that day the town indulges in a friendly but unrestrained tomato fight, using the surplus tomatoes from their main crop as projectiles to throw at their neighbors.

TOP FIVE Proverbs About Travel

1. **Adonde fueras, haz lo que vieras.** Wherever you might go, do what you see. (That is, imitate local customs and try to blend in.)

2. **Martes, ni te cases ni te embarques, ni de tu familia te apartes.** On Tuesdays, don't get married or go on a boat trip, nor journey too far from your family. (This warns of the dangers of traveling on a Tuesday, the bad-luck day in Hispanic culture, in contrast to the North American superstition about Fridays that fall on the 13th.)

3. **Preguntando se llega a Roma.** By asking questions, you get to Rome. (Curiosity and boldness are needed to get what you want out of travel.)

4. **Quien no ha visto Sevilla, no ha visto maravilla.** He or she who hasn't seen Seville hasn't seen a wonder (marvelous thing). (This expresses the natural pride of place that people feel for their home territory.)

5. **Quien no ha visto Granada, no ha visto nada.** He or she who hasn't seen Granada hasn't seen anything at all. (This affirms pride of place along with the common sense of rivalry among neighbors, because it was obviously modeled as a comeback to the previous proverb about Granada's neighbor, Sevilla.)

Rehearsal Time

¡Vamos a festejar! (Let's celebrate!) What have you learned about Hispanic celebrations? Circle the letter of the correct option for each statement. Check your answers in the Answer Key.

1. You've heard about Mardi Gras, celebrated in spring in New Orleans. The Hispanic equivalent is celebrated at the same time in many parts of Spain and Latin America. It is called:
   a. Carnaval
   b. Cuaresma
   c. Vendimia

2. An international windsurfing show is held every year at the end of February as part of the festival called *Cabarete Alegría* in:
   a. Cuba
   b. Colombia
   c. the Dominican Republic

3. The famous *Día de los Muertos* is celebrated every year in Mexico on November 1 with songs, decorated altars, and skull candies called:
   a. calaveras
   b. ofrendas
   c. velas

4. In their capital city of San Juan, Puerto Ricans greet the spring solstice on June 24 with dancing, drinking, prayers, and costume parades that culminate in the dramatic moment at midnight when they
   a. shoot off fireworks
   b. form a giant circle
   c. enter the sea

5. The sun festival, *Inti Raymi*, takes place in a dramatic setting: high up in the Andes mountains near Cuzco, Peru, in the ruins of an ancient stone fortress built centuries ago by the
   a. mayas
   b. guaraní
   c. incas

6. The *fiesta de San Fermín*, one of the most dangerous and well-known festivals in the world, occurs every July 6 in the north of Spain when people run ahead of wild bulls through the town of
   a. San Sebastián
   b. Pamplona
   c. Valencia

7. Pageantry and piety mix together in the south of Spain in Sevilla during the reenactment of the passion of Jesus Christ that is held shortly before Easter during
   a. la Semana Criolla
   b. la penitencia
   c. la Semana Santa

8. The Spanish proverb that is an equivalent of the English "When in Rome, do as the Romans do" is
   a. Adonde fueras, haz lo que vieras.
   b. Preguntando se llega a Roma.
   c. Quien no ha visto Granada, no ha visto nada.

TUNE-UP
6

De compras

Shopping and Money

1. What's the first thing you should do when you walk into a store?

2. How do you ask how much something costs?

3. What is sold at a *quiosco*?

4. How do you say "Just looking" or "Can I try it on?"

5. When should you bargain for an item and when should you definitely not?

6. What is *el qué dirán*?

7. If someone says that he is *hasta el gorro* or *como niño con zapatos nuevos*, what does he mean?

8. Why go to a *casa de cambio*?

9. What do the words *lana*, *guita*, and *pasta* have in common?

10. What do *hijo de papá* and *niño bien* have in common?

"Money makes the world go round," "I feel like a million dollars," "That's my two cents on the matter": these are all common sayings in English. Luis Valdez, the famous movie director and writer of Mexican-American descent, says this about the Latino view of money:

Para ganar dinero, uno tiene que prepararse. Y hay gente—entre ella, muchos latinos—que no se prepara para ser próspera, sino sólo para ser pobre. Tenemos una cultura, una historia y una tradición de pobreza. Hasta podríamos decir que en la cultura latina, la pobreza es una cosa noble. Sufrimos calladamente todas las opresiones de la vida. Sin embargo, para poder fun-

To earn money, you have to prepare yourself. And there are people—among them many Latinos—who do not prepare themselves to be prosperous, but rather to be poor. We have a culture, history, and tradition of poverty. We could even say that in Latino culture, poverty is a noble thing. We suffer silently all the oppressions of life. However, in

cionar, el hombre... debe saber que nada en la vida es material. Que todo es espiritual. Que todo es ilusión, incluso el dinero. Así es que para que una persona pobre se transforme en próspera, debe sentir esa vibración, creer en uno mismo. Todo proviene del Creador, por lo que de ahí viene la riqueza del mundo. «Creer es crear», como dicen los descendientes de los mayas.

order to function, man . . . must know that nothing in life is material. That everything is spiritual. That everything is illusion, including money. So for a poor person to transform himself or herself into a prosperous one, he or she must feel that vibration, believe in himself or herself. Everything comes from the Creator, from thence comes the wealth of the world. "To believe is to create," as the descendants of the Mayas say.

—«EL CISCO KID CABALGA DE NUEVO», *HOMBRE*, ABRIL 1994, PÁGINA 15

There are other historical roots for this point of view. In the beginning of the last century, the essay *Ariel* by Uruguayan writer José Enrique Rodó advised Latin Americans to avoid materialistic values in favor of spiritual values, and not to judge people by what they have but by who they are. The essay was a huge best-seller, and this point of view became known as *arielismo* (from Ariel in *The Tempest*, as opposed to the rather beastly Caliban). Latin Americans who followed this school of thought proclaimed that art and literature and spiritual pursuits were more desirable than commercial and money-oriented endeavors, and these *arielistas* had a great deal of influence on their societies.

Nevertheless, money has a place in all cultures, and of course this is also true in Spain and Latin America. First, let's look at some ways to spend (or save!) it.

En el mercado: ¡Qué ganga!

¡Qué ganga! ("What a deal!") No matter where you go in the Hispanic world, chances are that sooner or later you'll want to seek out local traditions or crafts or just find the perfect gift for a special someone. In Spain and Latin America, handicrafts (*las artesanías*) are many and varied, and the *artesanos* and *artesanas* who make them are highly respected individuals. Craftsmanship of everything from fine cheese or wine to leather purses or belts is considered an art, not just a job. Prices can be amazingly low in some areas if you know how to look for bargains. A good place to buy things at low rates is the *mercado*, which may have everything from basic food-stuffs to souvenirs. Some famous ones are the Rastro in Madrid, San Telmo in Buenos Aires, and La Lagunilla in Mexico City.

TOP TEN Things You May Hear in a Marketplace

1. **Déme medio kilo de queso, por favor.** Give me a half kilo(gram) of cheese, please (a little over a pound).

2. **Un poco más, por favor. Así está bien.** A little more, please. That's good.

3. **¿A cómo son los melones?** How much are the melons?

4. **¿Están maduros(-as)?** Are they ripe? (Ask rather than touching the fruit, which may get you some very negative attention from vendors. Usually they'll be happy to find ready-to-eat fruit or vegetables for you.)

5. **¿Cuánto cuestan (valen) los collares?** How much are the necklaces?

6. **Ese florero vale (cuesta) 200 pesos.** That vase costs 200 pesos.

7. **Entonces me lo (la) llevo.** Then I'll take it.

8. **Me voy a llevar éste (ésta).** I'll take this one.

9. **¿Cuánto es?** How much is it?

10. **¿No tiene cambio? ¿Tiene cinco pesos?** Don't you have change? Do you have five pesos?

Bargaining

You can save a lot of money if you know how to *regatear* ("bargain"). This is not normally done in stores or places where the merchandise has price tags—and *precios fijos*, "fixed prices"—but it is very common in marketplaces. Here are some basic rules:

When the seller quotes a price, praise the item but say you can't afford it and offer about half of the price quoted. For example:

Es muy bonito, pero no tengo mucho dinero. (No puedo gastar tanto dinero. Es un poco caro para mí.) ¿Podría aceptar... ? (Le podría ofrecer...) It's very pretty, but I don't have a lot of money. (I can't spend so much money. It's a little expensive for me.) Could you accept ... ? (I could offer you ...)

A very common expression is *No me alcanza el dinero* ("My money doesn't reach," won't stretch to cover that amount). That's probably the most common way of saying "I can't afford it" in this kind of situation, so if you say this you'll sound savvy, not like a greenhorn out to market for the first time. The seller will usually come back with another price, probably around two-thirds or three-fourths of the original price. You can then buy the item or continue bargaining if you feel the price is still too high. Know that *el regateo* is a very common practice in the Hispanic world, and many Latinos enjoy it. However, if you don't feel comfortable with the idea of naming your own price, you can also say something like *¿Me lo puede dejar a menos?* ("Can you give it to me for less?")

To say that something is expensive, people say *Está por las nubes* ("It's in the clouds," meaning it's sky high) or *Cuesta más que un ojo de la cara* ("It costs more than an eye from the face," meaning it costs a fortune). If you get a good price, you can say that it is *una ganga* ("a bargain"), *casi regalado* ("almost given away").

Rehearsal Time

¡Lógico! You're in a marketplace in South America and you hear people talking. Choose the logical response to each question. Check your answers in the Answer Key.

1. ¿A cómo son las papayas?
   a. Están maduras.
   b. Quince pesos el kilo.

2. La carne está cara, ¿verdad?
   a. Sí, está por las nubes.
   b. Sí, casi regalada.

3. ¿Por qué no llevaste el poncho?
   a. Porque era una ganga.
   b. Porque no me alcanzó el dinero.

4. ¿No te lo pudieron dejar a menos?
   a. No, el precio era fijo.
   b. No quería menos.

En la tienda: ¡Está en oferta!

¡Está en oferta! ("It's on sale!") In stores, where prices are fixed, there is normally no bargaining, but you can still find excellent buys. Remember, however, that in some places stores may be closed

from noon to about two o'clock in the afternoon for the large mid-day lunch, so if you see a sign *Cerrado a mediodía* on the door of a shop, you know that you can go back later that day. Stores are often specialized, as in English-speaking countries.

TOP TEN Kinds of Stores

1. **la librería** bookstore

2. **la farmacia** drugstore

3. **el almacén** department store

4. **la zapatería** shoestore

5. **la joyería** jewelry store

6. **el quiosco** kiosk (usually for magazines, sweets)

7. **la juguetería** toy store

8. **la tienda de regalos** souvenir shop

9. **la tienda de artículos deportivos** sporting goods store

10. **la tienda de música** music store

Don't forget to greet the salesclerk when you enter a small shop or store—this is customary and in fact it's rather rude not to do so. A simple *Buenos días* or *Buenas tardes* will do, but remember to say something, because in the Hispanic world the *saludo* ("greeting") is very important. In fact, there is a saying, *Dime cuantas personas te saludan y te diré quién eres.* ("Tell me how many people say hello to you and I'll tell you who you are.") Forgetting to say hello to someone is considered rude and "dehumanizing." In cities or towns, people tend to walk rather than drive and stay in their local communities to shop. People often know the local merchants very well, and friendly small talk is common. Besides, this is a great time for you to practice your Spanish—the shopkeeper is a perfect captive audience.

TOP TEN Questions a Salesclerk May Ask You

1. **¿En qué le puedo servir?** How can I help you?

2. **¿Le puedo ayudar en algo?** Can I help you with something?

3. **¿Busca algo en especial?** Are you looking for something in particular?

4. **¿Qué medida quiere?** What size do you want?

5. **¿De qué talla? ¿Cuál es su talla?** What size? What is your size (for clothing)?

6. **¿Qué número necesita/usa?** What size do you need/use (for example, for shoes)?

7. **¿Algo más?** Anything else?

8. **¿Cómo quiere pagar?** How do you want to pay?

9. **¿Va a pagar al contado (con dinero en efectivo)?** Are you going to pay cash?

10. **¿Se lo envuelvo?** Shall I wrap it for you?

TOP FIVE Things a Salesclerk May Say to Help Clinch the Sale

1. **Es de muy buena calidad.** It's very high quality.

2. **El precio está rebajado.** The price is reduced.

3. **Le queda muy bien, perfecto.** It fits you very well, perfectly.

4. **El color le sienta bien.** The color looks good on you.

5. **Se puede pagar con tarjeta de crédito. También acepta-mos cheques de viajero.** You can pay with a credit card. We also accept traveler's checks.

TOP TEN Things You May Say to a Salesclerk

1. **Sólo estoy mirando.** I'm just looking.

2. **¿Me podría enseñar aquella camiseta, por favor?** Could you show me that T-shirt, please?

3. **No me gusta el color. El color no me sienta bien.** I don't like the color. The color doesn't look good on me.

4. **¿Hay otros colores (estilos)?** Are there other colors (styles)?

5. **¿Hay uno más barato (grande, pequeño)?** Is there a cheaper (bigger, smaller) one?

6. **¿Podría probármelo? (Me gustaría probarlo.) ¿Dónde está el probador?** Could I try it on? (I'd like to try it on.) Where's the fitting room?

7. **Necesito un número más grande (pequeño). Son anchos (estrechos).** I need a bigger (smaller) size. They're wide (narrow) (for example, shoes).

8. **Voy a pensarlo. No puedo decidirme.** I'll think about it. I can't decide.

9. **¿Dónde está la caja?** Where's the register?

10. **¿Me podría dar un recibo, por favor?** Could you give me a receipt, please?

TOP FIVE   Answers to the Question *¿De qué está hecho(-a)?* ("What's It Made Of?")

1. **Es de algodón (seda, pana, lana, terciopelo, poliéster).** It's cotton (silk, corduroy, wool, velvet, polyester).

2. **Está hecho(-a) de cuero (plástico, goma, madera, plata).** It's made of leather (plastic, rubber, wood, silver).

3. **Es oro puro de 24 quilates.** It's pure 24-karat gold.

4. **Es de barro (cerámica, porcelana), pintado(-a) a mano.** It's clay (ceramic, porcelain), painted by hand.

5. **Es de lino con encaje hecho a mano.** It's linen with hand-made lace.

TOP FIVE   Questions That May Save You Money

1. **Es un poco caro. ¿No tiene algo a precio más bajo?** It's a little expensive. Don't you have something lower in price?

2. **¿Hay algo más barato?** Is there something cheaper?

3. **¿Es de color permanente?** Is it colorfast?

4. **¿Se puede lavar a máquina?** Is it machine washable?

5. **¿Es de oro puro? ¿Son genuinas las esmeraldas?** Is it pure gold? Are the emeralds real?

It's usually less expensive to buy in areas where you see local people shopping. Airport stores or shops frequented mainly by tourists tend to be expensive, so when you see Bermuda shorts and cameras, it's better to move on. However, in many Latin American countries there are government-run shops for *artesanías* that have beautiful goods of excellent quality and at reasonable prices. The artisans are approved by the government, as are the prices. Find out if there is a government-run handicrafts store in the town you are visiting, especially if you are short on time or just don't want to spend a lot of time shopping.

What if you buy the wrong thing or someone else buys you something that you don't want? Here are some useful phrases:

TOP FIVE Ways to Complain About and/or Exchange a Purchase

1. **Quisiera devolver esta camisa. Es demasiado grande (pequeña, corta, larga).** I'd like to return this shirt. It's too big (small, short, long).

2. **No me queda bien.** It doesn't fit (me).

3. **¿Podría cambiarme este rollo de película, por favor? Necesito uno de 35 milímetros.** Could you exchange this roll of film for me, please? I need a 35-millimeter one.

4. **Lo siento, pero necesito devolver esta cámara. Aquí está el recibo.** I'm sorry, but I need to return this camera. Here's the receipt.

5. **No funciona. Está descompuesto(-a).** It doesn't work. It's broken.

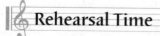

Rehearsal Time

¿En qué le puedo servir? Answer the following questions, then check your answers in the Answer Key.

1. What's the first thing you should do when you enter a shop or store in a Spanish-speaking area?

2. How do you say, "I'm just looking"?

3. What does *¿De qué talla?* or *¿Cuál es su talla?* mean?

4. How do you ask what something is made of?

5. What are two questions that may save you money in a store?

6. What do you say if you want to return something that doesn't work?

¡Vestido y calzado!

El qué dirán, a phrase that means "public opinion" (literally, "what they will say"), can be important in the Hispanic world, and so is appearance. Two common Spanish sayings are:

Como te ven, te tratan. "As they see you, they treat you." (People treat you according to what you look like.)

Si en tu tierra apellido, en la ajena tu vestido. "If in your own country, your last name; in a foreign one, your clothing." (Your clothing is your calling card, your introduction to others.)

People in Spanish-speaking countries tend to dress nicely and neatly in general, paying attention to matching colors and accessories. Clothes are typically ironed, and most middle- or upper-class women would not dream of going out to do an errand in tennis shoes or sweats. Just think of some of the most famous fashion designers of the past century: Fernando Peña, Oscar de la Renta,

Adolfo, Carolina Herrera, Paloma Picasso. One of the great ironies of the Argentinean financial crisis that began in 2001 was the photos of women in front of government buildings banging on pots to protest the bad economic conditions; the photos showed ladies dressed to the nines in elegant suits, cashmere sweaters, high heels, pearl necklaces, and so on. Even if one does not have a lot of money, one should be *vestido y calzado*, "dressed and shod" . . . properly. This is a matter of dignity, not a desire to show off—the cost of the clothing is not as important as its appropriateness. Those who do not adhere to this code are subject to a wide variety of verbal descriptions:

> *cursi* overly elegant in a tasteless way (also, too sentimental or syrupy, colloquial)
> *desordenado(-a)*, *descuidado(-a)* sloppy, disorderly
> *zarrapastroso(-a)* sloppy, badly dressed (colloquial)

For people who are way overdressed, there is the saying: *Si se quema la casa no pierde nada* ("If the house burns down, he or she won't lose anything"—because of all the jewelry and other things being worn). Conversely there are expressions about being well dressed:

> *estar como una reina* to look great, like a queen (for women)
> *ser elegante, fino(-a)*, *chic* to be elegant, fine, chic

Sizes

Buying clothing or shoes in Spain or Latin America may be a bit confusing because, in general, the sizes are not the same as in the United States or Canada. On the next page is a rough approximation of size differences between the United States and Spain.

Women's Clothing

Dresses/Suits

U.S.	6	8	10	12	14	16	18	20
Spain	36	38	40	42	44	46	48	50

Tops

U.S.	32	34	36	38	40
Spain	40	42	44	46	48

Shoes

U.S.	4	5	6	7	8	9	10
Spain	34-35	35-36	36-37	38-39	40-41	41-42	42-43

Men's Clothing

Suits

U.S.	36	38	40	42	44	46
Spain	46	48	50	52	54	56

Shirts (Neck)

U.S.	14	14.5	15	15.5	15.75	16	16.5
Spain	36	37	38	39	40	41	42

Shoes

U.S.	8	8.5	9	9.5	10	10.5	11
Spain	41	42	43	44	45	46	47

In Latin America, there are different sizings according to regional practice, so these will vary. In fancier stores or boutiques, there will usually be someone available to help you; however, traditional stores run by the owner are being swallowed up by the larger businesses just as they are north of the U.S.-Mexico border. Walmart, for example, has made huge inroads into Latin America in recent years. This process of globalization has been much debated, but no one denies that it will mean fewer products that are locally created and sold and more mass-produced imported items.

Not surprisingly, clothing has entered the Spanish language in many forms. Following are a few expressions you may hear.

TOP TEN Expressions with Names of Clothing Items

1. **a calzón quitado** openly, frankly (literally, with shorts or underwear taken off)

2. **con la camiseta puesta** very enthusiastic, a fan (used in Southern Cone; literally, with one's T-shirt on)

3. **colgar los guantes (los tenis)** to die (literally, to hang up one's gloves [tennis shoes]); in Costa Rica, you may hear *cerrar el paraguas*, to close one's umbrella

4. **como niño con zapatos nuevos** very happy (literally, like a kid with new shoes)

5. **estar hasta el gorro** to be fed up (used in Mexico, Central America, Spain; literally, to be up to the cap)

6. **donde el diablo perdió el poncho (y la diabla la chancleta)** very far away, in a godforsaken place (used in Southern Cone, Spain; literally, where the devil lost his poncho [and the she-devil her sandal])

7. **llevar bien puestos los pantalones** to impose one's authority, especially in a home setting (literally, to wear the pants well placed)

8. **quitarle hasta la camisa a alguien** to take the shirt off someone's back, rip someone off (*Me quitaron hasta la camisa.*)

9. **recoger el guante** to accept or rise to a challenge (literally, to pick up the glove)

10. **Zapatero, a tus zapatos.** Mind your own business. Stick to what you know. (Literally, Shoemaker, to your shoes.)

Rehearsal Time

Conversaciones. Complete the conversations with expressions using names of articles of clothing. Check your answers in the Answer Key.

SILVIA: Teresa, ¿dónde compraste ese vestido? Es muy bonito y te sienta muy bien el color.

TERESA: En una tienda en Soledad.

SILVIA: ¿Soledad?

TERESA: Es un pueblo en el norte, lejos, donde el diablo (1) _____. Fui allí para ver a mi prima Beatriz. Me perdí dos veces, y cuando llegué estaba hasta (2) _____. Pero es un lugar muy lindo.

MARTA: Hola, Alonso, ¿qué tal?

ALONSO: Estoy como niño con (3) _____, muy contento.

MARTA: ¿Y eso?

ALONSO: Compré una nueva casa.

MARTA: ¡Felicitaciones!

ALONSO: Sólo que tendré que tener mucho cuidado con el dinero ahora porque si no pago cada mes, me van a quitar (4) _____.

Don Dinero o el sueño de Picasso

According to a Spanish saying, *Poderoso caballero es don Dinero* ("A powerful gentleman is Sir Money"): Money is power. Or, as the Spanish philosopher Fernando Savater said: «*Mi sueño es el de Picasso: tener mucho dinero para poder vivir tranquilo como los pobres.*» ("My dream is the same as Picasso's: to have a lot of money so as to be able to live in peace [unworried] like the poor.") Here are some Spanish expressions about the "root of all evil."

TOP TEN Common Sayings About Money

1. **El dinero es como el agua; un poquito salva, y mucho ahoga.** Money is like water; a little bit (of it) saves you, and a lot drowns you.

2. **Paga lo que debes y sabrás lo que tienes.** Pay what you owe and you'll know what you have.

3. **Los hijos son la riqueza de los pobres.** Children are the riches of the poor.

4. **Quien más tiene, más quiere.** The person who has most wants more.

5. **El dinero todo lo puede.** Money can do anything.

6. **No hay mejor maestra que la pobreza.** There's no better teacher than poverty.

7. **La plata platica.** Money (literally, silver) talks.

8. **El crédito y las ostras son las cosas más difíciles de abrir.** Credit and oysters are the hardest things to open.

9. **No es oro todo lo que brilla (reluce).** All that glitters is not gold.

10. **Lo barato es (cuesta) caro.** Something cheap costs a lot (in the long run).

When traveling, you may need some expressions about finances; here are some important ones.

TOP FIVE Expressions About the Use of Money

1. **¿Dónde se puede cambiar un cheque de viajero?** Where can one (I) change a traveler's check?

2. **¿A cuánto está el cambio?** What's the exchange rate?

3. **¿Podría usted cambiar un billete de mil pesos? ¿Podría cambiar doscientos dólares?** Could you change a thousand-peso bill? Could you change two hundred dollars? (Note that you could use *Puede*... in these two questions, but it would be less polite. The conditional forms like *podría* are often used for politeness and can make you sound not only more courteous but more knowledgeable about the language.)

4. **Disculpe, pero sólo me dio veinte pesos de vuelta (de cambio).** Excuse me, but you only gave me twenty pesos change.

5. **Quédese con el cambio.** Keep the change.

Changing money is usually done in *casas de cambio*, places that specialize in changing currency, although many banks will also change money for you. Rates can vary a lot in some countries, where there may be a black market for dollars. Beware of changing money in hotels or other commercial establishments; if you do this, make sure you know what the rate will be before you hand over your check or cash. Be aware that it's much more common to buy in cash (*dinero en efectivo*) in Hispanic countries than to use credit cards—many places will not accept them. Many people do not use travelers' checks anymore, preferring to use ATMs and credit cards to get money in the local currency. However, if you do this, call before you leave home to make sure that your bank knows you will be taking out money overseas so that it doesn't put a hold on your account. Also, check rates for using the credit card at ATMs— sometimes they are extremely high (for instance, you might have to pay $10 to take out $100 in local currency).

Slang expressions for money abound. Here are some common ones.

TOP FIVE Slang Words That Mean "Money"

1. **la plata** (literally, silver)

2. **la lana** (literally, wool, from the time when raising sheep was highly profitable; used in Mexico, Central America, Cuba, Peru)

3. **la guita** (used in Ecuador, Peru, Southern Cone, Spain)

4. **la feria** (literally, fair; used in Mexico, Central America)

5. **la pasta** (literally, dough; used in Spain)

In English we also say "dough" (like *la pasta*) or "bread" referring to money, and there are a variety of slang expressions in Spanish meaning "money" that have to do with food: *el maíz* ("corn"), Cuba; *la lechuga* ("lettuce," used for dollar because it's green), Cuba; *el mango* ("mango"), Uruguay, Argentina; *la harina* ("wheat"), Costa Rica, Ecuador. In Argentina, people say *largar los mangos* ("to distance the mangos") meaning "to spend money." And then there is the ironic use of *dolores* ("pains, aches") in place of *dólares* (or pesos): *Me costó diez dolores.* ("It cost me ten pains" [dollars, pesos]).

Of course, there are also lots of slang expressions to describe people who have a lot of money or those who are barely getting by.

TOP FIVE Slang Expressions to Describe the Rich

1. **ricachón (ricachona)** rich

2. **platudo(-a)** wealthy (from *plata*)

3. **niños bien** children from well-off families; in Mexico, *niños bien* are referred to pejoratively as *niños popis* (rich brats)

4. **hijos de papá** kids whose wealthy dads will solve any problem they have

5. **la crema y nata** upper crust, highest social class (literally, cream and whipped cream)

TOP FIVE Slang Expressions to Describe the Poor

1. **ser pobre como una rata** to be poor as a (church) mouse

2. **no tener donde caerse muerto** to have nothing, not even a place to die in (literally, to not have a place to fall dead in)

3. **estar pelado(-a)** to be broke (literally, to be peeled; used in Central America, Caribbean, Colombia, Spain)

4. **estar sin cinco, no tener ni cinco** to be without a plug nickel (used in Mexico, El Salvador, Dominican Republic, Spain)

5. **andar comiéndose un cable** to be in a pinch economically (literally, to be going around eating a cable; used in the Caribbean)

If someone has come down in economic status but comes from a family that was "high class," there is a special expression used: *Mal suena el don sin el din* ("The title *don* doesn't sound good without the *din[ero]*"). In other words, nobility is nothing without money.

Good or bad, money will be around for a while. Here are two final thoughts about it:

No hay hermano
Ni pariente tan cercano
Ni amigo tan de verdad
Como el dinero en la mano
En cualquier necesidad.

There's no sibling
Or relative so close
Or as true a friend
As money in your hand
In any necessity.
—Cristóbal de Castillejo,
sixteenth-century Spanish
poet

El dinero es la única infelicidad que todos deseamos y de la cual no queremos librarnos jamás... Los ricos son modelo de ingratitud. Creen que a nadie sino que a sí mismos deben su fortuna. El dinero no se gana

Money is the only unhappiness that we all want and that we don't ever want to free ourselves from . . . The rich are a model of ingratitude. They think that they owe their fortunes to no one but themselves. Money is not

solo. Para que alguien gane, contribuyen muchos... No hay seguridad más inseguro que el dinero.

earned by itself. For someone to earn it, many contribute . . . There is no security so insecure as money.

—Pepita Turino,
MULTIDIÁLOGOS

 Rehearsal Time

Dinero, dinero, dinero. Answer the following questions, then check your answers in the Answer Key.

1. What's a *casa de cambio*? Why is it good to check about the exchange rate at a commercial establishment before changing money?

2. How do you ask what the exchange rate is?

3. How do you say "Keep the change"?

Sinónimos. Which of these words or expressions are synonyms? Note that most of them are colloquial, used informally, and that some are regional. Check your answers in the Answer Key.

1. el cambio   a. la guita

2. no tener cinco   b. estar pelado(-a)

3. los hijos de papá   c. la vuelta

4. ricachón   d. platudo

5. la lana   e. los niños bien

TUNE-UP

7

¿En serio
o en broma?

Understanding How Language, Culture,
and Humor Interact

1. If someone tells you in Spanish that they have their "soul in a thread" or that their new boss is "not a pear in sugar water," what are they saying?

2. Do you know what it means in Spanish if you're "bored as an oyster" or "sing like a clam"?

3. If someone tells you in Spanish that he was late because the sheets stuck to him, what happened?

4. You have a date with a cute person. The day before you are to meet, he or she says *No me dejes plantado(-a)*. What does this person not want you to do?

5. What's an *abogánster*? A *matasanos*?

6. What does the proverb *Donde manda capitán, no manda marinero* mean?

7. Why would you light one candle for San Miguel and another for the devil?

8. If you are in a Spanish-speaking area and you see a falling star, how many wishes will people tell you to make?

9. What happens if you open an umbrella in the house or spill wine?

10. If someone says to you *El gozo en un pozo* or *A otra cosa, mariposa*, what on earth do they mean?

¿En serio o en broma? ("Are you serious or joking?") Most Americans "get" Spanish humor once they get the hang of it, because many jokes translate well from Spanish to English (or vice versa). However, Spanish-speakers love word play and puns, and the language is peppered with sayings that may not be immediately clear to an English speaker. In this chapter, you'll see some of the many imaginative ways that Spanish speakers play with their language and how some expressions reflect folk beliefs and culture—that is, how language and culture interact.

La ironía y la exageración

One of the most common forms of humor in Spanish is the use of irony, saying one thing to mean something else. Here are some examples.

TOP TEN Ironic Expressions

1. **Lo harán cuando la rana eche pelos (o el 30 de febrero).** They'll never do it. (Literally, They'll do it when the frog sprouts hair [or the 30th of February].)

2. **Es muy especial.** He or she is very difficult. (Literally, He or she is very special.)

3. **Tiene cara de «yo no fui».** He or she looks guilty. (Literally, He or she has the face of "It wasn't me.")

4. **Lo conocen en su casa.** No one here knows him. (Literally, They know him at his house.)

5. **Es poco espléndido(-a).** He or she is tight-fisted, stingy. (Literally, He or she is not very splendid.)

6. **Porque la abuela fuma.** For no reason at all. (Literally, Because Grandma smokes; used in Spain.) In Mexico and Colombia: *Porque voló la mosca.* Because the fly flew away.

7. **Se casaron por detrás de la iglesia.** They didn't get married. (Literally, They got married behind the church.)

8. **¿Cuándo hemos comido en el mismo plato?** Since when are we bosom buddies? (Literally, When have we eaten from the same plate?; used in El Salvador.)

9. **bendito(-a)** darned (literally, blessed); for example, *La bendita computadora no está funcionando*. The darned computer isn't working.

10. **Es un mandilón.** He's a man whose wife bosses him around. (He's a big commander; used in Mexico, Central America.)

Related to this last item is the Mexican expression *el ministerio de guerra* ("war department") meaning one's wife, who might also be referred to as *la Santa Inquisición* ("the Holy Inquisition"). The man's mistress might be called his *segundo frente* ("second front"). And in Spain, you might hear the expression *menudo número* ("diminutive number/show") meaning "a pretty picture" or "fine state of affairs."

 Uses of Irony in Negative Expressions: *no es perita en dulce*

1. **Ese niño no es perita en dulce.** That boy is difficult, not sweet or easy. (Literally, That boy is not a little pear in sugar water.)

2. **Ana no da su brazo a torcer.** Ana is no pushover. (Literally, Ana doesn't give her arm to twist.)

3. **No me chupo el dedo.** I'm not naive, wasn't born yesterday. (Literally, I don't suck my thumb.)

4. **No calentó el asiento allí.** He or she didn't last long there (for example, in a job). (Literally, He or she didn't warm the seat there.)

5. **No es cojo ni manco.** He's competent, experienced. (Literally, He's neither lame nor one-handed.)

6. **No come un huevo por no perder la cáscara.** He or she's a real miser. (Literally, He or she doesn't eat an egg so as not to waste the shell.)

7. **Ese hombre no ha roto un plato en su vida.** That man acts like he's never made a mistake (although of course he has). (Literally, That man hasn't broken a plate in his life.)

8. **No soy plato de segunda mesa.** I'm not playing second fiddle. (Literally, I'm not a dish of a second table.)

9. **No es nada del otro mundo.** It's mundane, nothing special. (Literally, It's nothing from the other world.)

10. **No es el santo de mi devoción.** He's not so much to my liking. (Literally, He's not the saint of my devotion.)

Exaggeration: *¡Se ahoga en un vaso de agua!*

The Spanish language is replete with hyperbole, exaggeration for effect. Here are ten expressions that exaggerate in order to make a statement.

TOP TEN Expressions Using Exaggeration

1. **Se ahoga en un vaso de agua.** He or she's incompetent. (Literally, He or she drowns in a glass of water.)

2. **Le da el pie y le toma la mano.** Give him an inch and he'll take a mile. (Literally, You give him your foot and he takes your hand.)

3. **Se caen los patos asados.** It's hot as Hades. (Literally, The ducks are falling roasted; used in Chile.)

4. **Tengo el alma en un hilo (o el corazón en un puño).** I'm really down in the dumps. (Literally, I have my soul in a thread [or my heart in a fist].)

5. **Es mortal (fatal, la muerte en bicicleta).** It's God-awful. (Literally, It's mortal [fatal, death on a bicycle].)

6. **El nuevo profesor está en pañales.** The new teacher is young and inexperienced. (Literally, The new teacher is in diapers.)

7. **El doctor Chávez es una reliquia.** Dr. Chávez is a fossil, up in years. (Literally, Dr. Chávez is a relic.)

8. **Adelante con la cruz.** Keep persevering. Hang in there. (Literally, Forward with the cross, a reference to the crucifixion.)

9. **Es una bacteria en el horizonte.** He or she is of no consequence, doesn't count. (Literally, He or she's a bacterium on the horizon; used in Spain.)

10. **Es más despistado que un pulpo en un garaje.** He's totally lost, off the track. (Literally, He's more lost than an octopus in a garage.)

Frequently these expressions include the word *más* as in the last example above and in the following: *más serio que un burro en lancha* ("more serious than a donkey in a boat"), *más lento que una caravana de cojos* ("slower than a caravan of lame people"), *más pesado que cargar un elefante* ("heavier than carrying an elephant"), *más loco que una cabra* ("crazier than a she-goat"), *más sordo que una tapia* ("more deaf than a wall"), *más largo que la esperanza del pobre* ("longer than the hope of the poor"). If the noun referred to is feminine, of course, the adjective ends in -*a*: *seria, lenta,* and so on.

And, in Spanish you can *llorar a mares* ("cry seas") or *morirse de risa* ("die of laughter").

🎼 Rehearsal Time

La pura verdad. What did the speakers of the following sentences really mean to say? Choose *a* or *b*, then check your answers in the Answer Key.

1. Enrique no ha roto un plato en su vida.
   a. Enrique acts like he's perfect.
   b. Enrique never washes the dishes.

2. Ariel es muy especial.
   a. Ariel is fussy, difficult.
   b. Ariel is my special friend.

3. No es nada del otro mundo.
   a. It's common.
   b. It's not an extraterrestrial.

4. Felipe no es el santo de mi devoción.
   a. Felipe's not very religious.
   b. I don't much care for Felipe.

5. Lo harán el 30 de febrero.
   a. They'll do it by the end of February.
   b. They'll never do it.

6. Pablito no es perita en dulce.
   a. Pablito can be a bit of a pain.
   b. Pablito is a sweet kid.

Comparisons: *como alma que lleva el diablo*

Oftentimes, Spanish speakers make comparisons in a humorous way, using similes (with *como*, meaning "like") or metaphors (more general comparisons) and colorful descriptions.

Similes

For fun, try to guess what these expressions refer to from their literal meanings, in parentheses. The answers are at the bottom of the page.

TOP TEN Similes with Humor

1. **como alma que lleva el diablo** (literally, like a soul that the devil takes)

2. **como cocodrilo en fábrica de carteras** (literally, like a crocodile in a wallet factory; used in Puerto Rico)

3. **como perro en canoa** (literally, like a dog in a canoe)

4. **como gallo en patio ajeno** (literally, like a rooster on someone else's patio)

5. **como nalga de lavandera** (literally, like a washerwoman's buttock; used in Nicaragua)

6. **como sardina en lata** (literally, like a sardine in a can)

7. **como chancho en misa** (literally, like a pig in mass [church])

8. **como entierro de pobre** (literally, like a poor person's funeral)

9. **como perros y gatos** (literally, like dogs and cats)

10. **como a un santo Cristo un par de pistolas** (literally, like a couple of pistols on a statue of Christ; used in Spain)

Answers: 1. very fast and/or agitated 2. very worried, anxious 3. very nervous 4. feeling very out of place 5. very cold 6. very crowded 7. very out of place, looking ridiculous 8. very fast, with no ado 9. at odds, fighting 10. totally absurd

TOP TEN Similes Containing Verbs

1. **aburrirse como una ostra** to be bored stiff (literally, to be bored as an oyster)

2. **vivir como escopeta de hacienda** to be always pregnant, like an old gun loaded and left in a corner (literally, to live like an old farm rifle; used in Nicaragua)

3. **estar alegre como unas castañuelas** to be happy as a clam (literally, to be happy as castanets)

4. **como pedir peras al olmo** like asking for the impossible (literally, like asking the elm for pears)

5. **cantar como una almeja** to stand out in a bad way, call attention to oneself and look bad (literally, to sing like a clam; used in Spain)

6. **fumar como chimenea** to smoke like a chimney

7. **pegar como guitarra en un entierro** to be out of time or place, to stick out like a sore thumb (literally, to stick like a guitar at a funeral; used in Spain)

8. **hablar como un papagayo** to talk a blue streak, be a big talker (literally, to talk like a parrot)

9. **tronar como ejote** to fail, wash out, end up badly (literally, to snap like a peapod; used in Mexico)

10. **como arar en el mar** like taking coals to Newcastle, doing something useless (literally, like plowing the sea)

And, if you are in the Southern Cone, you'll find that it's possible to *andar como bola sin manija* ("to go around like a ball without a string"), which means "to be going around in circles, very busy."

Metaphors: *¡Se cree la divina garza!*

Many expressions in Spanish make an allusion or reference to something. Here are ten such metaphors. The literal meanings are included.

TOP TEN Spanish Metaphors

1. **Esa mujer se cree la divina garza.** That woman thinks she's God's gift. (Literally, That woman thinks she's the divine heron.)

2. **Tomás es el as de la baraja.** Tomás is hard to get hold of. (Literally, Tomás is the ace of the deck.)

3. **Felipe está echando chispas.** Felipe is irritable, angry. (Literally, Felipe is throwing off sparks.) (You might also hear **echar humo**, "to throw off smoke or steam," or **echar rayos**, "to throw off thunderbolts.")

4. **Vamos a menear el esqueleto.** Let's dance. (Literally, Let's move our skeletons.)

5. **Voy a casa a planchar la oreja.** I'm going home to bed. (Literally, I'm going home to iron my ear.)

6. **Se me pegaron las sábanas.** I got up late. (Literally, The sheets stuck to me.)

7. **La dejó plantada.** He stood her up. (Literally, He left her planted.)

8. **Comieron la torta antes de la fiesta.** They enjoyed something before they should have, sometimes a reference to a pregnant bride. (Literally, They ate the cake before the party; used in El Salvador.)

9. **Es un pez gordo en el gobierno.** He's a big shot in the government. (Literally, He's a fat fish in the government.)

10. **Papá tiene una cara de teléfono ocupado.** Dad looks annoyed, upset. (Literally, Dad has a face like a busy telephone; used in Puerto Rico.)

Word Inventions: *el ridículum vitae*

Sometimes people invent words from known expressions or from putting two words together, like "workaholic" (*trabajólico* or *trabajólica* in Spanish, from *trabajo* and *alcóholico*). The Mexican comic and actor Cantinflas was famous for this and for his convoluted comical "spiels"; *cantinflear* means to talk humorously but not make a lot of sense. Here are some examples of the kinds of made-up expressions you hear everywhere in Spain and Latin America:

TOP TEN Plays on Words

1. **el ridículum vitae** ridiculum vita (instead of curriculum vita or résumé)

2. **el abogángster** lawyer that gets guilty rich guys off (*abogado* + *gángster*)

3. **el sistema jodicial** the judicial system, but with *jod-* of *joder*, "to screw," instead of *judicial*

4. **graduarse raspa cum laude** to graduate "raspa" cum laude (*raspar* is "to fail" in parts of the Caribbean, where this expression is used)

5. **el/la matasanos** doctor (literally, killer of the healthy)

6. **el/la chupatintas** paper pusher, drudge (literally, ink-sucker)

7. **la preocupabilidad** worry and guilt (*preocupación* + *culpabilidad*)

8. **lentejo(-a)** dope (sounds like *lento*, "slow," + *pendejo*, vulgar for "idiot")

9. **la pitopausia** male menopause (*pito* is slang for the male organ in some places)

10. **el matricidio** matrimony; sounds like *matrimonio* and *suicidio* (used in Costa Rica)

If you are in Mexico, you might hear someone called an *analfabestias*, an ignorant redneck, from *analfabeto* and *bestia* ("illiterate" and "beast"). This person may have a *trompabulario*, from *trompa* ("elephant's trunk," colloquial for "mouth") and *vocabulario*; in other words, he or she uses bad language. Worse yet, he might be *en cuernavaca* ("in [the town of] Cuernavaca," but referring to *en cueros*, or "naked"). Originally, these were probably *albures*, spontaneous word plays, but they were repeated and became commonly used.

 Rehearsal Time

Imágenes. What's in a metaphor? Match these Spanish sentences with their meanings in English—try to picture what the Spanish portrays. Check your answers in the Answer Key.

1. María se cree la divina garza.   a. Gabriel is making himself scarce.

2. Se les pegaron las sábanas.   b. My parents were fuming.

3. Gabriel es el as de la baraja.   c. They went home to sleep.

4. Mis papás estaban   d. They overslept.
echando chispas.

5. Vamos a menear el   e. María thinks she's God's gift.
esqueleto.

6. Fueron a casa a planchar   f. Let's dance.
la oreja.

Las adivinanzas y los dichos

While riddles (*adivinanzas*) are found in many cultures, they seem particularly abundant in Spanish, especially in Mexico and Central America. Ask any Mexican person about riddles, and he or she is sure to know many of them. Here are five that contain their own answer (it's embedded in the riddle itself); see if you can figure them out. The answers are at the bottom of page 196.

TOP FIVE Riddles That Contain Their Answer

1. **Oro parece; plata no es. ¿Qué es?** It looks like gold; it's not silver. What is it?

2. **Verde por fuera, amarilla por dentro; si quieres saber, espera.** Green on the outside, yellow on the inside; if you want to know, just wait.

3. **Ya ves, ya ves, el que no lo adivine muy tonto es.** Now you see, now you see, he who doesn't guess it is very silly.

4. **Me dicen algo y no soy nada, me dicen don y no lo soy.** They call me something and I'm nothing; they call me don (a title of respect) and I'm not that.

5. **Te lo digo, te lo digo; te lo vuelvo a repetir.** I tell it to you, I tell it to you; I repeat it to you again.

Here are ten more riddles, but these do not have an answer embedded in them. See if you can guess what they are. The answers are at the bottom of page 197.

TOP TEN Common Riddles

1. **Cuando seca, se moja.** When it dries, it gets wet.

2. **Sube el cerro y baja y siempre está en el mismo lugar.** It climbs the hill and goes down and is still in the same place.

3. **Dos muertos cargando a un vivo.** Two dead ones carrying a live one.

4. **El que lo hizo no lo quiso, el que lo compró no lo usó, y el que lo usó no lo vio.** He who made it didn't want it, he who bought it didn't use it, and he who used it didn't see it.

5. **Son hermanos muy unidos, donde quieren van juntitos.** They're very close siblings; they go everywhere together.

6. **Alto más que un pino y espeso más que la selva, pero menos que un comino pesa.** Taller than a pine tree and thicker than the forest, but it weighs less than a cumin seed.

Answers: 1. **el plátano** "banana" (*plátano es*) 2. **la pera** "pear" (*es pera*) 3. **las llaves** "keys" (*ya ves*) 4. **el algodón** "cotton" (*algo* + *don*) 5. **el té** "tea" (*Te lo...*)

7. **Da sin tener manos y anda sin tener pies.** It gives without having hands and walks without having feet.

8. **A pesar de que tengo patas, yo no me puedo mover; llevo encima la comida y no me la puedo comer.** Even though I have feet, I can't move; I carry food and can't eat it.

9. **Paso por la casa, voy a la cocina, meneando la cola como una gallina.** I pass through the house, I go to the kitchen, wagging my tail like a chicken.

10. **Vuela sin alas, silba sin boca y no se ve ni se toca.** It flies without wings, whistles without a mouth, and it's neither seen nor touched.

Some riddles are usually in the form of questions. For instance:

¿Qué le dijo la luna al sol? What did the moon say to the sun?
¿Tan grande y no te dejan salir de noche? So big and they don't let you out at night?

¿Qué cosa nunca puedes alcanzar y siempre está contigo? What thing can you never reach and is always with you?
Tu sombra. Your shadow.

Along with riddles, proverbs (*proverbios* or *dichos*) are very common in daily language in Spanish. First, here are five that "sound Hispanic."

Answers: 1. **la toalla** towel 2. **el camino** road 3. **los zapatos** shoes 4. **el ataúd** coffin 5. **los dedos** fingers 6. **el humo** smoke 7. **el reloj** clock (In Spanish, a clock "walks" instead of "runs" and "gives" the hour, *da la hora.*) 8. **la mesa** table (*Patas* are feet or legs of furniture or of animals, but are used colloquially for people also.) 9. **la escoba** broom 10. **el viento** wind

TOP FIVE Proverbs That "Sound Hispanic"

1. **Hay moros en la costa.** Watch out—there's danger. (Literally, There are Moors on the coast.) Spain was ruled by the Moors, who invaded the country from North Africa and governed for many centuries (the Reconquest wasn't completed until 1492), so this goes back to historical roots.

2. **Al nopal lo van a ver sólo cuando tiene tunas.** People call on other people only when they are prosperous or doing well. (Literally, They only go to see the nopal cactus when it has *tunas*, "fruits"; used in Mexico.)

3. **Peor es chile y agua lejos.** Things could be worse, said with resignation. (Literally, Worse is chili and water far away; used in Mexico and Central America.)

4. **No se puede negar la cruz de tu parroquia.** You can't deny your roots; you can take the boy out of the country, but you can't take the country out of the boy. (Literally, You can't deny the cross of your parish.)

5. **No se ganó Zamora en una hora.** Rome wasn't built in a day—i.e., some things take time. (Literally, Zamora, Spain, wasn't won in an hour.)

TOP TEN Useful Proverbs

1. **Ojos que no ven, corazón que no siente.** What you don't know won't hurt you. (Literally, Eyes that don't see, heart that doesn't feel.)

2. **Donde manda capitán no manda marinero.** Just relax, because there's nothing one can do. (Literally, Where the cap-

tain is in command the sailor is not in command; phrase of resignation.)

3. **Dios sufre a los malos, pero no para siempre.** They'll get their due some day. (Literally, God tolerates bad people, but not forever; phrase said when there is an injustice.)

4. **Ya que la casa se quema, vamos a calentarnos.** Let's make the best of a bad situation. (Literally, Now that the house is burning, let's warm ourselves.)

5. **Unos nacen con estrella y otros estrellados.** Some people are born with good luck and others are jinxed; said when either type of luck presents itself. (Some people are born with a [lucky] star and others are born "starred" or seeing stars—literally, dashed or smashed in the form of a star.)

6. **El que no llora no mama.** The squeaky hinge gets the grease—i.e., speak up. (Literally, He who doesn't cry doesn't suckle.)

7. **Más sabe el diablo por ser viejo que por ser diablo.** Experience and age are important. (Literally, The devil knows more because he's old than because he's the devil.)

8. **Más hace una hormiga andando que un buey echado.** Let's do what we can. (Literally, An ant that's moving does more than an ox lying down; used in Mexico.)

9. **Hijos no tenemos y nombres les ponemos.** Let's not count our chickens before they hatch. (Literally, We don't have children and we're naming them.)

10. **En boca cerrada, no entran moscas.** Sometimes it's better to keep quiet. (Literally, In a closed mouth, flies do not enter.)

TOP FIVE Proverbs You Will Probably Hear Only the First Half Of

1. **Hablando del rey de Roma... y se asoma.** Speak of the devil and he appears. (Literally, Talking about the king of Rome . . . and he appears.)

2. **Agua que no has de beber... déjala correr.** If it's not for you, let it be. (Literally, Water that you shouldn't drink . . . let it run.)

3. **Cuando el río suena... piedras lleva.** Where there's smoke, there's fire. (Literally, When the river makes a sound . . . it's carrying stones.) Note that there are several variants to the last part: *es que agua lleva* (in Mexico), *es porque algo trae* (in Cuba and Puerto Rico), *piedras trae* (in Chile). But you'll probably just hear the first part anyway!

4. **Como dijo Herodes... te jodes.** As Herod said . . . you're screwed. (Used in Mexico, Spain, and some other countries; vulgar)

5. **Dios los cría... y ellos se juntan.** Birds of a feather flock together, but with a negative connotation. (Literally, God creates them . . . and they get together.)

Rehearsal Time

Proverbios. What Spanish saying could you use in each of these situations? Choose from the options on the right and check your answers in the Answer Key.

1. Están hablando de su amigo Jaime en una fiesta; de repente usted da la vuelta ("suddenly you turn around") y ahí está él.

   a. No se ganó Zamora en una hora.

2. Usted le cuenta a un amigo que por mala suerte acaba de perder su trabajo, pero que hay gente que tiene mejor suerte.

b. Ojos que no ven, corazón que no siente.

3. Un amigo ve a una chica bonita por la calle, pero usted le dice que ella no es para él porque ya tiene novia.

c. Hablando del rey de Roma y se asoma.

4. La mamá de su mejor amigo no sabe que él empezó a fumar cigarrillos. Usted le aconseja a su amigo que no le diga nada; lo que ella no sabe no le hace daño ("doesn't hurt her").

d. Unos nacen con estrella y otros estrellados.

5. Hay un trabajo que hacer, pero no se puede hacerlo en un día. Usted le dice a sus amigos que habrá que hacerlo poco a poco.

e. Agua que no has de beber, déjala correr.

La suerte y las creencias

Many expressions are based on beliefs that come out of tradition. For instance, in English we might blame bad luck on "Friday the thirteenth" or tell someone that he or she "got up on the wrong side of the bed" (which originally referred to the left or "sinister" side). The same is true in Spanish.

Saints Alive!

Because Spain and Latin America are predominantly Catholic, the saints play a large role in culture and language. Traditionally, you pray to San Antonio to recover something you lost or—for a girl—to find Mr. Right. You might pray to Santa Barbara to protect you in a storm or to San Judás for lost causes, and each person has a special patron saint to apply to (for instance, if you were born on March 8, your saint is San Juan de Dios). Many people remember Saint Christopher's medals; San Cristóbal was the protector of travelers until he was decanonized by the church because they decided he was legendary, not real. There are many Spanish expressions that invoke the *santos*; here are ten that are usually said "tongue-in-cheek," although they do reflect strong religious traditions.

TOP TEN Expressions Invoking the *santos*

1. **Se me fue el santo al cielo.** I had good intentions, but things went awry, usually said when something has not been accomplished. (Literally, My saint went up to heaven.)

2. **Santo que no me quiere, basta con no rezarle.** There's no need to bother with someone who doesn't care about me. (Literally, Saint that doesn't like me, it's enough not to pray to him.)

3. **Sara se quedó para vestir santos.** Sara never married. (Literally, Sara stayed behind to dress statues of saints.)

4. **Andrés pone una vela a San Miguel y otra al diablo.** Andrés is keeping his options open so as to profit from either of two people or groups. (Literally, Andrés is lighting one candle for San Miguel and another for the devil.)

5. **Tengo el santo de espaldas.** I'm having bad luck. (Literally, I have my saint turning his back on me.) **Tengo el santo de**

9. **Si quieres evitar la mala suerte, puedes tirar sal sobre el hombro izquierdo tres veces.** If you want to avoid bad luck, you can throw salt over your left shoulder three times.

10. **El martes trece es un día de mala suerte.** Tuesday the thirteenth is an unlucky day.

Rehearsal Time

Dichos y supersticiones. Answer the following questions, then check your answers in the Answer Key.

1. What Spanish expression can you use if you forget to do something or don't fulfill an obligation—for instance, you plan to be on time at a café meeting with your friends but you see an interesting shop, go in, and lose track of the hour?

2. If someone says to you *Tengo el santo de espaldas*, are they having a good day or a bad day?

3. If you do something *en un santiamén*, are you doing it quickly or slowly?

4. If you are in a Spanish-speaking country, what day is unlucky, according to local superstition? What supposedly happens if you open an umbrella inside the house? If you spill wine? If you break a mirror? If you see a falling star, what can you do?

Rhyming Expressions: Are You *tiquis miquis? Feliz como una lombriz?*

"See you later, alligator." "After a while, crocodile." You probably recognize these English expressions. Similar ones abound in Spanish, whose speakers are very creative and love to play with rhyme. If you ask how someone is, you might get the reply *Feliz como una lombriz* ("Happy as a worm") or *Sana como una manzana* ("Healthy as an apple"). The latter is for a woman, of course, who might also say *Soy como Santa Elena, cada día más buena* ("I'm like Saint Elena, better each day"). In Venezuela, someone might say *Chao, pesca'o* ("Good-bye, little fish") in farewell, and in some places at the end of a party you might hear *Calabaza, calabaza, cada uno para su casa* ("Pumpkin, pumpkin, each one to his or her house"). In Spain, if someone calls you *tiquis miquis*, that means "fussy" or "stuck up," but if you are *guay del Paraguay*, that's really cool. And in Mexico or Colombia, an affirmative answer might be *Okei maguey* ("O.K., cactus plant") or *Iguanas ranas* ("Iguanas—which sounds like *igual*—frogs" meaning "The same for me" or "Me too"). For example: *¿Quieres ir al cine? —Okei maguey.* ("Do you want to go to the movies?" "Okey-doke.") *Quiero un helado de chocolate. —Iguanas ranas.* ("I want a chocolate ice cream cone." "Me, too. The same for me.") Needless to say, all of these are very informal and colloquial.

For some reason, there are many rhymes to express a negative response:

Nada, pescadito mojado. Nothing. Zip. (Literally, Swim, little wet fish.) *Nada* means "nothing" as well as "swim."

Nel pastel. No way. (Literally, No cake; used in Mexico, Central America.)

Nada, nada limonada. Nothing. Zip. (Literally, Nothing, nothing, lemonade.)

Uno y no más, Santo Tomás. Never again. (Literally, Once and no more, Saint Thomas.)

De eso nada, monada. No way! Nothing doing! (Literally, Of that nothing, monkey [cute] face; used in Spain.)

¡Nones para los preguntones! Nothing for those who ask too many questions! (often used with children) Also, *¡Botones para los preguntones!*

Here are some of the most common rhymes you might hear in the Spanish-speaking world. See if you can guess what they mean from the literal meanings that are given in parentheses. The answers are at the bottom of page 208.

TOP TEN Common Rhyming Expressions

1. **El gozo en un pozo.** (Enjoyment in a well.)

2. **A otra cosa, mariposa.** (To another thing, butterfly.)

3. **Sin padre, ni madre, ni perro que me ladre.** (Without father or mother or dog to bark for me.)

4. **Si no lo veo, no lo creo.** (If I don't see it, I don't believe it.)

5. **Lo mismo es Chana que Juana.** (Chana is the same as Juana.)

6. **Sepa Chepa.** (Perhaps Chepa knows.)

7. **Te conozco, mosco.** (I know you, fly.) A variant in Spain: *Te conozco, bacalao, aunque vengas disfraza'o.* (I know you, codfish, although you come in disguise; cod was an inexpensive source of protein in Spain until recently, so it was prepared in many kinds of dishes.)

8. **Fuimos de la Ceca a la Meca.** (We went from Ceca to Mecca.)

9. **Sin ton ni son.** (Without tone or sound.)

10. **En eso no tengo arte ni parte.** (I have neither art nor part in that.)

Some rhymes seem to be made to instruct or chastise. Here are five of them:

TOP FIVE Rhymes with a Moral: Poetic Sarcasm

1. **El burro delante, para que no se espante.** The burro first, so he isn't frightened, doesn't get startled. (Said to someone who goes first or names himself or herself first, sort of like "Age before beauty." Often you'll just hear the first part, *El burro delante*.)

2. **El maestro Ciruela, que no sabe leer y pone escuela.** Master Ciruela, who can't read and has a school. (Said to censure someone who is talking about something he or she doesn't know much about.)

3. **Comida hecha, amistad deshecha.** Meal finished (done), friendship finished (undone). (Said to censure someone who "eats and runs.")

4. **¿Dónde va Vicente? Donde va toda la gente.** Where is Vicente going? Where everyone else goes. (Phrase expressing the lack of initiative of someone, saying that he or she is just a follower.)

5. **¿Quién te mete, Juan Bonete?** Who brings you into this, Juan Bonete? (This isn't your affair. None of your business!; used in Nicaragua.)

Answers: 1. Expression of sadness, something like "It's all down the drain." 2. Forget it. Let's change the subject. 3. Alone, without support. 4. I wouldn't believe it if I weren't seeing it for myself. 5. It's the same thing, six to one or half a dozen to the other. 6. Who knows? 7. I see your intention, know what you're up to. 8. We went from pillar to post, all over the place. 9. Without rhyme or reason. 10. That has nothing to do with me; I have no part in that.

Well, you get the picture—there is a rhyme for almost anything you want to say, and you'll hear many of these in informal Spanish. Just try to get the gist: *¿Me entiendes, Méndez?*

Rehearsal Time

Rimas. What rhyming expression could you use in each of these situations? Check your answers in the Answer Key.

1. Someone asks how you are and you respond that you're very happy.

2. As far as you're concerned, two things are just alike.

3. Someone pushes in front of you as you go through a door.

4. A friend has come for dinner and wants to leave right away—you'd like him or her to stay, so you make a humorous remark about "eating and running."

5. You say you have no part at all in the party an acquaintance is planning.

6. You are very surprised to see something happening—you wouldn't believe it if you hadn't seen it with your own eyes.

TUNE-UP
8

De la casa a la plaza

The Intimate Life of Family and Friends

--- Preview ---

1. Where would you meet the "godparents of the rope"?

2. What are the two meanings of the word *novio*?

3. How would you ask about someone's aunt and uncle?

4. When would a Mexican say, *¡Híjole!* ("Child to you!")?

5. What does the word for "father" mean when used as an adjective in Mexico?

6. Why are there two words for children?

7. Where do they answer the phone by saying *Dígame* instead of *Hola* or *Aló*?

8. What does *compadrazgo* mean?

9. What is the difference between *Te amo* and *Te quiero*?

10. How do you say that you love chocolate?

Marriage is the cornerstone of Spanish and Latin American societies. You only have to look at the Spanish word *casarse* ("to get married"), to see *casa* ("house," "home") inside of it.

Casa + *r* + *se* = to get married (a reflexive verb meaning literally, "to take a house to yourself")

El matrimonio y la familia

Getting married in these cultures means settling down with serious intent, *hasta la muerte nos separe* ("till death do us part"). Divorce occurs and is now legal everywhere (since Chile finally made it legal in 2004), but it is not as common as in North America and is still looked down upon in more traditional circles. The complicated rituals in a typical Mexican wedding ceremony underscore the respect and honor given to marriage. There are often five or six different *padrinos* ("godparents"): male and female pairs that include, of course, a *padrino* ("godfather") and a *madrina* ("godmother"). For example, there are *los padrinos del libro* who carry the Bible and *los padrinos de las monedas* who distribute coins to the children for good luck. One of these pairs, *los padrinos del lazo*, carry a large rope up to the altar and at the appropriate moment literally tie the bride and groom together! After a wedding like that, what couple can even think of splitting up?

And speaking of the bride and groom, they are called the *novio* and the *novia*, the same words used for boyfriend and girlfriend, which shows you why a young man may become rather nervous when he goes to his girlfriend's house for the first time to pick her up for a date and has to meet *los viejos* ("the old ones," i.e., parents).

TOP FIVE Proverbs About Marriage

1. **Antes que te cases, mira lo que haces.** Before you marry, take a look at what you are doing.

2. **El matrimonio y la mortaja, del cielo baja.** Marriage and the shroud, come down from on high.

3. **Baje la novia la cabeza y cabrá por la puerta de la iglesia.** Let the bride lower her head (become submissive) and she will fit through the church door.

4. **A marido celoso, poco reposo.** For a jealous husband, little repose.

5. **Casa sin mujer, cuerpo sin alma viene a ser.** A house without a woman becomes a body without a soul.

A Different Concept of Family Life

The importance of family is one of the best-known hallmarks of Spanish and Latin American cultures. That is why Canadians and Americans doing business south of the U.S. border are instructed to be sure to greet their Latino associates and then to ask them, *¿Cómo está su familia?* ("How is your family?"), a common courtesy not always obvious to people from English-speaking cultures where "business is business." Observers comment on the closeness of the Latino family, which is often described as *muy unida* ("very close") or even, in Mexico, as *amueganada* ("melted together like sticky candy"), and this is pointed out as a strong advantage for them when they emigrate to other countries. Relatives visit among themselves frequently, depend on each other for help in tough times, and keep in constant contact.

The very concept of what constitutes family is different from that of most Americans and Canadians because in Spanish-speaking society, the basis is the *familia extensa* ("extended family"). As an Argentine-Canadian once commented, "Here in Canada when someone talks about his family, he means his wife and children, possibly his mother and father, too, but for me the family is vast and may include even the great-aunt of my wife's cousin." Because family is so important, it is always polite to ask people how their family is doing and, in general, family is an accepted and interesting topic for conversation.

TOP TEN Questions to Ask About Someone's Family

1. **¿Cómo está su (tu) familia?** How is your family? (A question almost always asked by friends, especially when meeting after a separation.)

2. **¿Es grande o pequeña su (tu) familia?** Is your family big or small?

3. **¿Cuántos hermanos tiene usted (tienes)?** How many brothers and sisters do you have?

4. **¿Dónde viven sus (tus) padres?** Where do your parents live? (Notice that padres means "parents" and "fathers.")

5. **¿Dónde viven sus (tus) abuelos?** Where do your grandparents live?

6. **¿Tiene usted (Tienes) muchos tíos? ¿Dónde viven?** Do you have a lot of aunts and uncles? Where do they live?

7. **¿Tiene usted (Tienes) muchos sobrinos? ¿Hay más sobrinas o más sobrinos?** Do you have a lot of nephews and nieces? Are there more nieces or more nephews?

8. **¿Tiene usted (Tienes) muchos primos? ¿Dónde viven?** Do you have a lot of cousins? Where do they live?

9. **¿Tiene usted (Tienes) hijos (nietos)? ¿Cuántos años tienen?** Do you have children (grandchildren)? How old are they?

10. **¿Es muy unida su (tu) familia?** Is your family very close?

Notice that when it comes to family talk, Spanish is sometimes more concise than English, because to ask, "How are your aunt and uncle?" you can simply say, *¿Cómo están tus tíos?* The same holds true for "your nieces and nephews" (*tus sobrinos*) or "your sisters and brothers" (*tus hermanos*), although some people use the word "siblings."

Some of the vocabulary used for relatives can be tricky. For instance, the actual word for "relatives," *parientes*, is a false cognate because it closely resembles the English word "parents." So, make an effort to remember that relatives are *parientes* and parents are *padres*, the plural of the word for "father." *Un niño necesita a sus dos padres* ("A child needs both his parents," not both his fathers). Family relations become more complicated after marriage when the spouse's family appears on the scene. In English, we say the "in-laws"; in Spanish, *la familia política*. There is specialized vocabulary for mother-in-law, father-in-law, brother-in-law, sister-in-law (*suegra, suegro, cuñado, cuñada*), but to keep it simple you can use *madre política, padre político, hermano político, hermana política*, and so on.

The priority of the family is reflected in Spanish slang that is used to express some of the deepest human emotions through words for family members. The literal meanings are included.

TOP TEN Strong Slang Expressions Referring to Family Members

1. **¡Híjole!** Wow! Good heavens! Darn! (Literally, Child to you!; very common in Mexico, parts of Colombia, and parts of Central America to express surprise or emotion about something very good or very bad.) *¡Híjole, qué buenas noticias!* Wow, what great news! *¡Híjole, qué desastre!* Darn, what a disaster!

2. **Hijo de su...** SOB, son of a gun (Literally, Son of your . . .; slightly vulgar insult in most of Spain and Latin America, a euphemism for stronger insults referring to the mother of the person in question.) *¿Dónde aprendió a manejar, hijo de su... ?* Where did you learn how to drive, you son of a gun?

3. **a toda madre** at full blast, going strong, "to the max" (Literally, at full mother; this is said in parts of Colombia, Central America, and Mexico when talking about something—either good or bad—that is going strong, full blast.) *Tengo un catarro a toda madre.* I have a full-blown cold. *¿Qué tal la fiesta? —¡A toda madre!* How was the party? To the max, fantastic!

4. **No tiene madre.** It has no equal. It's the best or the worst. (Literally, he, she, or it doesn't have any mother; used in Mexico and parts of Central America.) *Ese actor no tiene madre.* That actor is the best. *Ese estafador no tiene madre.* That con man is the worst.

5. **Me vale madre.** I don't give a damn about it. (Literally, It is worth mother to me. This expression is so common in Mexico and parts of Central America that it has given its name to a whole attitude: *el valemadrismo*, the I-don't-care attitude.) *¡Este trabajo me vale madre!* I don't give a damn about this work! Take this work and stuff it!

6. **un desmadre** a terrible botched-up mess or confusion (Literally, an un-mothering; typical way of describing a messy place or situation in Spain, Mexico, and other parts of Latin America.) *¡Qué desmadre hay en esta casa!* What a mess there is in this house!

7. **¡Qué padre! ¡Padre!** Marvelous, fantastic, wonderful (Literally, What a father! Father!; used in Mexico.) *¡Qué padre tu nueva casa!* How gorgeous your new house is! *¡Este carro está padre!* This car is fantastic!

8. **padrísimo(-a)** the very best, out of this world (Literally, the father-est, the most father; used in Mexico. This takes the word "father" to the nth degree and, of course, means something is the best, super.) *¡Felicitaciones, querido, elegiste un hotel padrísimo!* Congratulations, dear, you chose a hotel that's out of this world!

9. **mano, mana** pal, buddy (short for *hermano* or *hermana*; literally, brother or sister; used in Mexico, Dominican Republic, parts of Colombia, and Central America for a close friend, common as a form of address.) *¿Qué pasa, mana?* What's happening, gal pal? *¿Adónde vas, mano?* Where are you going, bro?

10. **¡Tu abuela!** Your grandmother! (Expression of anger and insult, impugning the honor of someone's grandmother, common in Spain and some parts of Mexico and Central America.) *¿No tienes el dinero? ¡Tu abuela!* You don't have the money? Heck with you!

Rehearsal Time

El matrimonio y la familia. Choose the correct words from the list to complete the following proverbs and statements about marriage and family. Check your answers in the Answer Key.

1. The couple who tie up the bride and groom at the altar in Mexico are called the _____ *del lazo*.   cabeza

2. In Spanish the word for the bride and groom is _____.   celoso

3. The word for "relatives," which often misleads English speakers, is _____.   familia

4. An old proverb warns you to be careful about whom you marry: *Antes que te cases, mira lo que* _____.   haces

5. Another one says that if a girl wants to get married, she has to at least pretend to be submissive: *Baje la novia la* _____ *y cabrá por la puerta de la iglesia*.   madre

6. A different way of saying "my brother-in-law," besides *mi cuñado*, is *mi hermano* _____.   novios

7. Then there's the proverb that warns about the fate of the jealous husband: *A marido* _____, *poco reposo*.   padre

8. When businessmen get together in Spain and Latin America, one of the first questions they ask each other is: *¿Cómo está la* _____?   padrinos

9. A party in Mexico that is going very well is *una fiesta a toda* _____.   parientes

10. To compliment a couple on their home, Mexicans might say: *¡Es muy* _____ *su casa!*   político

Después de la luna de miel: los altibajos

Just because families are close, it doesn't mean that life is a bed of roses. After the *luna de miel* ("honeymoon") is over, married life has its usual *altibajos* ("ups and downs"—all in one word in Spanish).

TOP TEN Ways of Describing Married Couples and Their *altibajos*

1. **un matrimonio** a married couple; marriage is considered so normal that the word for matrimony also means married couple. *¿Viene el matrimonio García esta noche?* Are the Garcías coming tonight?

2. **una pareja** a couple; this can refer to married people, people who are not married but living with each other (*las uniones de hecho*), or people just going together. The word is also used to refer to one of the two people who make up the couple. *¿Cuántas parejas van al banquete?* How many couples are going to the banquet? *Iban cinco, pero Manuela va sin su pareja.* There were going to be five, but Manuela is going without her partner.

3. **un matrimonio (bien avenido** or **mal avenido)** a harmonious (or conflictive) married couple; the common way of describing a couple that appears to be successfully married (or not), with no exact equivalent in English. This comes from the verb *avenirse* "to agree with each other." *Se avienen bien Mario y Matilde, son un matrimonio muy bien avenido.* Mario and Matilde get along well; they are a harmonious married couple (one that will probably last).

4. **los esposos** the husband and wife (spouses); women refer to *mi esposo* and men to *mi esposa* or, in some places, to *mi señora*. Interestingly, in the feminine, *las esposas* means "handcuffs."

5. **marido y mujer** husband and wife (literally, woman); the opposite of English, in which it is common to talk about "man and wife," this expression means "husband and woman." In Spanish, women speak of *mi marido* but there is no feminine form of this term, and instead the men speak of *mi mujer*. These terms are just as common as *mi esposo(-a)*.

6. **los hijos, los niños** the children; while both of these words mean "children," there is a difference. *Hijos* are your sons and daughters. *Niños* are children in general. *Hay muchos niños aquí esta noche, pero no vinieron mis hijos.* There are a lot of children here tonight, but my children didn't come.

7. **tener celos, ser (estar) celoso(-a)** to be jealous; the word for "jealousy" in Spanish is plural, *celos*, and it is something you have. *Tengo muchos celos cuando mi novio mira a otras mujeres.* I'm very jealous when my boyfriend looks at other women. The adjective *celoso* can also be used with either *ser* or *estar* depending on context. These words refer to the kind of jealousy you feel when your lover is attracted to someone else. It does not refer to the green-eyed monster of envy as the word "jealousy" can in English. For that kind of jealousy (envy), use the words *envidia* or *envidioso(-a)*.

8. **ponerle los cuernos a alguien** to cheat on someone (literally, to put horns on someone; a common term used for either men or women). *¡Pobre Lalo! Su mujer le pone los cuernos con su ex-novio.* Poor Lalo! His wife is cheating on him with her ex-boyfriend. *¡Pobre Daniela! Roberto le ha puesto los cuernos muchas veces.* Poor Daniela! Roberto has cheated on her many times. Some people go wild with jealousy at certain moments, and in Spain and some parts of South America this is called *un ataque de cuernos* (a horn attack).

9. **pelear, tener diferencias (disputas, discusiones, peleas)** to fight, have differences, disputes, quarrels, arguments (a few of the many ways of describing marital disagreements). *Los*

González-Méndez pelean mucho. Siempre hay diferencias, disputas o discusiones. The González-Méndez family fights a lot. There are always quarrels, disputes, or arguments.

10. **hacer las paces, arreglar el pastel** to make peace (to make up after a fight); the second expression means, literally, to fix the cake, and is used mostly in the Southern Cone. *Juan y María estaban bien enojados pero ayer hicieron las paces (arreglaron el pastel).* Juan and María were very angry, but yesterday they made up.

Children: *los hijos y los niños*

What we feel for our own children is so much more intense than what we feel for other people's children. Some folks confess that they didn't even like children until they had their own, who seem like little saints with halos on them. So it isn't surprising that Spanish, with its tendency to emotional nuance, has two different words for these categories.

TOP FIVE Proverbs About Children

1. **Cada niño llega con el pan (la torta) debajo de su brazo.** Every child arrives with his bread under his arm.

2. **Hijo de tigre sale rayado.** The tiger's child comes out with stripes.

3. **Los niños pequeños son tan lindos que quieres comértelos—y cuando crecen, ¡qué lástima que no lo hayas hecho!** Small children are so darling you want to eat them up—and when they get older, what a shame that you didn't do it!

4. **El que no tiene hijos los mata a palos.** The person with no children of his own beats them to death.

5. **Los hijos son la riqueza de los pobres.** Children are the wealth of the poor.

Rehearsal Time

De padres e hijos. What could you say? Match each of the following descriptions to the appropriate lettered phrase. Check your answers in the Answer Key.

1. You are visiting an older couple and want to comment to another guest on how happy and well-adjusted your hosts seem.

    a. Cada niño trae el pan debajo del brazo.

2. A friend begs you to tell him the truth about his girlfriend, who you and everybody else knows is running around with another guy.

    b. Es un matrimonio muy bien avenido.

3. Although you are not married, you want to introduce your partner to a group of friends.

    c. Hija de tigre sale rayada.

4. You try to encourage your friend and his wife to have a child even though they are worried about their finances.

    d. Desgraciadamente, te pone los cuernos.

5. You are at a typical Latino party, where there are people of all ages, when a single man begins to complain about how active and noisy the children are.

    e. El que no tiene hijos los mata a palos.

6. Your colleague introduces you to her daughter, who looks just like her and is studying for the same career.

f. Quiero presentarles a mi pareja.

Los lazos de la amistad

In general, the people of Spain and Latin America are a friendly and outgoing lot. They spend a great deal of time in *tertulias* (regular reunions with a close group, often in a café or bar) and attending the many social events of their relatives and friends such as *bautizos* ("baptisms"), *quinceañeras* (lavish parties in honor of a daughter's fifteenth birthday), *bodas* ("weddings"), *el Día de la Madre* (usually considered very important and always celebrated on May 10), *fiestas de cumpleaños* ("birthday parties") and other celebrations.

In addition to birthdays, many people celebrate annually *el día de su santo* (their Saint's Day) since the calendar of the Catholic church has a special day every year to commemorate each saint. For example, March 19 is the feast of St. Joseph so anyone named José or Josefina will probably receive gifts, invitations, and congratulations on that day. In Mexico, the custom exists to wake up the person whose birthday or saint's day it is by singing the beautiful celebration song *«Las mañanitas»* ("The Little Morning Song"), in one of its versions and with a few of its innumerable verses. This can be done by bringing a group of friends to sing a serenade outside the window, calling up on the phone, or dropping by.

Amazingly (at least to those from other cultures), despite all these activities, there is somehow always time to *tomar un cafecito* ("have a little cup of coffee") with a new acquaintance. You never know when a new friendship (*una nueva amistad*) may take root, for friendship is an important element in Latino life.

TOP TEN Proverbs About Friendship

1. **Vino y amigo, el más antiguo.** With wine or friends, (choose) the oldest one.

2. **A casa de mi novia llevé a un amigo; él se quedó dentro y yo despedido.** To my girlfriend's house I brought a friend; he stayed inside and I was sent away.

3. **Amigo de muchos, amigo de ninguno.** Friend of many, friend of no one.

4. **Amistad que dice no, amistad que se perdió.** Friendship that says no, friendship that is lost.

5. **A buen amigo, buen abrigo.** For a good friend, a good coat.

6. **Amigo no es el que te hace reír con la mentira, sino el que te hace llorar con la verdad.** A friend is not the one who makes you laugh with lies, but the one who makes you cry with the truth.

7. **Amigo no es el que seca tus lágrimas, sino el que impide que caigan.** A friend is not the one who dries your tears, but the one who prevents them from falling.

8. **Amigo es uno mismo en otro cuero.** A friend is your own self in another skin.

9. **La amistad hace lo que la sangre no hace.** Friendship does what blood relations won't.

10. **Amistades que son ciertas mantienen las puertas abiertas.** Friendships that are true keep the doors open.

¡Dame un telefonazo! How to Call Up a Friend

If you make friends while visiting in a Spanish-speaking country, they may offer you their telephone number and ask you to give them a *telefonazo* or, in Argentina or Uruguay, *un golpe de teléfono* (slang for a phone call, but literally, "a hit with the telephone"). This seems like a challenge, but after a few tries, you will find that it isn't so hard. It helps if you know in advance what to expect. In English, most people answer the phone by saying, "Hello." In the Spanish-speaking world the ways of answering the phone vary from country to country. Here are the most common ones:

TOP TEN Common Ways of Answering the Telephone in Spanish

1. **¿A ver?** What's happening? (Literally, Let's see? Used in Colombia and parts of Central America.)

2. **Aló. Aló, ¿con quién hablo?** Hello. Hello, with whom am I speaking? (Used in many parts of Latin America.)

3. **Bueno.** Good. Well. (The normal way of answering the phone in Mexico.)

4. **Diga.** Say. Tell. (The normal way of answering the phone in Spain.)

5. **Dígame.** Say to me. Tell me. (A variation on the above, often used in Spain.)

6. **¡Hola!** Hi! (The normal way of answering the phone in Uruguay and Argentina.)

7. **Oigo.** I hear. (Used in Cuba and Miami.)

8. **¿Quién es?** Who is it? (A common way of answering the phone in some parts of Colombia and Spain.)

9. **Casa de la familia Alomá.** Home of the Alomá family. (An alternate way of answering the phone, occasionally heard in various places.)

10. **Residencia de los Domínguez Malvárez.** Domínguez-Malvárez residence. (Another way of answering the phone heard at times in many places.)

Once the phone has been answered, you ask to speak with your friend. Here are some ways to do that:

TOP FIVE Phrases for Asking to Speak to a Friend on the Telephone

1. **Hola, quisiera hablar con Margarita.** Hello, I'd like to speak with Margarita. (The word *quisiera* is the past subjunctive of the verb *querer* and is very polite. In general, it is a good way to ask for almost anything.)

2. **Buenos días, me gustaría hablar con Daniel.** Good morning, I would like to speak with Daniel. (*Buenos días* is used until noon. The expression *me gustaría* is the conditional of the verb *gustar* and is another very polite expression that can be used for general requests.)

3. **Buenas tardes, ¿podría hablar con Beto, por favor?** Good afternoon, could I please speak with Beto? (*Buenas tardes* is used after noon until it gets dark. Here the conditional of the verb *poder* is used. You can always add the word *por favor* to mean "please," even though it is not necessary because the verb form itself is polite.)

4. **Hola, ¿me hace el favor de ponerme con el señor Martín, por favor?** Hello, would you do me the favor of putting me (in contact) with Mr. Martín, please? (This is a somewhat formal and polite phrase. When asking for someone on a last-

name basis, be sure to put the definite article—*el* or *la*—in front of *señor[a]*, *señorita*, *doctor[a]*, or other titles.)

5. **Buenas noches, con la señora Rubio, por favor.** Hello, with Mrs. Rubio, please. (The expression *Buenas noches* is used once it is dark outside. This is the shortest way of asking for someone and works very well, especially if you are feeling nervous and don't want to say too much.)

What comes next? Once you have asked in Spanish for your friend, you have made a big step, especially if you have been understood. However, your friend may or may not be the one answering. It could be a roommate, a relative or friend, or perhaps the house maid. Many house maids come from the countryside and have a different way of speaking. Here are some of the responses to your request that you can expect to hear:

TOP FIVE Responses to a Phone Request

1. **¿De parte de quién?** May I ask who is calling? (Literally, On behalf of whom? Respond to this by identifying yourself with your name, for example, *De parte de John Smith [Mary Jones]*, or, *Soy John Smith [Mary Jones]*.)

2. **¿Quién lo (la) llama?** Who's calling (him or her)? (Answer in the same way as above.)

3. **No se encuentra en este momento.** He or she is not here now. (There can be many other ways of saying this, for example, *Salió con su hija hace tres horas*, *Ya se fue muy tempranito*, etc. If you don't quite understand, simply ask, *¿A qué hora*

regresa? What time is he or she coming back? Then listen hard
for the time [*a las tres, a las cuatro*], etc.)

4. **Con él. Con ella.** You are speaking with him or her. (Literally, With him. With her. The first part is understood here.
This means you have had a stroke of good luck [*un golpe de
suerte*] and your friend has answered.)

5. **Él (Ella) habla.** He (She) is speaking. **Soy yo.** It's me. (Literally, I'm I. Both ways of answering let you know that you are
speaking with your friend.)

Rehearsal Time

Hablando por teléfono. Pull it all together and complete the missing words for the following phone conversations. Check your
answers in the Answer Key.

Conversación A (en España)

—Diga.
—Hola, Buenos (1) _____. Me (2) _____ hablar
    con (3) _____ señor López.
—¿De parte de (4) _____?
—De (5) _____ de Mary Jones.
—Un momento, señorita.

Conversación B (en México)

—Bueno.
—(6) _____ tardes. (7) ¿_____ hablar con
    Conchita, por favor?
—Con (8) _____. ¡Hola, amiga!

Conversación C (en Venezuela)

—Aló.

—Hola. Quisiera hablar con Alejandro.

—El señor no se (9) _____. Salieron todos muy temprano.

—¿A qué hora (10) _____ Alejandro?

—Como a las seis y media, señor.

La amistad y el sistema de compadrazgo

Spaniards and Latin Americans maintain contact with their extended families, which includes cousins, uncles, aunts, in-laws, grandparents, great-aunts and great-uncles, and so on. As if this weren't enough to occupy their attention, most of them, to varying degrees, honor the system of *compadrazgo* ("compadre-ship"), which is a way of extending one's family even more. The root of this system is in the religious rite of baptism that requires the appointing of *padrinos* (*un padrino y una madrina*), "a godfather and a godmother," for a child who has recently been born.

The godparents have a moral obligation to watch over their godchild and give advice or help if it is needed. Usually they attend birthday parties and other important events. These *padrinos* also acquire a new relationship with the parents of the child, and this is where the extending of the extended family comes in because they become *compadre* and *comadre* (like a "co-father" and "co-mother") with the child's parents. This is even closer than just being an *amigo* and *amiga*.

Even without this formal relationship through baptism of one's child, many young men with or without children choose certain friends to be their *compadres*, and young women choose from their circle certain ones to be their *comadres*, which is to say, their special, very close friends, the ones you can say anything to, the ones who will help you when you are in need and rejoice when you do well. So, in many places, that is what these words mean: very close friends.

There are many other words for friends, and these vary from region to region. Here are some common ones:

TOP FIVE Ways of Referring to Friends

1. **mi cole** (short for *colega*) colleague (used by men and women in Spain and Mexico)

2. **mi compa** (short for *compadre*) good friend (used by Latin American men for close male friends)

3. **mi compinche** (a variant of *compa*) buddy (used in many parts of Latin America by men for close male friends)

4. **mi pana** (from *panal*) honeycomb (used by both men and women in Colombia, the Dominican Republic, Ecuador, Puerto Rico, and Venezuela for a close pal or buddy)

5. **mi socio(-a)** associate or club member (used by men and women in Colombia, Chile, Cuba, and Mexico for a close friend)

Moving from *usted* to *tú*

The general parameters for using the formal *usted* or the informal *tú* are explained in Appendix A, but in some cultures people may find that they suddenly wish to change from one form to the other. There can be a magic moment when you feel the wish to *tutear* (speak in the *tú* form) to a colleague or acquaintance you have been speaking to always in the *usted* form. Or it can happen that as you travel you meet someone and start out with one form of address but decide to switch.

The best approach is to ask if he or she agrees. You can ask in a formal way: *¿Me permitiría tutearlo(-la) a usted?* ("Would you allow me to use the *tú* form with you?") Or you can ask in an informal way: *¿Qué tal si nos tuteamos?* ("How about if we call each other by *tú*?") Then start using the *tú* form. If the other person follows suit, fine, but if he or she continues with the *usted*, no offense taken. It may be that his or her upbringing was more rigid and the use of the *tú* in that situation is uncomfortable. In some parts of Spain and Chile, it is common to use the *tú* form very soon after meeting someone, but this is not the case in most parts of Central America. In certain regions of Latin America, the word *vos* is used for informal talk instead of the *tú* form, and special verb forms are required. (See Appendix A for more on regional differences.)

Rehearsal Time

La amistad al estilo latino. Choose the correct option to complete each sentence. Check your answers in the Answer Key.

1. In Spain and Latin America most people have two special days of the year that their friends celebrate with them: su cumpleaños y
   a. su quinceaños
   b. el día de su tertulia
   c. el día de su santo

2. The proverb *La amistad hace lo que la sangre no hace* means
   a. Friendship lasts till death.
   b. Blood is thicker than water.
   c. Friends help when family won't.

3. The message of the proverb *Vino y amigo, el más antiguo* is
   a. You should drink wine with your friends.
   b. Old friends are the best friends.
   c. People in the past had better friendships.

4. A proverb similar to the English saying "A friend in need is a friend indeed" is
   a. A buen amigo, buen abrigo.
   b. Amigo es uno mismo en otro cuero.
   c. Amigo de muchos, amigo de ninguno.

5. If a woman becomes the *madrina* of another woman's son, she and that woman become
   a. comadres
   b. compadres
   c. padrinos

6. In Spain or Mexico, you can call a man or woman you work with
   a. mi compa
   b. mi maestro
   c. mi cole

7. In the north of Latin America or in the Caribbean, people refer to a very close friend as
   a. mi madrina
   b. mi pana
   c. mi vale

8. If someone says to you, *¿Qué tal si nos tuteamos?*, it means that they want to
   a. use the informal *you* with you
   b. invite you out to dinner
   c. address you in Spanish as *usted*

Los verbos para decir «Love»

> One word is too often profaned for me to profane it,
> One feeling too often disdained for thee to disdain it . . .
> —PERCY BYSSHE SHELLEY

Now, of course, the famous romantic poet Shelley was referring to the word *love*. But if he had been speaking in Spanish rather than English, he would have had to say, "Two words are too often profaned . . ." because Spanish has two verbs for love: *amar* and *querer*. Naturally, this can be a bit confusing to English speakers. The best way to learn to use the two verbs is by listening and reading and getting the feel of them in context, but there are a few guidelines that can help.

The verb *amar* is more spiritual than *querer*. It sounds somewhat literary and it is not used for trivial things, except as a joke. *Amar* implies admiration, even a bit of adoration. Use *amar* to speak of your love for God and country, for things transcendent or people you consider sublime, almost sacred. The verb *querer* (which is also the most common way to say "want" or "desire") is more physical and down-to-earth. It implies affection, the kind of love that grows over time through familiarity, or, in certain circumstances, strong sexual attraction.

Use *querer* to talk about the love you feel for your friends, colleagues, or neighbors, if you have a very special feeling for them and want to say that you love them, or to express the love you feel for your family: *Quiero a mi hermano. Quiero a mis abuelos. Quiero a mi familia.* You could say *Amo a mi familia*, at some dramatic moment to show your total commitment to them, but this is not a normal use.

Both verbs can be used to say "those three little words" (which in Spanish are two little words: *dos palabritas*) to the object of your affection, but there is a difference. After saying *Te quiero*, the next step may be hugs and kisses of affection or it may be the bedroom, but if a woman hears, *Te amo*, she will start looking for the engagement ring. Naturally, most of the time, true lovers will say both of these phrases to each other.

So, which one do you use to say "I love chocolates"? Neither, absolutely not either one. The concept is too trivial for *amar* (even if they are Belgian chocolates), and if you were to use *querer* it would mean you "want" chocolates, not that you love them. It's best to use *Me encanta(n)* to express that you love some food or object. Literally, this says "It is (or they are) enchanting to me."

TOP TEN Ways to Say What You Love with *amar, querer,* and *encantar*

1. **Amo a Dios, la patria, la justicia y la libertad.** I love God, my native country, justice, and liberty.

2. **Amo la música. Para mí, es el lenguaje sublime del alma.** I love music. For me, it is the sublime language of the soul.

3. **Amo a mi familia: a mis padres, hijos, hermanos, primos.** I love my family: my parents, children, brothers and sisters, cousins. (Use this only in exceptional circumstances to emphasize your deep spiritual love and commitment. It is not the normal use.)

4. **Te amo, María (Juan) con todo mi corazón. Quiero pasar la vida a tu lado.** I love you, María (Juan), with my whole heart. I want to spend my life at your side.

5. **Quiero a mis vecinos, a mis compañeros de clase, a mis amigos.** I love my neighbors, my classmates, my friends.

6. **Quiero a mi familia: a mis padres, hijos, hermanos, primos.** I love my family: my parents, children, brothers and sis-

ters, cousins. This is the normal everyday use. At the end of a phone conversation, you might say, *¡Te quiero!* I love ya'! or *¡Los quiero mucho!* I love you guys!

7. **Quiero mucho a mis mascotas (a mi perra, a mi gato).** I love my pets (my [female] dog, my [male] cat). Oddly, by adding *mucho* this sounds more normal, and it seems to lessen the force of the word *querer* rather than strengthening it. It would sound really ridiculous to use *amar* here.

8. **Te quiero, María (Juan), con todo mi corazón. Quiero hacer el amor contigo.** I love you, María (Juan), with my whole heart. I want to make love to you.

9. **¡Me encantan los chocolates! ¡Qué delicia!** I love chocolates! What a treat!

10. **Me encanta tu nuevo auto. ¡Es estupendo!** I love your new car. It's super!

Liking and Disliking, Attraction and Repulsion: *gustar* Versus *caer bien, mal, gordo*

No soy monedita de oro para caerle bien a todo el mundo.
I'm not a gold coin so that I will be liked by everyone.
—OLD SPANISH PROVERB

Friendship and love start with attraction. Sometimes you simply want to say that you like someone or something. The standard verb to translate the English idea of "liking" is *gustar*, but this is a little tricky because in English the attraction starts in the person doing the liking and in Spanish it emanates out of the object of the liking. That is to say, if I like cheese, I feel that liking inside of me, but in

Spanish *el queso me gusta* means "the cheese is pleasing to me." The action starts in the cheese. It's the cheese that pleases. That's why the verb changes to plural if the thing being liked is plural: *las manzanas me gustan* ("apples are pleasing to me"). Word order is flexible in Spanish, so often you say, *Me gusta el queso, me gustan las manzanas*. ("I like cheese, I like apples.")

Now most of the time you don't want to use this wonderfully expressive verb *gustar* when referring to a person you like because it suggests a sensory attraction that can be interpreted as sexual. If a woman is talking about her new boss (who is a man) and wants to say "I like my new boss," she says, *Mi nuevo jefe me cae bien*. (Literally, "My new boss falls well to me.") If she wants to say she doesn't like him or dislikes him, she says, *Mi nuevo jefe no me cae bien; mi nuevo jefe me cae gordo*. (Literally, "My new boss does not fall well to me; my new boss falls fat to me.")

If she were to say *Me gusta mi nuevo jefe*, people would probably think she meant *Me gusta mi nuevo jefe como hombre*, that is, "I am physically attracted to my new boss." Of course, the same thing would be true with a man saying, *Me gusta mi nueva profesora*. Better to say, *Me cae muy bien mi nueva profesora*.

So use *gustar* (or *no gustar*) to talk about liking or disliking things, groups of people, or attributes of people, but when referring to liking one person, use *caer bien* (or *gordo*) or that good old standby, *encantar*.

TOP FIVE Ways to Say You Like Julia, from Weak to Strong, with No Sexual Implication

1. **No me cae mal.**

2. **Me cae bastante bien.**

3. **Me cae bien.**

4. Me cae muy bien. Me encanta.

5. Me cae de las mil maravillas. Me fascina.

TOP FIVE Ways to Say You Don't Like el señor Gruñón (Mr. Grumpy), from Weak to Strong, with No Sexual Implication

1. No me cae bien.

2. No me cae bien en absoluto.

3. Me cae mal.

4. Me cae gordo.

5. Me cae muy gordo, gordísimo.

Now, on the other hand, if you want to ask your sister if she feels physically attracted to Mr. Grumpy, you say, *¿Te gusta el señor Gruñón?* If you want her opinion specifically on his sex appeal, you can add, *¿Tiene pegue?* ("Is he sexy?") (Literally, "Does he have glue?")

Rehearsal Time

Cómo decir «I love» o «I like» con amar, querer, gustar, encantar y caer bien/mal. Complete the statements of opinion in Spanish. For some, there is more than one right answer. Check your answers in the Answer Key.

1. I love coffee. _____ *el café.*

2. Oh, Romeo, I love you and I always will! *Oh, Romeo,*
   ¡ _____ para siempre!

3. I love my dogs. _____ *a mis perros.*

4. I don't like my new math teacher very much. *No*
   _____ *mi nuevo profesor de matemáticas.*

5. I love you madly, my darling! Let's go to bed.
   ¡_____ locamente, mi cielo! Vamos a acostarnos.

6. I love carrots, don't you? _____ *las zanahorias, ¿y a*
   ti?

7. I love my nieces. They are so cute! _____ *a mis*
   sobrinas. ¡Son tan monas!

8. I like my boss a lot. He's very fair. _____ *mi jefe. Es*
   muy justo.

9. My mother likes my new boyfriend. *A mi madre*
   _____ *mi nuevo novio.*

10. My friends and I like that new restaurant. *A mis amigos y a mí*
    _____ *ese nuevo restaurante.*

11. You are an idiot. I really dislike you. *Eres idiota. Me*
    _____.

12. Do you like hot food? *¿Te* _____ *la comida picante?*

¿Qué significan realmente? What are the real meanings behind the proverbs? Look through the chapter and find the Spanish proverbs with meanings close to those of the following messages. Check your answers in the Answer Key.

1. The woman is the heart of the home.

2. A real friend tells you the truth.

3. Like father, like son. (Like mother, like daughter.)

4. Marriage (and funerals) are made in heaven.

5. Just like in the "Tennessee Waltz," my friend stole my loved one from me.

6. Children are a gift from God.

7. A friend is someone who never lets you down.

El español: voz de muchos pueblos

The Many Ways of Speaking Spanish

Preview

1. What's the difference between the Spanish of Spain and the Spanish of Latin America?

2. How many ways can you say "bus" in Spanish?

3. If a man tells you he is suffering from *el ratón*, what does he mean and where is he from?

4. If someone in Spain invites you to *la senda de elefantes* ("the elephants' path"), are you going to the zoo?

5. When a Mexican says you are very *abusado* (or *abusada*), should you feel insulted or say thank you for the compliment?

6. How do you talk about having fun?

7. When is it important not to step on a bug (*bicho*)?

8. Where do you have to be careful about asking for a *papaya*?

9. What does it mean if someone gives you "the fat look" (*la vista gorda*)?

10. If your friends come back from a party and say *lo pasamos bomba*, did they have a good time or a bad time?

Genio y figura... ¡hasta la sepultura! "Temperament and appearance . . . until the grave!" This is an old Spanish proverb that points out how unique every person is. The same thing can be said for countries, and even at times for regions. Twenty-one different countries on four continents, with many different regions in each one . . . that can make for a lot of differences. The language spoken in all of these places is Spanish, but naturally there are many small variations in vocabulary, grammar, and pronunciation. Fortunately, these do not prevent communication any more than the differences between British, Irish, Australian, New Zealand, Canadian, or U.S. English keep people from those places from talking with each other. In fact, these very differences give a special flavor and character to the language of each place, which is part of what makes learning Spanish so much fun! Let's examine some of the special ways of speaking Spanish.

La gran variedad: Variations in Grammar and Pronunciation

The most immediate and obvious difference is between the Spanish of Latin America and the Spanish of Spain, because many Spaniards pronounce the *z* and the *c* before *e* or *i* as the *th* in the word "teeth" rather than as an *s*. Therefore, in Spain they pronounce *zapatos* ("shoes") as "thapatos" and *bicicleta* as "bithicleta." (This has given rise to a myth that people in Spain lisp, which is not at all true because they pronounce their *s* very clearly, just as English speakers do.) In addition, they use two extra pronouns for "you" and special verb forms to go with these. In some Latin American countries there are also special types of pronunciation and grammar that are characteristic. (For more information about this, see the appendixes at the end of this book.)

Países diversos, palabras diferentes: objetos y lugares

Even more noticeable than differences in grammar and pronunciation are the variations in vocabulary throughout the Spanish-speaking world. Of course, standard words will be understood almost universally, especially in large cities or tourist areas. Still, it is useful to learn about the regional variations so you can recognize them when they are used around you or when people respond to you. They also help to give you an idea of the diversity and flavors of the various cultures. Let's examine how some objects and places are spoken of in different places.

TOP TEN Ways to Say "Bus" in Spanish

1. **el autobús** The common word that is understood everywhere. No matter where you are, you can always say, *Voy a tomar el autobus* (I am going to take the bus) and be understood.

2. **el bus** A short version of the above.

3. **el bondi** School bus in Argentina.

4. **el camión** The normal way to say "bus" in Mexico, this word also means "truck" in Mexico and in other places. To specify that you mean a "truck" and not a "bus" in Mexico, say **un camión de carga**.

5. **la camioneta, la combi** Both of these words mean "van" and in some places they can refer to large publicly operated vans that pick up passengers along set routes.

6. **el colectivo** The normal way of referring to a small bus or taxi-van in Argentina and Chile, a bus that operates along certain routes, picking up passengers and dropping them off at designated points.

7. **la guagua, la guaguita** The normal ways of saying "bus" in Puerto Rico, Cuba, and the Dominican Republic. The form ending in -*ita* can be used for a small bus or a van.

8. **el microbús** A small public bus in Mexico, Chile, and some other countries.

9. **la micro** A short version of the above used in Latin America.

10. **el ómnibus** The normal way of saying "bus" in Uruguay and Argentina.

A Misunderstanding: *la crueldad de los estudiantes*

The story goes that years ago in Ecuador some Puerto Rican tourists were discussing recent political demonstrations on the island. When asked by some Ecuadorians if anything serious had happened they replied, «*Pues, no fue nada serio. Sólo los estudiantes que quemaron unas guaguas.*» ("Well, it wasn't anything serious. Only students who burned a few buses.") They couldn't understand why their Ecuadorian friends reacted with shock and horror until the next day, when they found out that in Ecuador the word *guagua* means "small child"!

In fact, quite a number of common objects and experiences have very different names in different places. Here are a few of them:

TOP TEN Common Things with Regional Variations in Spanish

1. beer: **una cerveza** (general), **una chela** (a light-colored beer in Mexico and other parts of Latin America), **una caña** (a draft beer in Spain), **una fría** (Cuba, Puerto Rico, and other parts of Latin America)

2. car: **el auto** (general), **el coche** (Spain and parts of Latin America), **el carro** (Mexico, other parts of Latin America), **la máquina** (Cuba)

3. glasses: **los anteojos, los lentes** (general), **las gafas** (Spain), **los espejuelos** (Cuba)

4. hangover: **la cruda** (literally, rawness, in Mexico and Central America), **(tener) la resaca** (literally, undertow, in Spain and parts of Latin America), **(tener) el guayabo** (literally, guava tree, in Colombia), **el ratón** (literally, the mouse gnawing inside your head, in Venezuela)

5. job: **un trabajo, un puesto** (general), **un curro** (Spain), **una chamba** (Mexico, Central America, northern South America), **un camello** (parts of Mexico and in other parts of Latin America), **un laburo** (Southern Cone)

6. gasoline: **la gasolina** (Spain, most of Latin America), **la nafta** (Argentina, Peru, Uruguay), **la bencina** (Chile)

7. ballpoint pen: **la pluma** (Mexico), **el bolígrafo, el boli** (Spain, most of Latin America), **la lapicera, el lapicero** (Southern Cone, Peru, Bolivia)

8. soft drink (soda pop): **una gaseosa** (Spain, Argentina, El Salvador), **un refresco** (most of Latin America), **un chesco** (slang in Mexico), **una bebida no alcohólica** (a nonalcoholic drink in general)

9. straw: **paja** (Spain), **popote** (Mexico, El Salvador), **sorbete** (Puerto Rico), **pajilla** (Venezuela and other parts of Latin America)

10. stuff, things, thingamajigs: **las baratijas** (Spain), **los cachivaches** (Latin America), **las chingaderitas** (slightly vulgar, Mexico), **las chucherías** (Spain, Puerto Rico, Dominican Republic, some other parts of Latin America), **los chunches** (Central America), **las vainas** (Caribbean islands, Central America, Colombia, Venezuela), **los volados** (El Salvador)

Although *una caña* means "a draft beer" in Spain, it refers to a strong liquor made from sugar cane in some parts of Latin America. Also, if you order *un tinto* (which literally means "ink"), you will usually get a glass of red wine, but not in Colombia! There you will be presented with a cup of black coffee.

A Misunderstanding: *¡Qué lindos chiches tiene usted!*

A Uruguayan diplomat was invited to dinner at the home of a Guatemalan family. He could not help but admire the charming knickknacks with which the home was decorated. At the end of a delightful meal he wanted to compliment his hostess and so leaned over and said to her, «*Señora López, ¡qué lindos chiches tiene usted!*» ("Mrs. López, what lovely knickknacks you have!") It amazed him when she turned red in the face and suddenly ran out of the room. For a long time he thought that Guatemalans were very unpredictable and rude people until one day someone explained to him that in Guatemala the word *chiches* is common slang for "breasts"!

Just like things, places may also have regional variations on their names. Here are a few examples:

TOP FIVE Places Where You Might Find Yourself

1. backyard: **el patio** (general), **el jardín** (also means "garden," Latin America), **el solar** (Colombia), **el fondo** (Uruguay), **el batey** (Puerto Rico), **la yarda** (Chicano)

2. farm or ranch: **la granja** (general for "farm"), **la finca** (small farm or rural property in Latin America), **la hacienda** (general for a big farm), **el rancho** (a small ranch in Mexico), **la ganadería** (a big cattle ranch in Latin America), **la chacra** (a moderate-sized farm in some parts of Latin America; hovel in Mexico), **la quinta** (a small farm in Latin America), **la estancia** (a large cattle or sheep ranch in Argentina and Uruguay)

3. party: **la fiesta** (general), **la jarana** (Spain, Mexico, Peru, Argentina, Uruguay), **la pachanga** (Mexico, Central America, Argentina, Cuba, Paraguay, Uruguay), **el bailongo** (Argentina, Uruguay), **el bayú** (Puerto Rico), **el bembé** (Caribbean), **la charanga** (El Salvador, Colombia, Costa Rica), **el fandango** (literally, flamenco dance, in Argentina, Uruguay), **la farra** (Spain, Southern Cone, Ecuador), **la reunión de amigos** (general), **la quedada** (get-together in Spain)

4. night club, bar, disco: **el club nocturno, el bar, la disco** (general), **el antro** (a club that is not very fancy, a dive, in Spain, Mexico, Argentina, Uruguay), **el garito** (a gambling place in Spain, Southern Cone), **el boliche** (Argentina, Uruguay), **la senda de elefantes** (literally, the elephants' path, an area with lots of bars where you can get *trompa*, a word that means both "trunk of an elephant" and "drunk" in Spain)

5. slums: **las villas miseria** (poverty towns in general), **los suburbios** (literally, the suburbs, but in a different context from the English meaning, in Spain, Uruguay), **los cinturones de miseria, las ciudades perdidas** (literally, misery belts, lost cities, in Mexico), **los tugurios** (Colombia, Uruguay), **los cantegriles** (Uruguay), **las ciudades callampas** (literally, mushroom cities, in Chile)

Places and the words that describe them vary from one region to another, in part due to differences in customs. For example, there are many equivalents to the English "backyard" because, traditionally, the Spanish home did not have a backyard, but rather it had an inner courtyard in the center called a *patio*. This word has been drafted into modern speech for *backyard*, along with other words in different regions such as *solar* ("family homestead"), *jardín* ("garden"), *fondo* ("place in the back"), *batey* ("storage area in a sugar refinery").

Similarly, parties, like homes, are different in the two cultures. The concept of a "party" in the North American sense is probably best expressed by the two expressions mentioned at the end of item 3 in the previous list: *la reunión de amigos* or *la quedada* because usually these get-togethers consist of talking, eating, and drinking. For most Latinos, a *fiesta* is a more active celebration in which dancing, singing, and playing music have a major role. There are numerous Spanish words for parties and many of them refer to different types of music or dance. When a party really gets going in the United States or Canada, people say it's "a blast "or "a bash," and there's an expression for that in Mexico and Central America, too: *un reventón de primera* (literally, "a first-class blowout"). The tradition of the stag party for a groom on the night before his wedding day exists in many places, and in some parts of Latin America it is also common to give a good-bye party for the bride: *la despedida de soltera*, "the good-bye to singlehood."

History offers another reason for lexical variation. Spanish and Latin American cities have evolved differently from those in North America, and this explains the contrast between the image of the affluent "suburbs" and that of the impoverished *suburbios*. In Spanish-speaking countries, the outskirts have attracted poor migrants from the countryside who set up shacks in *cinturones de miseria* ("belts of poverty") that surround the cities, while their centers often have remained strong and vital, providing residences for the rich and middle class. This, of course, is the direct opposite of the historical process of Canadian and U.S. urban centers.

 Rehearsal Time

Diferencias de vocabulario: objetos y lugares. Check your knowledge of the different ways of referring to some objects and places in various parts of the Spanish-speaking world. Write the letters of the correct options before each statement. Check your answers in the Answer Key.

1. The normal way to say "bus" in Mexico is
   a. guagua
   b. ómnibus
   c. camión

2. If someone refers to his or her car as a *máquina* ("machine"), that person is probably
   a. Cuban
   b. Paraguayan
   c. Panamanian

3. In Spain they fill up their gas tanks with *gasolina*, but in Argentina, Peru, and Uruguay, they call it
   a. bencina
   b. petróleo
   c. nafta

4. A very large cattle ranch in Spain and most of Latin America can be called a *ganadería* or a *hacienda*, but in Argentina and Uruguay, it is usually called
   a. una granja
   b. una estancia
   c. un rancho

5. If a Spaniard invites you to *la senda de elefantes*, it means that you will be spending some time
   a. exercising
   b. buying
   c. drinking

Países diversos, palabras diferentes: la gente y sus acciones

Now let's look at some vocabulary variations that refer to people, what they're like, and what they do. First, there's the way they are referred to in different cultures.

TOP TEN　Types of People and What You Call Them in Different Places

1. attendant (at a garage, store, hotel, train station, etc.): ¡**Señor!** ¡**Señorita!** (general), ¡**Joven!** (Mexico and Colombia)

2. baby: **el (la) niño(-a), el (la) nene(-a), la criatura** (general, also means "child"), **el bebé, la bebita** (most of Latin America), **el** or **la chichi** (parts of Mexico and Central America), **el tierno, la tierna** (El Salvador, Nicaragua, Guatemala), **la guagua** (Bolivia, Ecuador, Chile, Peru), **una chancleta** (liter-

ally, sandal, but used only for a baby girl in Argentina, Uruguay)

3. farmer, person from the country: **el (la) granjero(-a)** (owner of a small or medium-sized farm in general), **el (la) ganadero(-a)** (owner of a large cattle ranch in general), **el (la) hacendado(-a)** (owner of a large farm or ranch in general), **el (la) estanciero(-a)** (owner of a large farm or ranch in Argentina, Uruguay), **el (la) campesino(-a)** (farm worker who usually works on a very small parcel of land that often is owned by someone else), **el (la) paisano(-a)** (someone living in the country in Argentina, Uruguay), **el gaucho** (man working on a ranch or farm in Argentina, Uruguay), **el (la) guajiro(-a)** (person from the country in Cuba), **el (la) jíbaro(-a)** (person from the country, sometimes pejorative, in Puerto Rico), **el (la) comunero(-a)** (member of one of the new agricultural cooperatives in Mexico)

4. cowboy: **el vaquero** (general), **el charro** (Mexico), **el gaucho** (Argentina, Uruguay), **el huaso** (Chile), **el llanero** (Venezuela)

5. driver: **el chófer** (Spain), **el chofer** (Latin America), **el motorista**, **el conductor** (bus driver in general)

6. guy and gal: **el chico y la chica** or **el muchacho y la muchacha** (general), **el chavalo y la chavala** (Mexico, parts of Central America), **el chavo y la chava** (Mexico, parts of Central America, and northen South America), **el tío y la tía** (literally, the uncle and the aunt, Spain), **el tipo y la tipa** (literally, the type, slightly pejorative, Latin America), **el chamo y la chama** (Colombia, Venezuela)

7. jerk: **un(-a) sinvergüenza** (general; literally, without shame), **un mal nacido** (general; literally, badly born), **un sangrón, una sangrona** (Mexico, Central America, Cuba, Colombia), **una persona de sangre pesada** (literally, person of heavy

blood, Mexico), **una persona de mala leche** (literally, a person of bad milk, Spain)

8. kids: **los niños, los nenes** (general), **los bichos** (literally, the bugs, Spain, El Salvador), **los chamacos, los chavitos** (Mexico and other parts of Latin America), **los chibolos** (Peru), **los buquis** (Chicano), **los pibes** (Colombia, Argentina, Uruguay), **los pelados, los sardines** (literally, the baldies, the sardines, Colombia), **los chiquilines** (Argentina, Uruguay), **los gurises** (Uruguay), **los chicocos, los chincoles** (Chile), **los cipotes** (El Salvador, Guatemala, Honduras, Nicaragua), **los guambras** (Ecuador), **los güilas** (Costa Rica), **los chiris** (Guatemala)

9. maid: **la sirvienta, la criada** (general, but not used much because it is considered impolite), **la muchacha** (Mexico), **la criada, la asistenta** (Spain, parts of Latin America), **la mucama, la chica** (Argentina), **la empleada, la asistenta** (Chile, Uruguay)

10. waiter, waitress: **el (la) camarero(-a)** (Spain), **el (la) mesero(-a)** (Mexico, El Salvador, Colombia, Bolivia), **el (la) mozo(-a)** (Southern Cone, Peru, Bolivia, other parts of Latin America)

For the door man, the gardener, the service station attendant, the security guard, or a man in any other position of service (including a waiter), in Mexico, the common word of address to use is *¡Joven!*, which literally means, "Young man!" It doesn't matter if he is much older than you—he can be in his twenties or in his sixties. While this sometimes is misinterpreted by tourists as lack of respect or condescension, Mexicans assure us that they feel flattered by the term. In many Latin American countries the term *¡Mozo!* or *¡Moza!* is used to call the attention of an attendant, but it is generally used for a young person, as its literal meaning suggests ("Young person!"). As a tourist, you can't go wrong by using *¡Señor!* or *¡Señorita!* This more or less translates to "Sir!" Or "Miss!" *¡Señorita!* is preferable to *¡Señora!* even if the woman in question is older, because it implies youth and therefore is flattering.

It's hard to translate "farmer" to Spanish because the reality of rural life is different from that of the north. In many places there are extremely large farms and ranches owned by rich families who hire or lease to rural workers. The owners may be called *hacendados*, *ganaderos*, *estancieros*, or, if the operation is fairly small, *granjeros*, depending on the region. Most people who live in the country are hired workers or owners of miniscule plots of land providing only subsistence farming and they are called *campesinos*, a word that in the past was translated as "peasants" but today could be "people from the countryside."

Similarly, there is not a one-word equivalent of "cowboy" or "cowgirl." The word *vaquero(-a)* refers to a person who works with cattle, cows, and horses. Many regions also have a long tradition of cowboys who are adept at riding and taming horses and many rodeo skills. The Mexican cowboy tradition had a great influence on the cowboy culture and vocabulary of the American and Canadian West. The figure of the brave and handsome *charro* in his fancy silver-plated outfit, riding on horseback, was an adored romantic icon for many years in Mexican movies, song, and pop culture. Then, sometime in the 1960s, there was a reversal and he turned into a figure of ridicule so that the word *charro(-a)* in common slang became the equivalent of "corny" or "silly." Now, fashion has swung back to a middle position and the Mexican cowboy is respected but not lionized. Farther to the south in Uruguay and Argentina the mythical figure of the *gaucho* lives on still in literature, song, and folklore: the solitary, brave, and independent hero of the *pampas*, loyal, simple, and true to his word. To this day, someone asking a friend for a big favor will say, *¿Me podrías hacer una gauchada?* Venezuela has its own tradition with *el llanero*, a similar figure of the plains (*los llanos*), and Chile has *el huaso*.

In general, the term "jerk" refers to someone nasty who hurts others on purpose or because he doesn't care. In certain places, such as Mexico and Uruguay, some people believe that individuals like this have heavy blood that causes them to behave that way. This is the origin of expressions like *persona de sangre pesada*, *sangrón(a)*, or *persona de mala sangre*.

A Misunderstanding: *¡Cuidado de los «bichos»!*

A Peruvian couple were vacationing in El Salvador. They rented a car and were driving along a mountain road when their Salvadoran friends warned them from the back seat, *«¡Cuidado! Hay que ir despacio porque acá a veces hay bichos en el camino.»* ("Be careful! You have to go slow because sometimes there are kids on the road around here.") The Peruvian man did not slow down and commented that he didn't care if he hit a few *bichos*, to which the Salvadorans replied, *«¡Cómo! ¿No te importa atropellar a unos niños?»* ("What?! You don't mind running down some children?") It took a few minutes before the visitors realized that in Salvadorian slang *los bichos* ("bugs") are "kids"!

Just as the words referring to people vary from place to place, so do the words used to describe them.

TOP FIVE Descriptions for People, with Some Regional Variations

1. short: **bajo(-a)**, **bajito(-a)** (general), **chaparro(-a)**, **chaparrito(-a)** (Mexico, Central America, parts of Caribbean, Colombia), **petizo(-a)** (Southern Cone), **enano(-a)** (literally, dwarf, Mexico, Spain, parts of Latin America), **chiquitico(-a)** (literally, teeny tiny, Costa Rica, Colombia, Venezuela), **tapón, taponcito** (literally, plug, little plug, Argentina, Uruguay), **tapón de alberca** (literally, swimming pool plug, Mexico)

2. blond: **rubio(-a)** (general), **güero, güerita** (Mexico), **catire** (Bolivia, Colombia, Peru, Venezuela), **mono(-a)** (literally, monkey, Colombia), **chele** (Costa Rica, El Salvador, Nicaragua)

3. brave: **valiente, tener agallas** (general; literally, brave, to have guts), **ser un gallo** (literally, to be a rooster, Spain, Mexico, parts of Central America), **guapo** (Cuba, Dominican Republic, Puerto Rico, Southern Cone), **tener huevos** (literally, to have eggs, Spain, Mexico, other parts of Latin America), **tener pelotas** (literally, to have balls, Spain, Argentina, Uruguay), **tener bolas** (literally, to have balls, Argentina, Uruguay), **tener bien puestos los calzones** (literally, to have your underpants well-placed, Mexico, Central America, Chile), **tener los cojones bien puestos** (literally, to have your balls well-placed, Spain, Dominican Republic), **tener narices** (literally, to have nostrils, a euphemism for "balls," Spain); all of the expressions that refer to eggs or balls are slightly vulgar.

4. crude, boorish: **bruto(-a), bestia, grosero(-a), ordinario(-a)** (general; literally, brute, beast, vulgar, low-class; notice that *ordinario(-a)* is a false cognate because "ordinary" is not derogatory in English), **cafre** (Spain), **naco(-a), barbaján(-a)** (Mexico), **cazado(-a) a boleadoras** (literally, hunted with a slingshot, i.e., an animal, Argentina, Uruguay), **el patán** (used only in the masculine in Mexico, Nicaragua, Argentina, Uruguay), **analfabestia** (literally, illiterate beast, Mexico, Colombia), **grasa, groncho(-a)** (Argentina)

5. smart, clever: **inteligente, listo(-a)** (general), **ser un coco, ser zorro** (general, except Southern Cone; literally, to be a coconut, to be a fox), **ser un bocho** (Argentina, Uruguay), **avispado(a)** (general, except Southern Cone; literally, waspish), **abusado(-a)** (literally, abused, Mexico), **buzo** (literally, diver, Mexico, Central America), **fino(-a) como un coral, más listo(-a) que el hambre, tener mucho coco** (literally, fine as coral, sharper than hunger, to have a lot of coconut, i.e., "a lot of head," Spain),

pillo(-a) (literally, rascal, Spain, Mexico, other parts of South America), **picudo(-a)** (literally, with a big beak, Mexico, El Salvador), **bocho(-a)** (Argentina, Uruguay)

A Misunderstanding: *la importancia de ser «corajudo»*

A Chilean man working in Mexico called up his sister to tell her how much the Mexicans admired him. He was surprised to find that everywhere he went people remarked on how brave he was. "You mean they say that you are *valiente*?" she asked. "No," he explained, "they say *Siempre tiene coraje. Es corajudo*." ("He always has courage. He's very brave.") His sister laughed and replied, "You dope! In Mexico *tener coraje* means 'to be angry' and calling you *corajudo* means they think you're a hothead!"

TOP FIVE Actions and Some Different Ways of Expressing Them

1. flatter, butter up: **adular** (general), **hacerle la barba a alguien**, **serle barbero** (literally, to do the beard/be the barber for someone, Mexico), **lamerle el trasero a alguien** (literally, to lick someone's backside, Spain, Mexico, El Salvador, Southern Cone), **lamer ojo** (literally, to lick the eye, Puerto Rico, Colombia), **ser chupamedias** (literally, to be a stocking sucker, Bolivia, Peru, Southern Cone), **endulzar a alguien** (literally, to sweeten up someone, Uruguay)

2. goof up (make a mistake): **meter la pata** (general; literally, to put in the paw), **regarla** (literally, to water it, Mexico), **pringarla** (literally, to grease it, Spain), **embarrarla** (literally, to muddy it up, parts of Latin America), **no dar una** (literally, to not give one, Spain, Mexico, Uruguay, Puerto Rico, Dominican Republic), **cometer una burrada** (literally, to act like a donkey, Spain, Mexico, other parts of Latin America)

3. have fun, have a good time: **pasarlo bien, divertirse a sus anchas** (general; literally, to spend it well, to enjoy yourself to your wide parts), **echar relajo** (literally, to throw a rumpus, Mexico, El Salvador, Colombia), **darse la buena (gran) vida** (literally, to give yourself the good [great] life, Mexico, Dominican Republic, Puerto Rico, Southern Cone), **pasarla padrísimo** (literally, to spend it very fatherly, Mexico), **pasarla de peluche** (literally, to spend it like a stuffed animal, Mexico, El Salvador), **pegarse la vida padre** (literally, to stick to yourself the father life, Spain), **pasarlo bomba** (general; literally, to spend it bomb, Spain, Argentina, Chile), **disfrutar a lo loco** (literally, to enjoy like crazy, Argentina, Uruguay), **reventar la noche** (literally, to blow open the night, Uruguay)

4. pay attention to him or her: **prestarle atención, hacerle caso, echarle ojo** (general; literally, to lend attention to, to make a case for, to throw an eye at), **echarle un taco de ojo** (literally, to throw an eye taco at, Mexico), **darle bola** (literally, to give him or her a ball, Southern Cone), **darle boleto** (literally, to give him or her a ticket, Chile, Uruguay), **pelarle** (literally, to peel him or her, Mexico), **pararle bolas** (literally, to stop balls, Ecuador, Nicaragua, Uruguay, Venezuela)

5. pay a bribe: **pagar un soborno** (general), **dar chayote** (literally, to give prickly squash, Mexico), **pagar la mordida** (literally, to pay the bite, Mexico), **dar una coima** (Peru, Southern Cone), **hacer un acomodo** (literally, to make an accommodation, Argentina)

Many actions are expressed differently in different countries. For example, the verb *conducir* is generally used for "to drive" in Spain but *manejar* is used in Latin America. Both verbs will be understood everywhere, and they both mean "to drive" in the sense of actually steering the car, so if you want to say "drive" in the sense of passively riding in a car, you have to use another verb, such as *pasear (ir) en coche. No caminemos. Vamos a pasear (ir) en coche.* ("Let's not walk. Let's drive.") An equivalent of "giving someone a ride" doesn't exist in most places so usually the idea is expressed this way: *¿Puede usted llevarme a la fiesta?* ("Can you give me a ride (take me) to the party?") Mexico, however, does have an expression for the noun "ride": *aventón*, so Mexicans might ask, *¿Puede usted darme un aventón a la fiesta?*

To convey the idea of "being ignored," one of the many expressions for *paying attention* can be used in the negative: *No me hacen caso (dan boleto, paran bolas).* Or, you can use the expression *pasar por alto* ("pass over above") or the colorful *hacer la vista gorda* ("make the fat look"): *Me pasan por alto* or *Me hacen la vista gorda.* All of these mean the same thing: They are ignoring me.

♪ Rehearsal Time

Diferencias de vocabulario: la gente y sus acciones. Check your knowledge of the different ways of talking about people and what they do in various parts of the Spanish-speaking world. Circle the letter of the correct option for each statement, then check your answers in the Answer Key.

1. If a Mexican refers to someone as *una persona de sangre pesada*, it means that he considers that person
   a. a hero
   b. an athlete
   c. a jerk

2. In Chile the rodeo cowboy is called a
   a. charro
   b. huaso
   c. gaucho

3. If a Mexican says that a man is *chaparrito*, it means that he is
   a. short
   b. tall
   c. handsome

4. A Colombian (or Mexican or Salvadoran) who plans to have fun might say, *¡Vamos a echar relajo!* What might an Argentinian say? *Vamos a*
   a. dar el chayote
   b. pasarlo bomba
   c. pararle bolas

5. When someone gives you "the fat look" (*la vista gorda*), it means he or she
   a. ignores you
   b. admires you
   c. insults you

¡Cuidado con las groserías!

This does not mean "Careful with the groceries!" even though it might appear like that at first glance and actually could have that meaning to people speaking "Spanglish" (the curious combination of English and Spanish used in some places where the two languages co-exist). In fact, as was pointed out earlier in this chapter, the word *grosero(-a)* means "rude" or "vulgar" and is related to the English cognate "gross." *Groserías*, then, are words and expressions that are considered vulgar, at least in certain contexts. These abound in Spanish as they do in English, and many are quite colorful.

Of course, there is a time and place for using "bad words," which are sometimes called *malas palabras* but more frequently *palabrotas*.

They are sometimes used as insults, or to express strong emotion (either positive or negative), or even for fun and friendship, but usually they are not encouraged for use by children. In Mexico, a child who is always saying *palabrotas* and *groserías* is told: *Oye, niño(-a), traes la boca llena de culebras.* ("Listen, child, you have your mouth full of snakes.") But just as each country has its own flora and fauna, including its native snakes, it also has its own brand of bad words. What surprises many Latinos when they travel is finding that some of the strongest obscenities from home are totally inoffensive in a different Spanish-speaking country. This is also true for English, of course, as many people in North America have realized in recent years when certain British comedies revealed that the word "shag" does not just refer to carpets.

TOP TEN Words That Are Ordinary in One Spanish-Speaking Culture and Obscene in Another

1. **cachar** In Mexico and Central America this is the word for "to catch (a ball)" and parents use it when they play with their kids. *¡Voy a cacharte!* ("I'm going to catch you!") In Peru and the north of Chile, however, it is an obscene word similar to the f-word in English. There, parents say, *¡Voy a atraparte!* ("I'm going to trap you!")

2. **la cachucha** In Mexico and Central America this is the word used for "baseball cap." But not in Puerto Rico or Uruguay, where it refers to the female sex organ and is definitely not used in polite company. So, if you leave your baseball cap in a Puerto Rican restaurant, don't go back and say, *¡Busco una cachucha!*

3. **cajeta** This is a popular Mexican and Spanish dessert made from cooking goat's milk and sugar that is also sometimes called *dulce de leche*, the name it goes by in Argentina and Uruguay, where it is made with cow's milk and is also very

popular. The trouble is that in Argentina and Uruguay the word *cajeta* has a different meaning: the female sex organ. So, if you decide to have this dessert in Buenos Aires or Montevideo, do not mention *cajeta*. Instead, you can order like this: *Para el postre, quisiera el dulce de leche.* ("For dessert, I'd like the sweet milk pudding.")

4. **chingar** This word meaning "to break down," "tear," or "rip" is ordinary and innocuous in Spain, the Southern Cone, and many parts of Latin America, but it is the big-time, number-one swear word in Mexico and parts of Central America, equivalent to the English f-word. So, in Spain you may hear a little old lady say, *Se chingó el coche* ("My car broke down"), but you will not hear this in polite company in Mexico, where there is even an arm movement with the closed fist that means *chingar* as applied to someone's mother, a very strong insult. In general, when used to swear, the word does not have much to do with sex, but rather it relates to violence and causing harm. Of course, like all powerful words, in the right context it is also used for jokes among friends.

5. **coger** In Spain, Puerto Rico, and certain parts of Latin America, this is a very common verb used in everyday speech to mean "to take," "grab," or "catch." For example, *Voy a coger el autobús. ¿Puedes coger la pelota?* ("I'm going to take the bus. Can you catch the ball?") But in Mexico, Central America, and the Southern Cone, it is a strong word meaning to have sexual intercourse. So, to be on the safe side, it is better as a tourist in Latin America to use *tomar*, unless you are in Puerto Rico. A Mexican couple on holiday on the island found themselves laughing all the time because the language seemed so scandalous. The Puerto Ricans not only use the verb *coger* for catching taxis, trains, and buses, but also *montar* ("to mount," "climb on") for getting on them (another verb avoided in Mexico for its sexual connotation, where *subir* or *abordar* are used instead). By the end of the trip, the husband teased his wife,

saying, "No wonder you like Puerto Rico so much. Whenever we come here, we have to *coger* and *montar*!"

6. **concha** In Spain and most parts of Latin America, this beautiful word designates a sea shell, especially the scallop shell. In Mexico it is also a common name for a woman, along with its diminutive *Conchita*. You will not find these names in use in the Southern Cone, however, where they signify—what else?—the female sex organ. In fact, the vulgar expression *¡La concha de tu madre!* (roughly equivalent to SOB) is common as an insult or even as a joking salute among male friends. If you go to the beach, you may want to say, *Me interesan las conchas* ("I'm interested in sea shells"), but don't say that in Argentina, Chile or Uruguay! It's better to say *las conchas marinas* or *los caracoles*.

7. **joder** This is a word meaning "to bother" or "pester" that is vulgar in some places, where it has a sexual connotation. Like the English word "screw," the meaning depends on the context, so you can say that a project *se jodió* ("got all screwed up") or you can talk about a movie in which everyone *estaba jodiendo* ("was getting laid"), but *joder* is not nearly as strong as the f-word in English. Spaniards sometimes use it as an expletive: *¡Joder! Está lloviendo otra vez.* ("Damn! It's raining again.") In most parts of Latin America it is used simply in the sense of "to bother": *No me jodas, porfa. Estoy estudiando.* ("Don't bug me, please. I'm studying.")

8. **papaya** This delicious fruit has the same name in English and in Spanish, but in Cuba and Nicaragua, it is better not to say it because *papaya* there is associated with the female organ. If you want to buy it in the market, you can ask for *una fruta bomba*, a common euphemism.

9. **pico** The word *pico* (meaning "beak of a bird," "sharp point," "peak") is used for "nose" or "mouth" in many places. *Sólo inserto mi pico en este asunto para echarles una mano.* ("I only put my nose into this matter in order to give you a helping hand.")

Abre el pico Luisito. ("Open your mouth, Louie, dear.") It also has other common meanings, such as *el pico de la montaña* ("the mountain peak") or *Nos vemos a las siete y pico.* ("We'll see each other at sevenish" [a little bit after seven].) None of these examples would occur in Chile, Costa Rica, El Salvador, or Guatemala, however, where *el pico* refers to the male sex organ and is an obscene word. Chileans, in particular, are very careful to avoid it. Instead of saying, *Te debo mil y pico* ("I owe you a little bit more than a thousand"), a Chilean might say, *Te debo mil y un poquito más.* ("I owe you a thousand and a little bit more.")

10. **los trastes** After supper, Mexicans have to *lavar los trastes* (wash up the dishes and pans), but farther to the south in Chile, Uruguay, and Argentina, the word *traste* has a different meaning: rear end or backside. This can lead to misunderstandings.

A Misunderstanding: *¡No voy a lavar los trastes!* (I'm Not Going to Wash the Dishes!)

A Mexican woman moved to Buenos Aires and hired a maid. She was explaining to her the household duties that she would like performed each day and came to the task of washing up after supper. «*Y, después de la cena usted tiene que lavar los trastes.*» ("And after supper, you have to wash the dishes.") The maid looked horror-stricken and quickly replied, «*Bueno, de usted y de sus hijas, está bien, pero del señor, no!*» ("Well, yours and the girls', O.K., but your husband's, no!") In Argentina the word *trastes* means "backsides."

Many other common Spanish words, even some you would not expect, can have a strong meaning in certain places. For example, the word *¡Hostia!* ("Host!"—the sacred wafer in the Catholic religious ceremony of the mass) in Spain is a common swear word, something akin to "God dammit!" The word *madre* ("mother") in Mexico is a forceful insult when used in the phrase *¡Tu madre!*

264 TUNE UP YOUR SPANISH

("Your mother!"—implying that her honor might be questionable). For this reason it is better to use the term *mamá* whenever combining it with *tú*. Perhaps the reason for this is that the things we hold most sacred carry a certain power that can add force to our emotions, whether positive or negative.

Even a word that seems ordinary and innocent, such as *paloma* ("dove") has a vulgar meaning in Central America and five South American countries, where it refers to the male sex organ. Yet in Mexico it simply means "dove," and it is also the name used there for the drink called "margarita" in the United States and Canada. So, in Mexico you don't have to hesitate to say to the waiter, *Me gustaría una paloma*. ("I would like a dove [margarita drink]").

A book could be written on the diverse styles and uses of swear words and off-color slang in Spanish, or perhaps several books. It's generally better to avoid using vulgar terms unless a native friend gives you explicit instructions on how to use them correctly in the right country and context. So, what to do if you stub your toe or lose your plane tickets and want to vent your emotions verbally but without sounding vulgar and offensive? Here are some mild expressions that can be substituted for the big *palabrotas*. Many of them are euphemisms (softened forms) for vulgar words, so they start out sounding like the bad word and then turn into something mild. This is like using "Heck!" instead of "Hell!" or "Shoot!" instead of "Shit!" in English.

TOP TEN Acceptable (Nonvulgar) Expletives to Use for Venting Emotions

1. **¡Ah, chirrión!** Oh, tasteless bread! Used in Mexico, it is similar to "Heck!" A euphemism for *chingar* (the Mexican f-word). This comes from the saying: *Me dio el chirrión por el palito.* ("He gave me tasteless bread for the good bread.")

2. **¡Caracoles! ¡Caray!** Snails! Similar to "Darn it!" in Spain, Mexico, other parts of Latin America. Both are euphemisms for *¡Carajo!* (male sex organ).

3. **¡Caramba!** Oh my goodness! A somewhat old-fashioned expression but still used in general. Similar to "Darn it!" A euphemism for *¡Carajo!* (male sex organ).

4. **¡Chispas! ¡Chin!, ¡Chihuahua!** Sparks! (the latter word being the name of a state in Mexico) Similar to "Heck!" in Mexico. Euphemisms for *chingado* ("screwed").

5. **¡Miércoles!** Wednesday! A slightly old-fashioned way of saying "Heck!" in general. A euphemism for *¡Mierda!* ("Shit!")

6. **¡Ostras!** Oysters! Similar to "Heck!" or "Darn!" in Spain. A euphemism for the vulgar and somewhat sacrilegious expression *¡Hostias!* ("Hosts!")

7. **¡Pucha!, ¡La pucha!** Shoot! More or less like "Darn it!" in the Southern Cone and some other Latin America countries. Euphemisms for the vulgar expressions *¡Puta!* or *¡Puta madre!* ("Whore!", "Mother whore!")

8. **¡Qué barbaridad! ¡Qué bárbaro!** What barbarity! How barbarous! Used in general more or less like "Good heavens!" or "Good grief!"

9. **¡Qué macana!** What a stupid act or lie! Roughly equivalent to "What the heck!" or "Oh, nuts!" in Argentina, Bolivia, Uruguay.

10. **¡Sopas!** Soups! Similar to "Wow!" or "Good heavens!" in Mexico. This may come from the phrase *Eso pasa*.

These expletives can be used to express anger or surprise, even at times a pleasant surprise, so they are roughly equivalent to

"Wow!" or "Oh, my God!" In Spain and Latin America, *¡Dios mío!* is often used to express surprise and implies no disrespect, as is also true of the expression *¡Ave María!* ("Hail Mary!")

A Misunderstanding: *¿Cómo te atreves a decirme «chingada»?* (How Dare You Say "chingada" to Me?)

A Mexican woman went to a party in Montevideo, Uruguay. A well-dressed lady approached her and said, *«Quiero decirle que usted trae la falda chingada.»* ("I want to tell you that the skirt you are wearing is screwed up.") The Mexican woman reacted as if she had been slapped in the face, asking the other why she was trying to insult her. How dare she use the word *chingada*! But the Uruguayan woman was completely taken aback. She thought for a moment and then pointed to the large tear in the Mexican's skirt and asked, *«¿Pero no ve usted que su falda se le chingó?»* ("But don't you see that your skirt got torn?") That's when it dawned on the Mexican woman that the verb *chingar* has a totally different meaning in Argentina, and *chingada* simply means "torn" or "ripped"!

Rehearsal Time

Las palabrotas y sus variaciones. How much do you remember about differences in swear words and obscenities in the Spanish-speaking world and how this can produce misunderstandings? Circle the letter of the correct option for each statement. Check your answers in the Answer Key

1. A synonym for *groserías* is
   a. palabrotas
   b. supermercado
   c. comida

2. In most places, you can use the word *cachucha* for baseball cap, but not in
   a. Mexico
   b. Peru
   c. Puerto Rico

3. To order a sweet milk dessert in Buenos Aires, be careful to ask for
   a. postre con crema
   b. dulce de leche
   c. cajeta

4. A word that is very strong and vulgar in Mexico and Central America but is an ordinary word meaning "broken" or "torn" in Spain and the Southern Cone countries is
   a. chingado
   b. atrapado
   c. roto

5. In Mexico and Central America the verb *coger* means "to have sex," but in Spain, Puerto Rico, and certain other places it simply means
   a. observar
   b. perder
   c. tomar

6. Where would a woman named *Conchita* find that people react strangely to her name?
   a. Ecuador
   b. Honduras
   c. Uruguay

7. Although the verb *joder* has a sexual connotation in some places, in most of Latin America it means
   a. to bother
   b. to cheat
   c. to insult

8. *Pico* means "beak," "nose," or "mouth" in most places but is considered very vulgar in
   a. Cuba
   b. Chile
   c. Paraguay

9. *Los trastes* means "backside" or "rear end" in the Southern Cone, but in Mexico it means
   a. clothing
   b. dishes
   c. furniture

10. A handy expletive used in many places that means "Snails!" (and is a euphemism for a vulgar word) is
    a. ¡Bichos!
    b. ¡Macanas!
    c. ¡Caracoles!

11. A name of one of the days of the week that is sometimes used to express strong emotion is
    a. ¡Domingo!
    b. ¡Miércoles!
    c. ¡Viernes!

12. A Spaniard who spills his coffee or stubs his toe might yell out the name of a shellfish
    a. ¡Camarones!
    b. ¡Langostas!
    c. ¡Ostras!

TUNE-UP
10

Don Quijote, La Malinche, Bolívar...

Understanding Icons, Heroes, and Antiheroes

Preview

1. Who was *el manco de Lepanto*?

2. What is *malinchismo*?

3. If someone tells you in Spanish that you have a lot of wood when referring to your character, what does he or she mean?

4. How did *El Che* get his name?

5. What does it mean to be *el diablo vendiendo cruces* ("the devil selling crosses")?

6. Who was *la Libertadora del Libertador*?

7. Why is José Martí a hero to all Cubans, regardless of their politics?

8. If someone tells you that she is *entre la espada y la pared* ("between the sword and the wall"), what does she mean?

9. Is it a good thing to *salir de Guatemala para entrar en Guatepeor*?

10. What's up with someone who tells you he is *metido en un rollo* ("put in a roll")?

Every culture has its heroes, and Spain and Latin America are no exception. They also have their villains. Then there are those who are heroes to some and villains to others. In this chapter, you'll look at some of these emblematic Spaniards and Latin Americans and examine the language people use to talk about them.

Don Quijote y el sueño imposible

What image is more quintessentially Spanish than that of Don Quijote with his squire Sancho Panza, probably the most famous literary pair of all time? The nobleman from La Mancha has read so many books about chivalry, about knights and villains and ladies in distress, that he goes mad and leaves home in search of the hero's life. The English word "quixotic," of course, derives from his name. Sancho (whose last name Panza means "belly") is the exact opposite of the Don: practical, earthy, concerned about his own skin and about comforts and conveniences. The two go off, Sancho riding an ass and the Don on his horse Rocinante, with the Don endeavoring to imitate the knights of old by rescuing the weak and helpless and defending the honor of hapless maidens. As all knights need a lady (the knight without love is compared to a tree without leaves or fruit), Don Quijote finds his in the form of a local washerwoman, Aldonza Lorenzo, who he dubs Dulcinea del Toboso. One of his adventures involves windmills that he takes to be giants; the expression *comulgar con molinos de viento* ("to commune with windmills") means to believe anything, however incredible. The idealistic Don in his madness has many an adventure as he tries to live out his dream.

Don Quijote's creator, Miguel de Cervantes Saavedra, was a war hero of sorts himself. In 1571 he fought valiantly in the Battle of Lepanto against the Turks and lost the use of his left hand. Several naval battles later, he landed in a Turkish prison. There he tried courageously but unsuccessfully to escape four times; he was finally ransomed by his family and others after five years in captivity. Back in Spain at the court of Felipe II, he petitioned for a post in the Americas but was turned down. A life of poverty awaited him. Unjustly imprisoned later in life, it was in jail that he began his great masterpiece *El ingenioso hidalgo don Quijote de la Mancha*.

It has often been said in jest that Shakespeare used many traditional expressions or commonplaces; the same could be said for Cervantes, who was his contemporary (both men died on April 23, 1616). Here are some famous words from *el manco de Lepanto* ("one-handed man of Lepanto"), a name Cervantes is sometimes known by:

TOP TEN Quotations by Cervantes

1. «**Más vale una palabra a tiempo que cien a destiempo.**»
   "Better a timely word than a hundred untimely [inopportune] ones."

2. «**Donde una puerta se cierra, otra se abre.**» "Where one door closes, another opens"—i.e., new opportunities will arise.

3. «**Más vale el buen nombre que las muchas riquezas.**» "A good name is better than many riches."

4. «**Confía en el tiempo, que suele dar dulces salidas a muchas amargas dificultades.**» "Trust in time, which tends to give sweet outcomes to many bitter difficulties."

5. «**Amistades que son ciertas nadie las puede turbar.**» "No one can upset or disturb true friendships."

6. «**Al bien hacer jamás le falta premio.**» "Doing good never lacks reward"—i.e., a good deed is always rewarded.

7. «**Por la calle del ya voy, se va a la casa del nunca.**» "Through the street of I'm coming/just a minute, one goes to the house of never"—i.e., don't put things off.

8. «**El año que es abundante de poesía suele serlo de hambre.**» "The year that is abundant in poetry is often one of hunger."

9. «**Sólo hay dos familias en este mundo: los que tienen y los que no.**» "There are only two families in this world: the haves and the have-nots."

10. «**Tienes que desconfiar del caballo cuando por detrás de él, del toro cuando estés de frente; y de los clérigos, de todos los lados.**» "You have to distrust the horse when you're behind it, the bull when you're in front of it, and clergymen from all sides."

Was the Don's impossible dream madness? Perhaps, but on the other hand Cervantes writes: «*[La ilusión es] manjar que quita el hambre, agua que ahuyenta la sed, fuego que calienta el frío, frío que templa el ardor, moneda general con que todas las cosas se compran... *» ("[Illusion is] the promise of reality, food that takes away hunger, water that quenches thirst, fire that heats cold, cold that tempers heat, general currency with which all things are bought . . .") The human spirit is capable of great things, as history has often proved.

The hero's life involves taking great risks and combatting evil, as the Don talked much of. Here are some related Spanish expressions:

TOP TEN Expressions About Courage or Strength of Character

1. **hacer de tripas corazón** to pluck up one's courage (literally, to make heart of one's guts)

2. **ir (nadar) contra la corriente** to go (swim) against the current

3. **tener agallas** to have guts, nerve (literally, to have galls)

4. **tener bien puestos los calzones** to be worthy, have character or valor, colloquial (literally, to have one's underwear well-placed; used in Mexico and Central America)

5. **defender a capa y espada** to back someone up; to defend vehemently (literally, to defend with cape and sword)

6. **no darse por vencido(-a)** to not give up (literally, to not give oneself for overcome)

7. **no tirar la toalla** to not throw in the towel

8. **tener mucha madera** to have strength of character (literally, to have a lot of wood; used in Spain, parts of Latin America)

9. **ser una persona de confianza** to be a trustworthy person, one someone can trust or confide in

10. **ser cumplido(-a)** to be responsible, do what one promises to do

There are also a large number of slang expressions in Spanish relating courage to having or not having testicles (commonly referred to as *huevos*, *cojones*, or, in the Southern Cone, *bolas*). *Tenerlos por corbata* ("to have them as a tie") can mean to be frightened, very scared. While vulgar, these expressions are extremely common, used for women as well as men, and there are many variants.

Courage, or the lack thereof, has inspired many quotations in Spanish throughout the centuries.

TOP TEN Quotations About Courage or Fear

1. «**El valiente tiene miedo del contrario; el cobarde, de su propio temor.**» "The courageous person is afraid of his adversary; the coward, of his own fear." —Francisco de Quevedo, Spanish writer

2. «**El miedo es natural en el prudente, y el vencerlo es lo valiente.**» "Fear is natural in the prudent person, and overcoming it is courage." —Alonso de Ercilla y Zúñiga, Spanish poet

3. «**La primera cosa contra la que el hombre tiene que batallar desde su nacimiento es el miedo. Es la gran represión, la gran dictadura.**» "The first thing man has to battle from birth is fear. It's the great repression, the great dictatorship." —Miguel Bosé, Spanish singer

4. «**El valor espera; el miedo va a buscar.**» "Valor waits; fear goes out to search." —José Bergamín, Spanish writer

5. «**El miedo no es más que un deseo al revés.**» "Fear is nothing more than desire in reverse." —Amado Nervo, Mexican writer

6. «**Todas las desgracias sociales derivan del miedo.**» "All social ills [misfortunes] derive from fear." —Antonio Buero Vallejo, Spanish dramatist

7. **Donde hay amor, no hay temor.** Where there is love, there is no fear. —proverb

8. **«Una retirada no es una derrota.»** "A retreat is not a defeat." —Miguel de Cervantes

9. **«Las masas humanas más peligrosas son aquéllas en cuyas venas ha sido inyectado el veneno del miedo... del miedo al cambio.»** "The most dangerous masses of humans are those in whose veins fear has been injected . . . fear of change." —Octavio Paz, Mexican writer

10. **Más vale decir «Aquí corrió que aquí murió.»** Better to say "Here he ran" than "Here he died." —proverb

Rehearsal Time

Dichos. What would you say to a friend in each of these situations? Choose from the answers that follow (*a* to *d*), then check your answers in the Answer Key.

1. You want to encourage your friend to ask a girl he likes out on a date.

2. Your friend has a job interview but doesn't get hired; you tell him that other opportunities will come up.

3. Sometimes it's better to take a risk.

4. You tell him it's better not to put things off.

   a. Donde una puerta se cierra, otra se abre.
   b. Por la calle del ya voy, se va a la casa del nunca.
   c. Donde hay amor, no hay temor.
   d. Más vale decir «Aquí corrió que aquí murió.»

Un verdadero amigo. What's a true friend? Complete the sentences with an appropriate word from the right column. The answers are in the Answer Key.

1. Siempre se puede confiar en un verdadero amigo; o sea, es una persona de _____. corriente

2. Sabe que en esta vida a veces hay que hacer de tripas _____. corazón

3. Cuando usted tiene un problema, lo (la) defiende a capa y _____. confianza

4. A veces, cuando otra gente se opone a sus ideas, se encuentra nadando contra la _____. espada

5. Pero sigue firme en sus principios y no se da por _____. vencido

La Malinche: ¿Heroína o antiheroína?

From the point of view of the indigenous Americans, the conquest that began in 1492 when Columbus landed in Hispaniola was a disaster, and it created countless stories of heroism among the natives of the Americas who suffered from the Spanish invasion. Every American country has its tales of Indian heroes and heroines, but some are much more famous than others. If you go to Honduras, you will see the Indian chief Lempira on the currency that bears his name—he was valiant in trying to unite the local tribes to defend themselves and died heroically. If you are in Mexico City, you will see the statue of Cuauhtémoc, the last Aztec emperor, who surrendered to Hernán Cortés and is a hero to modern Mexicans. In Peru, you will hear about Atahualpa, the emperor of the Incas;

his story is one of the greatest betrayals of all time. The conquistador Francisco Pizarro's soldiers captured Atahualpa and then demanded a ransom; they got a room full of gold and two rooms of silver, but they executed their prisoner anyway. (The book *Guns, Germs, and Steel* by Jared Diamond devotes an entire chapter to how a small group of Spaniards managed to conquer the enormous Inca empire; the book's title is the answer. Horses, like guns, were used to frighten the Indians, but steel weapons and—later on—European diseases played a more important role.) Just as famous in Peru is the Inca Tupac Amaru, who defied the Spanish and met a cruel fate at their hands.

If you are in Mexico you will certainly hear the story of La Malinche, one of the most famous Indian women of all time. When the Spanish arrived in Mexico in the early sixteeenth century, they encountered the great Aztec Empire. The Aztecs had taken over a vast territory and conquered many local tribes, enslaving them, forcing them to pay tributes, and sacrificing many victims to the sun god. According to their beliefs, the god Quetzalcóatl (who was light-skinned and bearded) would return in the year 1519, and by an amazing coincidence the Spanish appeared in just that year, led by Hernán Cortés. The local chiefs on the Yucatán Peninsula, where Cortés landed, gave him gold and also female slaves to try to pacify him; among the slaves was an extraordinary woman called Doña Marina by the Spanish and La Malinche by others. La Malinche had been sold into slavery as a child and had learned both the Mayan and Náhuatl languages. She learned Spanish very quickly and became one of Cortés's chief advisors about the local Indians. The emperor Montezuma sent Cortés gifts of gold and other things from the Aztec capital, but these just attracted the Spanish to draw closer. With the help of La Malinche, Cortés eventually managed to make the enemies of the Aztecs his allies and by 1521 had conquered the entire empire. La Malinche was not only his translator but also his lover and the mother of his son (the beginning of the mestizos of Mexico). Because she aided Cortés so much in his conquest of the area, La Malinche was considered a traitor by the general public, and in Mexico *malinchismo* means "betrayal." Of late her name has begun to be cleared—she was a courageous and brilliant woman—but for many she is still an antiheroine.

An aside about antiheroes: Latin American history is replete with them, because a hero to one group can be an antihero to another. Let's look at two other very famous examples, beginning with Eva Perón. Born in 1919 the illegitimate daughter of an Argentinean landowner and his mistress, Evita grew up in poverty. She went to Buenos Aires as a young woman and became a radio soap-opera actress. There she met Juan Domingo Perón, a military man who eventually became president of Argentina. Evita helped him win over the poor with her charismatic personality, elegant looks and dress, and impassioned speeches in which she praised her husband to the skies. She set up the *Fundación de Eva Perón* and participated in many charitable events. Having been poor herself, she understood the problems of those in need. However, Perón was a fascist; although he sided with the workers on some issues and had their support, he allowed many Nazis to enter the country after their defeat in World War II, and items that had been confiscated from Jews in Europe were found in the Perón house. The upper classes despised Evita, but she was worshipped by the poor. She died of cancer in 1952.

Anyone who lived through the 1960s has seen posters, banners, and T-shirts featuring the polifaceted "Che" Guevara, held in esteem as a hero by many of his contemporaries. Born Ernesto Guevara in Argentina in 1928, he became a medical doctor and traveled and worked in various places in Latin America among the poor. These experiences galvanized him politically. While in Mexico he met Fidel Castro, the young Cuban lawyer who wanted to topple the regime of Fulgencio Batista, dictator of Cuba at the time. Their story is one of the most amazing in history: a group of only a little more than a hundred men sailed from Mexico to Cuba on a private American yacht that they had purchased for the "invasion of Cuba." When they landed, Batista's troops were waiting and killed all but twelve. Fidel and El Che were among those who managed to escape to the Sierra Madre, the high country, where they set about to create a revolution that finally did depose Batista in 1959. Of course, Fidel eventually became dictator of the country he was supposedly liberating. El Che received his name because of the Argentinean use of *che* to mean "pal" (for example, *Hola, che, ¿qué pasa?*). He was executed in Bolivia in 1967 after attempting to foster a Cuban-style revolution there.

In all stories about heroes or antiheroes there are bad guys: dictators, frauds, hypocrites, or traitors. Here are some words for these types of people:

TOP TEN Expressions for Bad Guys

1. **el/la malvado(-a)** bad guy, evil person

2. **un canalla** person who is abject, vile, lout (from canine, dog)

3. **el/la descarado(-a)** scoundrel (literally, faceless one)

4. **ser el mismísimo demonio** to be the devil himself, very perverse or cunning

5. **ser un cero a la izquierda** to be worthless, no good (literally, to be a zero to the left)

6. **ser el diablo vendiendo cruces** to be a hypocrite (literally, to be the devil selling crosses)

7. **el/la mal nacido(-a)** jerk, SOB (literally, badly born—i.e., illegitimate; somewhat vulgar)

8. **el/la estafador(-a)** fraud, con man or woman, cheat

9. **el/la tramposo(-a)** cheat

10. **el/la sinvergüenza** shameless person, jerk

Other expressions for undesirable people include *cabrón* (*cabrona*), which usually means "SOB" or "jerk" (vulgar, and the feminine form means "bitch"); *faltón* (*faltona*)—someone who doesn't do something they are supposed to, an irresponsible person; *sangrón* (*sangrona*)—an unpleasant or annoying person (used in northern Latin America); *bestia*—someone who is rude, a boor; and, in Mexico, *pelado(-a)*—someone who is rude, shameless. "Rude" is usually *grosero(-a)* or *mal educado(-a)*. There are many, many expressions like this, but these are some of the most common ones. A child who is "a little dickens" is *de la piel del diablo* ("of the devil's skin").

Finally, here are some expressions for the things that the *malvados* or *estafadores* do; these expressions abound in Spanish. The literal translations are included where appropriate.

TOP TEN Expressions for Evil Deeds and Deception

1. **hacerle una mala pasada a alguien, hacerle una trastada** to play a dirty trick on someone

2. **hacer polvo a alguien** to cause serious damage, destroy, ruin (literally, to make someone dust; used in Spain, Mexico)

3. **dar en la madre (romper o partir la madre)** to hit hard, hurt someone where he or she is vulnerable (literally, to give in the mother, to break the mother; colloquial, used in Mexico, Central America, Colombia)

4. **jugar con dos barajas** to act with duplicity (literally, to play with two decks)

5. **tirar la piedra y esconder la mano** to hurt someone but cover up one's action, propose an action but later deny having a part in it (literally, to throw the stone and hide one's hand)

6. **dar gato por liebre** to deceive someone, giving them something inferior (literally, to give cat for rabbit; the comparison

is like someone who passes off a cat in a bag claiming it is a tasty rabbit)

7. **madrugar** to get ahead of someone, to cut off at the pass, to beat to the punch (literally, to get up early)

8. **vender a alguien** to sell someone out (used in Mexico, Cuba, Colombia)

9. **serrucharle el piso a alguien** to undermine, often by severe criticism behind someone's back (literally, to saw off the floor from under someone—i.e., to saw a hole around the person so he or she would fall through)

10. **fregar(le)** to mess up, ruin, jerk around; to pester (literally, to scour, rub [the wrong way])

This last entry (which is common throughout Latin America but not used in Spain) has numerous much stronger equivalents, such as *joder* ("to screw," "bother," "bug") or, in Mexico, parts of Central America, and Colombia *chingar*, equivalent to the f-word in English. Both of these words have a near-infinite number of variants, some of which are not as vulgar as others.

Rehearsal Time

Problemas. What would you say in these situations? Choose the appropriate response, then check your answers in the Answer Key.

1. A usted le roban la cartera ("wallet") en la calle y pierde cien dólares.
   a. ¡Me vendieron!
   b. ¡Me fregaron!

2. Una persona casada lo (la) invita a salir.
   a. ¡Qué sinvergüenza!
   b. ¡Qué buena gente!

3. Usted compra un carro usado y resulta que el motor está en muy malas condiciones.
   a. ¡Me hicieron una mala pasada!
   b. ¡Qué mal educado!

4. Va de vacaciones y un colega habla con el jefe ("boss"), quejándose ("complaining") del trabajo de usted.
   a. Me serruchó el piso.
   b. Me dio gato por liebre.

De libertadores y poetas

La Guerra de Independencia, in which Spanish Americans fought against Spain and won their independence, forged many heroes and heroines. In the early nineteenth century in Hispanic America, society was highly stratified from the Spanish born in Spain at the top, to the *criollos* (Europeans born in Latin America) on the next rung, to all the various other groups, including Indians, Africans, and racial mixtures. To hold the most important government posts, you had to have been born in Spain. It was inevitable that the ideas of the *realistas* ("royalists," who supported Spanish control of Hispanic America) and the *republicanos* or *revolucionarios* would collide.

While each country has a national hero from the days of the war of independence of the early 1800s—for example, Bernardo O'Higgins of Chile and José de San Martín of Argentina—the most famous of them all is Simón Bolívar. Bolívar was born of an aristocratic family in Caracas, Venezuela, in 1783. He studied in Spain, then returned to Venezuela in 1802. From 1807 he fought passionately against the royalists until independence was finally obtained. He was called the "George Washington of Latin America," and he was also *Libertador y Dictador* of Venezuela, president of Colombia, *Padre y Salvador* of Peru, and *Presidente Vitalicio* ("president for life") of Bolivia, the country that was named for him. His lover Manuela Sáenz, a fascinating character and revolutionary in her own right, accompanied him on many journeys and even fought alongside him, saving his life on occasion. Bolívar called her *«la Libertadora del Libertador»*. Bolívar dreamed of a unified Hispanic America, but his dreams of course did not come true; he suffered exile and betrayal. *«La América es ingobernable»* ("ungovernable"), he declared.

The Pen and the Sword

Cuba was maintained as a colony of Spain for many more years; it did not win its independence until 1902. José Martí, revered Cuban hero and poet, was born in 1853 of humble origins; by the age of sixteen he had a newspaper called *La patria libre ("The Free Homeland")*. Arrested and sentenced to six years' hard labor, he was deported and sent to Spain after one year. There he was able to study at the University of Zaragoza. He returned to Cuba but his political activities led to exile again. In New York he founded the *Partido Revolucionario Cubano* in 1892. In 1895 he participated in the invasion of Cuba by revolutionaries and was killed in the battle of Dos Ríos. His poetry, essays, and newspaper articles inspired many to fight for freedom; he once said *«La única fuerza y la única verdad que hay en esta vida es el amor. El patriotismo no es más que amor... »* ("The only force and the only truth in this life is love. Patriotism is nothing more than love . . . "). His work endures for its great literary value—for instance, the famous song *«Guantanamera»* has lyrics based on poetry by Martí from his book *Versos sencillos*. The following is one of his most famous poems, which says a lot about his view of life:

Cultivo una rosa blanca	I Cultivate a White Rose
Cultivo una rosa blanca	I cultivate a white rose
En julio como en enero	In July as in January
Para el amigo sincero	For the sincere friend
Que me da su mano franca.	Who gives me his hand frankly.
Y para el cruel que me arranca	And for the cruel person who tears out
El corazón con que vivo,	the heart with which I live,
Cardo ni ortiga cultivo;	I cultivate neither nettles nor thorns;
Cultivo una rosa blanca.	I cultivate a white rose.

It's worth noting that writers and artists hold a high place in Hispanic society, and they are lionized, if not held as heroes. Writers are often interviewed on television and radio shows, and they are treated with a great deal of respect. Typically they command a great deal of attention and may have considerable influence on public opinion. A salient example is Peruvian author Mario Vargas Llosa, who ran for president of his country and lost by a narrow margin, despite his lack of experience holding political office.

The story of heroic deeds is often one of dangers and daring, of trials and tribulations. Here are some expressions related to these concepts:

TOP TEN Ways of Talking About Trials and Tribulations

1. **estar entre la espada y la pared** to be between a rock and a hard place, between two unfortunate choices, in a dilemma (literally, to be between the sword and the wall)

2. **escapar del trueno y dar con el relámpago** to escape one predicament and end up in another (literally, to escape the thunder and confront the lightning)

3. **huir del fuego y caer en las brasas** to go from the frying pan to the fire (literally, to flee the fire and fall into the coals)

4. **salir de Guatemala para entrar en Guatepeor** to go from the frying pan (from *Guatemala*) into the fire (*Guatepeor*); there is a pun on *mala*, "bad," and *peor*, "worse"

5. **entrar bizco(-a) y salir cojo(-a)** to have things go from bad to worse (literally, to come in cross-eyed and leave crippled)

6. **estar metido(-a) en un rollo** to be involved or stuck in a problem (literally, to be put in a roll)

7. **meterse en camisa de once varas** to bite off more than one can chew, get mixed up in something unnecessarily (literally, to put oneself in a shirt of eleven rods)

8. **meterse en la boca del lobo** to expose oneself to unnecessary danger, go into the lion's den (literally, to put oneself in the wolf's mouth)

9. **pender de un hilo, tener la vida en un hilo** to be in great danger (literally, to hang from a thread, have one's life by a thread)

10. **ir por lana y volver trasquilado(-a)** to have the tables turned, have a serious reversal (literally, to go for wool and come back shorn)

When a situation is really desperate and *no tiene remedio* ("has no remedy," is hopeless), people may use one of the following expressions.

TOP FIVE Expressions for a Situation That *¡No tiene remedio!*

1. **Estoy frito(-a).** I'm toast. (Literally, I'm fried.)

2. **Estoy en la olla.** I'm in hot water. (Literally, I'm in the pot.)

3. **Tengo la soga al cuello.** I'm up the creek without a paddle. (Literally, I have the noose at my neck.)

4. **Estoy en las astas del toro.** I'm in the eye of the storm. (Literally, I'm on the horns of the bull.)

5. **Estoy fregado(-a).** I'm in a fix. (Literally, I'm scrubbed.)

This last entry is sometimes translated as "I'm screwed," but it's not as strong; for that, people say *jodido(-a)* or, in Mexico and Central America, *chingado(-a)*, which are both vulgar. One last expression, from Chile: *Estoy donde las papas queman* ("I'm where the potatoes burn," in a real jam).

Sometimes problems are solved, usually after a bit of effort. Here are some expressions about saving the day.

TOP FIVE Ways of Saving the Day, Solving a Problem

1. **salvar el pellejo** or **salvarse por un pelo** to be saved by the bell, escape by a hair (literally, to save one's skin or to be saved by a hair)

2. **sacarle a alguien de un apuro** to get someone out of a jam

3. **bajar a todos los santos** to try everything in times of trouble (literally, to get all the statues of saints down—as if to pray to all of them at once; used in Mexico, Central America)

4. **jugar la última carta** to play one's last trick (literally, to play the last card)

5. **quemar el último cartucho** to go to the last resort (literally, to burn the last cartridge)

Sometimes when people tell you about their problems, about something bad that they thought would happen that did not actually come about or something good that was long awaited, you might want to express your relief or happiness about the situation. Here are some ways to do that.

TOP FIVE Expressions of Relief

1. **¡Qué alivio!** What a relief! *¿Encontraste tu cartera? ¡Qué alivio!* You found your wallet? What a relief!

2. **¡Gracias a Dios!** Thank God! *Gracias a Dios, todos estamos sanos.* Thank God, we're all healthy.

3. **¡Cuánto me alegro! ¡Qué alegría!** How happy I am! *Qué alegría saber que aprobaste el examen final.* How happy I am to know that you passed the final exam.

4. **Menos mal.** Just as well. (Literally, Less bad.) *Menos mal no pudiste ir con nosotros al concierto... no valió la pena.* Just as well you couldn't go to the concert with us . . . it wasn't worth it. *¿Esa carne tiene seis horas de estar en la mesa? Menos mal que no la comimos ahora.* That meat has been on the table for six hours? Just as well we didn't eat it now.

5. **¡Por fin!** Finally! *¿El cheque llegó hoy? ¡Por fin!* The check came today? Finally!

Heroes don't always succeed at what they attempt. How do you define success? What is "the good life"? Here are some Spanish sayings and quotations on this theme.

TOP TEN Sayings or Quotations About "the Good Life"

1. **Los fracasos son los pilares del éxito.** Failures are the pillars of success. —proverb

2. **«El que no sabe gozar de la ventura cuando le viene, que no se debe quejar si se le pasa.»** "He who does not know how to enjoy good fortune when it comes to him should not complain when it passes him by." —Miguel de Cervantes

3. **«¡Quítame, oh Dios, el oro y la fortuna, pero vuélveme a dar las ilusiones!»** "Take from me, oh God, gold and fortune, but give me back my illusions!" —Ramón de Campoamor, Spanish writer

4. **«[La clave para triunfar es] hacer feliz a la gente que la rodea a una. Nada más. Si eso se logra, lo demás llega corriendo solo.»** "[The key to success is] making the people who surround you happy. Nothing more. If you achieve this, everything else will follow on its own." —Marjorie Agosín, Chilean-American writer

5. **«El secreto de la felicidad es tener gustos sencillos y una mente compleja; el problema es que a menudo la mente es sencilla y los gustos complejos.»** "The secret of happiness is having simple tastes and a complex mind; the problem is often that the mind is simple and the tastes are complex." —Fernando Savater, Spanish writer

6. **«La felicidad es darse cuenta que nada es demasiado importante.»** "Happiness is realizing that nothing is too important." —Antonio Gala, Spanish writer

7. **No te pueden quitar lo bailado.** Enjoy life while you can. (Literally, They can't take away what has been danced.) —proverb

8. **«He cometido el peor pecado que uno puede cometer. No he sido feliz.»** "I have committed the worst sin that one can commit. I haven't been happy." —Jorge Luis Borges, Argentinean writer

9. **«La felicidad, a semejanza del arte, cuanto más se calcula, menos se logra.»** "Happiness is like art, the more it's calculated, the less it's obtained." —Enrique Jardiel Poncela, Spanish writer

10. **«El éxito no da ni quita la razón a las cosas.»** "Success doesn't make things right or wrong." —Antonio Cánovas del Castillo, Spanish politician and writer

---

Finally, here are some ideas for getting others to talk about famous people, whether they love them or loathe them.

TOP FIVE Questions That Will Get People to Talk

1. **¿Quién es la persona más famosa de este país, en su opinión?** Who's the most famous person from this country, in your opinion?

2. **¿Cuál es una persona famosa de este país que a usted no le gusta para nada?** Who's a famous person from this country that you don't like at all?

3. **En su opinión, ¿en este país hay un escritor o una escritora que tenga mucha influencia o que sea especial-**

mente importante? In your opinion, is there a writer in this country who is especially influential or important?

4. **¿Quién es una persona que haya contribuido mucho a este país?** Who's a person who has contributed a lot to this country?

5. **¿A quién admira usted mucho?** Whom do you admire a lot?

You can ask the person about *su país*, "their country," instead of *este país* if they are visiting from elsewhere. Of course you can ask more specific questions also, depending on where you are and what you know about the country and its famous people. And maybe take a minute to think: Do you have heroes? Who are they? What did they do to make life better for the rest of us? What could you tell someone about them in Spanish? If you don't have heroes, what celebrities do you most admire?

Rehearsal Time

Situaciones. Answer the following questions, then check your answers in the Answer Key.

1. How do you say "I'm in hot water" in Spanish?

2. Your friend tells you that his father was not on the plane that crashed yesterday after all; you want to express relief. What do you say?

3. What are two questions that will get people to talk about famous people?

4. Answer Question 3 for yourself.

Lo mismo es Chana que Juana. (Six to one, half dozen to the other.) Match the sentences that have similar meanings. Check your answers in the Answer Key.

1. Estoy frito.

2. Escapó del trueno y dio con el relámpago.

3. ¡Cuánto me alegro!

4. Jugaron la última carta.

5. No te metas en la boca del lobo.

a. ¡Qué alegría!

b. Estoy en la olla.

c. No te pongas en una situación peligrosa.

d. Huyó del fuego y cayó en las brasas.

e. Quemaron el último cartucho.

APPENDIX
A

Regional Variations
for "You"

It's generally acknowledged that Spanish is a more personal language than English, and one example of this is the various ways of saying "you" to those we are speaking with. Some of these depend on what corner of the Spanish-speaking world you are visiting.

TOP FIVE Ways to Say "You" in Spanish When Asking About People's Professions

1. **usted (Ud., Vd.): Perdón, ¿es usted el gerente?** Excuse me, are you the manager? (Used everywhere, this is the formal "you" with its two abbreviations, which both occur commonly in writing, but are pronounced always as *usted*. The reason for the *V* in *Vd.* is that the form originally was for the nobility and stood for *Vuestra Merced*—Your Grace. That is why it patterns with third-person verb forms, just as in English. You would

say, "Your Grace is [*not* are] ready for tea?" This was a way of showing respect, and still remains so.)

2. **ustedes (Uds., Vds.): Señores, ¿son ustedes profesores?** Gentlemen, are you [all] teachers? (Used everywhere as the plural of *usted*. The abbreviations are also used commonly in writing but pronounced as *ustedes*. In Latin America it is also used for the plural of *tú*—i.e., to a group of children or friends.) *Niños, ¿son ustedes estudiantes de primaria?* Children, are you elementary school students?

3. **vosotros, vosotras: Marco y Gabriela, ¿sois abogados?** Marco and Gabriela, are you lawyers? **Muchachas, vosotras sois estudiantes, ¿verdad?** Girls, you are students, right? (Used in most of Spain, but not in Latin America, as the plural of *tú* for talking to two or more children or friends, the form ending in *-os* is for males or a mixed male-female group and the form ending in *-as* is for an all-female group. Notice that these forms of "you" require the use of special verb forms used only in Spain.)

4. **tú: Mónica, es obvio que eres una buena abogada.** Mónica, it's obvious that you are a good lawyer. (Used in standard Spanish in Spain and Latin America for talking with one child or friend or a colleague with whom you are on informal terms.)

5. **vos: Vos sos comerciante, ¿no es cierto?** You are a businessman [businesswoman], right? (This form does not exist in standard Spanish but is used in parts of Latin America instead of the *tú* form for very close friends. It patterns in different ways with substandard forms of the verb.)

When traveling, it is safest to use *usted* for "you" when speaking to one person and *ustedes* when speaking to more than one, or at least to start out that way. This is especially true in Mexico, Colombia, and Central America. If someone begins to *tutear* you (to speak to you with the *tú* forms), then you may decide to follow suit. This often happens in Spain or the Southern Cone (Argentina, Uruguay, and Chile), for example, if you are talking to another adult who is a bit older than you because that person may say that your use of the *usted* form makes him or her feel old. In Costa Rica, the *usted* form is used a great deal, even to children, but in most places as an adult you would automatically use the *tú* form with a child. Usage varies a good deal from country to country and in some places the *usted* form is even used by children to their mothers or fathers. There are other regional variations, such as *su mercé* in regions of Colombia. There is no need to attempt to use the other forms of "you" besides *tú*, *usted*, and *ustedes*, but it is good to recognize them so you know what they mean.

Two other common ways of asking someone what he or she does for a living are:

> *¿A qué se dedica Ud.?* (Literally, To what do you dedicate yourself?)
>
> *¿En qué trabaja Ud.?* (Literally, In what do you work?)

Rehearsal Time

¿Usted, tú, vosotros... ? How much do you remember about grammar differences relating to the use of "you" in Spanish? Circle the letter of the correct option for each statement. Check your answers in the Answer Key.

1. What is the difference between the two abbreviations for *usted*?
   a. *Ud.* is more formal than *Vd.*
   b. *Vd.* is more formal than *Ud.*
   c. There is no difference.

2. What word for "you" would a Spaniard use when talking to several women friends?
   a. ustedes
   b. vosotros
   c. vosotras

3. What word for "you" would a Latin American use when talking to several women friends?
   a. ustedes
   b. vosotros
   c. vosotras

4. What word for "you" would a Spaniard use when talking to a mixed group of men and women friends?
   a. ustedes
   b. vosotros
   c. vosotras

5. What word for "you" would a Latin American use when talking to a mixed group of men and women friends?
   a. ustedes
   b. vosotros
   c. vosotras

6. When and where is *vos* used for "you"?
   a. in parts of Spain to one person
   b. in parts of Spain to more than one person
   c. in parts of Latin America to one person

7. How do you normally ask someone what he or she does for a living?
   a. ¿Qué hace usted para vivir?
   b. ¿A qué se dedica usted?
   c. ¿Cuál profesión juega su mercé?

APPENDIX
B

Pronunciation Around the Globe

Grammar is one way Spanish differs from region to region; pronunciation is another. You may have had the experience of not being able to understand an Irish or Australian movie or a joke told to you by a British visitor because of the difference in accent. The same problem exists in Spanish because every country, and even a region within a country, has its own particular accent. In some cases, there is a characteristic intonation, as in the case of certain parts of northern Mexico, where the ending of each sentence rises and then falls, or in the west of Argentina, where the inhabitants of the cities of Córdoba and Mendoza are known for their lilt and the slow pace of their speech. Mexicans in general speak slowly by comparison with many others, but in the city of Veracruz they talk so fast that some other Mexicans call *veracruzanos «los tíbiri-tábara,»* in imitation of their rapid speech.

In general, the biggest immediate obstacles to understanding are the different ways that certain letters are pronounced across the Spanish-speaking world. Let's take a look at some of them.

TOP FIVE Letters with Different Regional Pronunciations in Spanish

1. **c before e or i** In Latin America the *c* before an *e* or *i* is pronounced like the *s* in "sun," as in *cero* ("zero") or *cinco* ("five"), which are pronounced "sero," "sinco." This is called the *seseo*. In most of Spain, however, the *c* before *e* or *i* is pronounced like the *th* in "teeth." So, *cero* and *cinco* sound like "thero" and "thinco." This is called the *ceceo* (pronounced "thetheo") and it is not a lisp. Spaniards pronounce the letter *s* the way we do in English and have no trouble with it. In Spain the word *sincero* sounds like this: "sin-the-ro."

2. **z** The same difference exists in the way the letter *z* (pronounced *zeta*) is said. In Latin America it is like an *s* and in most of Spain like the *th* in "teeth." So, the words for "shoe" and "pencil" sound like this in Latin America: *zapato* ("sa-pa-to"), *lápiz* ("lá-pis"). In most of Spain they sound like this: *zapato* ("tha-pa-to"), *lápiz* ("lá-pith"). Notice that in no place in the Spanish-speaking world is the letter *z* pronounced like the English *z* in the word "buzz."

3. **ll** This has a distinctive sound in some parts of Spain. The double *l* is generally pronounced like the *y* in "yes" in Latin America. The Andean pack animal, the *llama*, is called a "ya-ma" and a chair, a *silla*, is called a "si-ya" (as in "See ya' later"). However, the *ll* in some areas of Spain is generally pronounced like the *ly* sound in the English word "million."

4. **ll and initial y** These are pronounced in a special way in Argentina and Uruguay. These letters sound like the *shz* sound

in "measure" in Buenos Aires and some other parts of Argentina and in all of Uruguay. Saying *Yo me llamo Guillermo* ("My name is Guillermo") sounds like this: "Shzo me shzamo Guishzermo." There is some variation in this so that many young people in Buenos Aires now use a *sh* sound instead and some individuals use a sound that is closer to the *j* in "jump."

5. **s at the end of words** This is not heard much in the Caribbean, especially in Cuba, Puerto Rico, the Dominican Republic, and in many rural areas of Spain and Latin America. The *s* is aspirated so that *todas las casas* ("all the houses") sounds like "todah lah cahah" or at times it disappears completely and becomes "toda la ca-a."

 ## Rehearsal Time

El español alrededor del mundo. How much do you remember about grammar and pronunciation differences in Spanish? Circle the letter of the correct option for each statement. Check your answers in the Answer Key.

1. Why do Mexicans from Veracruz have a reputation for speaking differently?
   a. They talk very fast.
   b. They talk very slow.
   c. They talk very loud.

2. How is the letter *c* before *e* or *i* pronounced in most of Spain?
   a. like the *s* in "mesa"
   b. like the *th* in "then"
   c. like the *th* in "theater"

3. How is the letter *z* pronounced in Latin America?
   a. like the *s* in "mesa"
   b. like the *th* in "then"
   c. like the *th* in "theater"

4. How are the initial *y* and the *ll* pronounced by many people in Uruguay and parts of Argentina, including Buenos Aires?
   a. like the *y* in "yes"
   b. like the *shz* sound in "treasure"
   c. like the *ly* sound in "billion"

5. In the Caribbean, what letter is often aspirated so that you don't hear it at the end of Spanish words?
   a. *c*
   b. *m*
   c. *s*

Answer Key

Ritmos

1. *plan*-tas

2. cho-co-*la*-te

3. es-pa-*ñol*

4. e-*xa*-men

5. bal-*cón*

6. ter-*mó*-me-tro

7. in-ter-na-cio-*nal*

8. u-ni-ver-si-*dad*

9. in-dus-*trio*-so

10. in-ter-pre-ta-*ción*

Presentaciones

1. nombre
2. Cúal
3. llamo
4. gusto
5. gusto
6. llamo
7. nombre
8. es
9. conocerlo
10. Encantado / Igualmente

La pronunciación

1. c
2. b
3. a
4. a
5. b
6. b
7. c
8. c
9. b
10. a

La buena educación

1. a

2. c

3. c

4. c

5. c

6. a

7. a

8. c

Iniciando una conversación

1. Disculpe

2. Oiga

3. correo

4. vista

5. dónde

Tune-Up 2: *Sonido y sentido*

¿Qué dice usted?

1. ¡Cuidado!

2. ¡Socorro!

3. ¡Ay! *or* ¡Huy!

4. ¡Tranquilo!

5. ¡Qué bonito!

¡Lógico!

1. c

2. b

3. a

4. c

Atajos

1. supermercado

2. abuelo *or* abuela

3. televisión

4. profesores

5. universidad

6. computadora

7. motocicleta

8. compadre

9. migración (INS)

10. Muchas gracias.

11. bicicleta

12. instituto

13. directora

14. película

15. depresión

16. por favor

Lo mismo es Chana que Juana (possible answers)

1. claro / por supuesto

2. Exacto. / Cierto.

3. No entiendo.

4. Ni a la fuerza. / Ni a palos. / De ninguna manera.

5. ¿Y después?

6. ¿Estás bromeando? / ¿Hablas en serio?

7. ¡Qué ridículo!

Situaciones (possible answers)

1. comprendo (entiendo) / despacio

2. quieras

3. Al contrario, no todos somos (son) ricos. No es verdad.

4. ¿De veras? ¡Qué interesante!

5. quiere decir la palabra *tapa*

Tune-Up 3: *¡Buen provecho!*

La lógica de la comida

1. b

2. a

3. c

4. b

5. a

6. c

Todo sobre las bebidas

1. amor

2. hierbas

3. tinto

4. descafeinado

5. con gas

6. rubia

7. jugos

8. gaseosa

¿Qué nos recomienda?

1. ¡Por favor! *or* ¡Señor!

2. appetizer; un entremés (Mexico: un antojito)

3. He wants to know what to serve you.

4. the daily special; el menú del día (Colombia: la comida corriente, Chile: la colación)

5. La sopa del día. La especialidad de la casa.

6. No. It means "All you can eat."

7. Answers will vary.

La invitación (possible answers)

1. ¡Qué gusto de verte!

2. Brindemos por el cocinero.

3. ¡Buen provecho!

4. muy rica (sabrosa, para chuparse los dedos)

5. poquito

6. satisfecho(-a)

7. trabajar mañana / levantarme temprano mañana, etc.

8. invitarme (la invitación)

9. Lo pasé muy bien (de maravilla).

La verdad sobre las comidas

1. V

2. V

3. F

4. V

5. F

6. F

Tune-Up 4: *Amor, pasión y aventura*

Palabras dulces

1. c

2. g

3. n

4. j

5. a

6. h

7. k

8. m

9. d

10. i

La pasión en palabras y poesía

1. aventura

2. verde

3. natural

4. enamorar

5. beso

6. locura

7. bodega

Invitaciones

1. b

2. b

3. b

4. a

5. b

6. b

7. a

8. c

9. c

10. a

Ritmos revueltos

1. son

2. cumbia

3. ranchera

4. tango

5. salsa

6. flamenco

Buscando el amor

1. b

2. a

3. a

4. c

5. b

Piropos and Contrapiropos

1. 8

2. 2

3. 2

4. 10

5. 1

El vocabulario del amor: sinónimos

1. c

2. e

3. i

4. a

5. f

6. h

7. g

8. d

9. b

El vocabulario del amor: antónimos

1. b

2. c

3. i

4. d

5. g

6. a

7. j

8. f

9. e

10. h

Tune-Up 5: *¡Viajar es vivir!*

Historia y geografía

1. b

2. b

3. c

4. a

5. c

6. b

7. c

8. b

9. a

10. a

¿Qué busca usted?

1. f

2. i

3. a

4. e

5. g

6. d

7. h

8. c

9. j

10. b

¿Qué necesita hacer?

1. g

2. c

3. d

4. a

5. e

6. f

7. b

El viajero experto

1. llave

2. cobra

3. dirección

4. baja

5. dejar

6. llave

7. ruido

8. gerente

¡Vamos a festejar!

1. a

2. c

3. a

4. c

5. c

6. b

7. c

8. a

Tune-Up 6: *De compras*

¡Lógico!

1. b

2. a

3. b

4. a

¿En qué le puedo servir?

1. Decir «Buenos días» («Buenas tardes»).

2. Sólo estoy mirando.

3. What size? What is your size?

4. ¿De qué está hecho(-a)... ?

5. Answers will vary.

6. Necesito devolver este... (esta...). No funciona.

Conversaciones

1. perdió el poncho

2. el gorro

3. zapatos nuevos

4. hasta la camisa

Dinero, dinero, dinero

1. currency exchange place; exchange rates vary

2. ¿A cuánto está el cambio?

3. Quédese con el cambio.

Sinónimos

1. c

2. b

3. e

4. d

5. a

Tune-Up 7: *¿En serio o en broma?*

La pura verdad

1. a

2. a

3. a

4. b

5. b

6. a

Imágenes

1. e

2. d

3. a

4. b

5. f

6. c

Proverbios

1. c

2. d

3. e

4. b

5. a

Dichos y supersticiones

1. Se me fue el santo al cielo.

2. A bad day.

3. Quickly.

4. Tuesday the 13. If you open an umbrella inside the house, you'll have a fight with someone. If you spill wine, you'll have good luck. If you break a mirror, you'll have bad luck. If you see a falling star, you can make three (not one, but three!) wishes.

Rimas

1. Feliz como una lombriz.

2. Lo mismo es Chana que Juana.

3. El burro delante, para que no se espante.

4. Comida hecha, amistad deshecha.

5. En eso no tengo arte ni parte.

6. Si no lo veo, no lo creo.

Tune-Up 8: *De la casa a la plaza*

El matrimonio y la familia

1. padrinos
2. novios
3. parientes
4. haces
5. cabeza
6. político
7. celoso
8. familia
9. madre
10. padre

De padres e hijos

1. b
2. d
3. f
4. a
5. e
6. c

Hablando por teléfono

1. días
2. gustaría

3. el

4. quién

5. parte

6. Buenas

7. quisiera / podría

8. ella

9. encuentra

10. regresa

La amistad al estilo latino

1. c

2. c

3. b

4. a

5. a

6. c

7. b

8. a

Cómo decir «I love» o «I like»

1. me encanta / me gusta

2. Te amo

3. Quiero mucho

4. me cae bien

5. Te quiero

6. Me encantan

7. Quiero

8. Me cae bien

9. le cae bien

10. nos gusta / nos encanta

11. caes gordo

12. gusta

¿Qué significan realmente?

1. Casa sin mujer, cuerpo sin alma viene a ser.

2. Amigo no es el que te hace reír con la mentira, sino el que te hace llorar con la verdad.

3. Hijo de tigre sale rayado.

4. Matrimonio y mortaja, del cielo baja.

5. A casa de mi novia llevé a un amigo; él se quedó dentro y yo despedido.

6. Los hijos son la riqueza de los pobres.

7. Amigo que dice no, amistad que se perdió. *or* Amistades que son ciertas mantienen las puertas abiertas.

Tune-Up 9: *El español: voz de muchos pueblos*

Diferencias de vocabulario: objetos y lugares

1. c

2. a

3. c

4. b

5. c

Diferencias de vocabulario: la gente y sus acciones

1. c

2. b

3. a

4. b

5. a

Las palabrotas y sus variaciones

1. a

2. c

3. b

4. a

5. c

6. c

7. a

8. b

9. b

10. c

11. b

12. c

Tune-Up 10: *Don Quijote, La Malinche, Bolívar...*

Dichos

1. c

2. a

3. d

4. b

Un verdadero amigo

1. confianza

2. corazón

3. espada

4. corriente

5. vencido

Problemas

1. b

2. a

3. a

4. a

Situaciones (possible answers)

1. Estoy en la olla.

2. ¡Qué alivio!

3. Answers will vary.

4. Answers will vary.

Lo mismo es Chana que Juana

1. b

2. d

3. a

4. e

5. c

Appendix A: Regional Variations for "You"

¿Usted, tú, vosotros... ?

1. c

2. c

3. a

4. b

5. a

6. c

7. b

Appendix B: Pronunciation Around the Globe

El español alrededor del mundo

1. a

2. c

3. a

4. b

5. c

Index of Top Five and Top Ten Lists

accept an invitation, ways to, 107–8

actions, ways of expressing, 256–57

agree, ways to, 56–57

altibajos, ways of describing married couples and their, 219–21

amar, ways to say what you love with, 234–35

animals, sounds made by, 16

Arabic, Spanish food words from, 66–67

arrival, things you might want after, 139–40

bad guys, expressions for, 279

beverage, ways to order, 75–76

"bus," ways to say, 243–44

Cervantes, quotations by, 271–72

character, expressions about strength of, 273

children, proverbs about, 221–22

city, places for travelers in a, 141–42

clothing items, expressions with names of, 175–76

complain about a purchase, ways to, 171

compliments you can give, 122–23

consonants, typical Spanish names containing tricky, 15

contrapiropos, how Mexican women talk back with, 121–22

conversation starters, 32–34

courage

  expressions about, 273

  quotations about, 274–75

courtesy, phrases for, 146–47

¿de qué está hecho(-a)?, answers to the question, 170

deception, expressions for, 280–81

declining an invitation

  when you really do not want to go, 108

  when you really *do* want to go but can't, 108–9

descriptions for people, 254–56

dinnertime expressions, 83–84

directions, ways to ask for, 143

disagree, ways to, 58

disbelief, ways to express, 58

drinks

  common expressions with names of, 92–93

  fruit, 73–74

  places to drink, 69–70

  ways to order, 75–76

eat, places to, 69–70

emergency, phrases for tourists in, 3–4

emotions, acceptable expletives for venting, 264–65

enamorar, techniques of Latin lovers to, 118–19

encantar, ways to say what you love with, 234–35

enthusiasm, ways to show, 56

evil deeds and deception, expressions for, 280–81

exaggeration, expressions using, 187–88

exchange a purchase, ways to, 171

expletives acceptable for venting emotions, 264–65

expressiveness with *-ísimo* endings, 6

family
    questions to ask about, 214–15
    strong slang expressions referring to, 216–17

fear, quotations about, 274–75

festivals to attend, 154–58

food
    common expressions with names of, 92–93
    special places for special, 70
    specialties from Spain and Latin America, 87
    ways to talk about preferences, 68–69
    with different names in Spain, 88
    words from Arabic for, 66–67
    words from native American languages for, 67–68

friends, ways of referring to, 230

friendship, proverbs about, 224

fruit drinks, 73–74

gestures and their meanings, 40–41

good life, sayings or quotations about, 288–89

"good-bye"
    ways people interact when saying, 25–26
    ways of saying, 29

greeting
    ways of, 22–23
    ways people interact when, 25–26

h, useful words with, 8–9

hesitation words used in place of "uh" or "um," 34

hopeless, expressions for situations that are, 286

host/hostess
    things said to welcome you by, 82
    things to say to, 84–85

hotel
    pairs of synonyms used in, 150
    things to do after you've settled in, 139–40
    things you might want after arriving in, 139–40
    typical problems in, 152

hotel desk clerk, handy phrases to say to a, 150–51

humor, similes with, 190

interjections
    one-word, 43
    with ¡qué... !, 44

introductions, phrases for, 19

invitation
    ways to accept, 107–8
    ways to decline when you really do not want to go, 108
    ways to decline when you really *do* want to go but can't, 108–9

invite someone out, how to, 106–7

ironic expressions, 185–86

irony, uses in negative expressions, 186–87

-ísimo endings, expressiveness with, 6

key, ways to ask for the, 27

Latin America
    famous places in, 18
    food specialties from, 87
    romantic musical traditions of, 112–13

leave, ways of taking, 29

letters with different regional pronunciations in Spanish, 298–99

like someone
    ways to say you, 236–37
    ways to say you don't, 237

linking words, common, 48–49

love
    proverbs about, 124
    sad steps in quadrangle of, 123–24
    ways to say what you, 234–35

lovers, techniques of Latin, 118–19

made of, answers to the question "what's
   it . . .?", 170
malentendidos, things to know to avoid,
   147–49
marketplace, things you may hear in,
   164–65
marriage, proverbs about, 213
married couples, ways of describing,
   219–21
meaning, word endings that change,
   12
meeting, ways people interact when,
   25–26
metaphors, 192–93
misunderstandings, things to know to avoid,
   147–49
money
   common sayings about, 177–78
   expressions about the use of, 178
   questions that can save, 80, 170
   slang words that mean, 179
moral, rhymes with a, 208
musical traditions of Spain and Latin
   America, 112–13

names
   to call your darling, 99–100
   to call your honey, and examples of
      "sweet nothings," 98
   typical Spanish, 15
native American languages, food words
   from, 67–68
needs, expressing your, 138
negative expressions, uses of irony in,
   186–87
no es perita en dulce, uses of irony in negative
   expressions, 186–87
¡no tiene remedio!, expressions for situations
   that, 286
not following, ways to tell someone you're,
   54–55
nouns, short forms of, 51

obscene, words that are ordinary in one
   Spanish-speaking culture but in
   another are, 260–63
one-word interjections, 43

people
   descriptions for, 254–56
   types of, and what you call them in
      different places, 250–51
piropos
   how Mexican women talk back to,
      121–22
   Mexican, 120–21
places
   to eat or drink, 69–70
   famous, in Spain and Latin America,
      18
   for special food, 70
   for travelers in a city or town,
      141–42
   where you might find yourself,
      247–48
plays on words, 193–94
poor, slang expressions to describe the,
   180–81
problems
   in hotels, 152
   ways of solving, 286–87
pronunciation, letters with different
   regional, 298–99
proverbs
   about children, 221–22
   about friendship, 224
   about love, 124
   about marriage, 213
   that "sound Hispanic," 198
   about travel, 158–59
   useful, 198–99
   you will probably hear only the first half
      of, 200
purchase, ways to complain about and/or
   exchange a, 171

¡qué... !, interjections with, 44
querer, ways to say what you love with,
   234–35

reductions, common word, 48–49
regional variations of Spanish
   common things with, 245–46
   different ways to say "bus,"
      243–44

letters with different pronunciations,
298–99
words that are ordinary in one Spanish-
speaking culture and obscene in
another, 260–63
relief, expressions of, 287
responses to a phone request, 227–28
rhymes, with a moral, 208
rhyming expressions, 207
rich, slang expressions to describe the, 180
riddles
common, 196–97
that contain their answers, 195–96
romantic musical traditions of Spain and
Latin America, 112–13

safety, phrases for, 146–47
saints, expressions invoking, 202–3
salesclerk
questions you may be asked by a, 168
things said to clinch the sale by a,
168–69
things you may say to a, 169
santos, expressions invoking, 202–3
sex, shameless Spanish terms relating to,
102
short forms of nouns, 51
similes
containing verbs, 191
with humor, 190
slang
expressions referring to family members,
216–17
expressions to describe the poor, 180–81
expressions to describe the rich, 180
words that mean "money," 179
slow down, ways to tell someone to, 54–55
soul mate, ways to describe, 116
sounds
animals make, 16
that have meaning, 41–42
Spain
famous places in, 18
food specialties from, 87
foods with different names in, 88
romantic musical traditions of, 112–13

Spanish. *See also* regional variations of
Spanish
reasons to learn, vii–viii
specialties from Spain and Latin America,
87
stores, kinds of, 167
stranger, ways to begin talking to a, 32
superstitions, 204–5
synonyms, common pairs used in hotels,
150

talk, questions that will get people to,
289–90
talking to a stranger, ways to begin, 32
telephone
asking to speak to a friend on the,
226–27
common ways of answering the,
225–26
responses to a request on the, 227–28
"thank you," ways to say, 28
toast, ways to make a, 76
tourists in need, phrases for, 3–4
town, places for travelers in, 141–42
travel, proverbs about, 158–59
travelers, places in a city or town for,
141–42
trials, ways of talking about, 284–85
tribulations, ways of talking about, 284–85

verbs, similes containing, 191
vowels, linking with, 49–50

waiter
things said to you by a, 78
things to say to a, 79
welcome, things your host or hostess may
say to you, 82
wishes, expressing your, 38
"wonderful!," ways to say, 5–6
word endings, examples that change
meaning, 12

"you," ways to say, when asking about
people's professions, 293–94